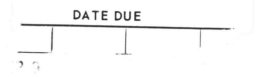

DATE DUE

History in Depth

Collections of documents come in all shapes and sizes. Many attempt to cover a very broad period; in consequence they rely heavily on illustrative material which is thought to be typical. In practice, this means a patchwork of often isolated snippets, with material torn out of context. Single documents or even fragments of documents have to bear the whole weight of a period, a problem, a theme. Students derive from such collections a mistaken impression of the nature of history, of the character of historical research, and very often, a false impression of the subject of study.

History in Depth is based on the belief that historical perception demands immediacy and depth. Working to the principle that true breadth of history can be achieved only by examining a concrete problem in depth, each volume in the series is devoted to either a particular event or crisis of considerable significance, such as the Peasants' Revolt of 1381; or to a trend or movement running through a coherent period of time, such as West African nationalism from the middle of the nineteenth century; or to a particular area of experience, such as Elizabethan Puritanism.

No artificial uniformity is imposed on the format of the volumes; each is shaped by the dictates of its subject. But there are certain basic elements common to all. The core of each book is a major collection of original material, translated into English where necessary, with editorial decisions on modernised punctuation and spelling governed by the nature of the subject. Each editor provides an introduction geared to the particular demands of his volume; each volume carries a full working bibliography, interpretative notes and an index.

This is a new approach to the teaching of history which has been evolved in response to a demand from practising teachers. The general editor has selected the subjects and the volume editors with care, so that each book stands in its own right and has something of the quality of a monograph.

History in Depth

GENERAL EDITOR: G. A. Williams

THE
INFIDEL TRADITION
from Paine to Bradlaugh

Edited by

Edward Royle
University of York

The work is done – The Press is free
The manner how – here look and see
Republican, vol. xiv (1826)

Macmillan of Canada/Maclean-Hunter Press

First published 1976 by
THE MACMILLAN PRESS LTD.
London and Basingstoke

First published in North America 1976 by
THE MACMILLAN COMPANY OF CANADA LIMITED
70 Bond Street
Toronto M5B 1X3

ISBN: 0–7705–1476–6

Printed in Great Britain

Contents

General Editor's Preface	ix
Acknowledgements	xiii
A Note on Presentation	xiv
Abbreviations	xiv
Preface	xv

PART ONE: THE TRADITION — 1

THE IMPACT OF PAINE — 3
1 The polarisation of opinion, 1792	6
2 The Committee of Secrecy, 1794	9
3 Another view of the conspiracy	10
4 The infidel metropolis	11

RICHARD CARLILE AND THE ZETETICS — 16
5 A call to action, 1819	20
6 Carlile's appeal for volunteers	23
7 The response	25
8 The Edinburgh Zetetic Society	31
9 Presents from Sheffield	32
10 The power of the press	33
11 The 'Infidel Mission'	34
12 The tradition continued	36

OWENISM — 38
13 The Association of All Classes	44
14 Reaction to persecution	47
15 The views of an infidel lecturer	49
16 Support from Carlile	52

17 The Anti-Persecution Union 54
18 The threat of redundancy 57
19 The need for a new infidel periodical 60

SECULARISM 63
20 Secular societies in 1852 71
21 The Leicester Secular Society 75
22 West Riding district organisation 78
23 Robert Cooper's militancy 81
24 The progress of freethought 84
25 The National Secular Society 86

PART TWO: THE MOVEMENT 91

FROM BELOW 93
26 The raw materials (1) 93
27 The raw materials (2) 95
28 The growth in class feeling 96
29 Rank and file – John Spencer 97

FROM ABOVE 99
30 Leadership – James Watson 99
31 Lectures – Joseph Barker's list 106
32 Preparations for a visiting lecturer 109
33 A lecturer on tour 111

LEISURE 115
34 A Paine birthday celebration 115
35 A Bradlaugh victory celebration 117
36 The Hall of Science classes 119
37 Huddersfield Secular Sunday School 121

PART THREE: THE SPRINGS OF PROTEST 123

DESTRUCTIVE PROTEST 125
38 Moral revulsion at the Atonement 125
39 A street-corner lecture on the Atonement 126
40 The horrors of the Bible 128
41 Anti-clericalism 131
42 A de-conversion 133

CONTENTS

CONSTRUCTIVE CRITICISM   136
  43 Biblical criticism   136
  44 Scientific criticism (1)   139
  45 Scientific criticism (2)   141
  46 The principles of naturalism   142
  47 An argument for atheism   143

THE NEW SYSTEM   147
  48 The Law of Nature   147
  49 The New Moral World   149
  50 The principles of Secularism   151

PART FOUR: THE POLITICS OF LIBERATION   153

DOMESTIC RADICALISM   155
  51 Paineite republicanism   155
  52 Carlile's republicanism   156
  53 An attack on apolitical Owenism   158
  54 A defence of apolitical Owenism   159
  55 Dreams of a new radicalism   160
  56 A plea for compromise   162
  57 In praise of Mr Gladstone   165
  58 Bradlaugh's election manifesto, 1868   168
  59 Republicanism for England   171
  60 The new socialism   174
  61 Secularism and socialism in Leicester   179

EUROPEAN REPUBLICANISM   181
  62 Hopes and fears in 1849   181
  63 Arms for Garibaldi   184

WOMEN'S RIGHTS   186
  64 A plea for divorce   186
  65 The Knowlton Pamphlet   187

PART FIVE: LAW AND PUBLIC OPINION   191

PERSECUTION AND PROSECUTION   193
  66 A history of persecution   193
  67 Blasphemy in Edinburgh   195

68 A problem for the Newcastle magistrates 204

CIVIL RIGHTS 208
69 Britain not a free country 208
70 The Bradlaugh case 210

PUBLIC OPINION 214
71 The suppression of infidel socialism 214
72 A Christian mob 215
73 Signs of progress 219

Sources and Further Reading 221

Index 225

General Editor's Preface

Historical perception demands immediacy and depth. These qualities are lost in attempts at broad general survey; for the reader of history depth is the only true breadth. Each volume in this series, therefore, explores an important historical problem in depth. There is no artificial uniformity; each volume is shaped by the problem it tackles. The past bears its own witness; the core of each volume is a major collection of original material (translated into English where necessary) as alive, as direct and as full as possible. The reader should feel the texture of the past. The volume editor provides interpretative notes and introduction and a full working bibliography. The volume will stand in its own right as a 'relived experience' and will also serve as a point of entry into a wider area of historical discourse. In taking possession of a particular historical world, the reader will move more freely in a wider universe of historical experience.

In this volume, Dr Edward Royle recreates the world of the radical 'infidels' of the nineteenth century, in a full, rich and fascinating exploration of what became one of the central traditions in the British popular, radical and labour movements. The reader is admitted to the experience of three generations, their modes of thought and action, the structure of their reasoning, the texture of their prose. In his rich documentation and in his cool but imaginative interpretation, Dr Royle reconstitutes this central theme in British radicalism. In our own day when a form of undemanding deism appears to have become universal,

this particular tradition has been elusive. Without an understanding of it, we lose our grip on populism and protest in the
last century. Through Dr Royle's admirable volume, we repos-
sess a frequently forgotten or under-valued world.

In 1831 the 'Chartist schoolmaster' Bronterre O'Brien denounced British working-class radicals to a congress of Owenite co-operators. They lacked any distinctive creed, he alleged;
they were content to mouth middle-class notions in a harsher
accent. Any reader of the *Poor Man's Guardian* will understand
what he meant; the very prose sometimes breaks down from
sheer inadequacy to the task it was called upon to perform.
Populist radicals failed to find a distinctive vocabulary, failed to
establish what our generation of dissidents calls a 'counter-
culture'. *Infidelity* offered the nearest approximation.

In many ways one sector of British populist radicalism in the
first generation of the nineteenth century represented, like its
big brother in the American Republic, a posthumous victory
for the Enlightenment. It was in these years that the Enlightenment, like the coffee house, was proletarianised in Britain,
struggling against the tide of the hegemonic ideologies of political economy and evangelicalism, dismissed by contemporaries
and historians alike as 'old-fashioned'. Its first lodgement had
been effected during the French Revolution, in the days of the
London Corresponding Society and Thomas Paine's *Age of
Reason*. Essentially French in inspiration, one of its major
instruments was Volney's *Ruins of Empires*, a rationalist fantasy
or piece of science fiction. Between 1793 and 1822 there were no
fewer than eleven English editions of Volney; it was even translated into Welsh and by a Baptist minister to boot. It came to
occupy a place in the world of popular and radical sensibility
not unlike that occupied by William Morris or Jack London in
a later generation. The great debate between Volney and that
other archetypal radical figure Joseph Priestley, the scientist
who clung to a Unitarian Christianity, assumed the trans-
Atlantic proportions proper to this phase of what was in truth
an Anglo-American tradition. At one point in the 1790s the
protagonists, both in exile, argued it out under the chair-
manship of that equally characteristic figure Thomas Jefferson
(whose sayings were to adorn British trade union banners) in
the hall of Benjamin Franklin's Philadelphia library before an

audience representing every wing of the British 'Paineite' movement in exile!

One of the great virtues of Dr Royle's book is the way in which it establishes the centrality of Richard Carlile in transmitting, indeed in some sense *creating* the Thomas Paine tradition in British radicalism. It was Carlile's massive, heroic, splenetic and idiosyncratic labours in the 1820s which in effect created the 'historical' Paine for British readers. Dr Royle argues a good case for a Paine–Carlileism to parallel Marxism–Leninism! Certainly, it was in that generation that *infidelity* was central to the 'silent insurrection' of working people struggling to establish a combative autonomy and presence in inimical circumstances. It was this which helped to give an anti-clerical, almost 'European' bite to the crisis of 1831–2, to put the bone of intransigence into populism. For it was intransigence which *infidelity* taught above all. Like the creed of Paine himself, *infidelity* had no particular relevance in itself to an industrial working class, except the essential function of enabling its militants to mark off their own Common Wealth of Reason in partial autonomy from the 'illusion of the epoch'. Carlile's Zetetic Societies were the nursery for a whole generation of working-class leaders.

Although many of *infidelity*'s instincts were diffused through an equally diffuse Owenism, Dr Royle clearly brings out the political and class ambiguity of freethought through the age of Holyoake and Bradlaugh, its essentially marginal relevance to the mass movements which grew in a later period (though Lenin himself, in despair at the development of working-class movements in the years before World War I, was to call for the reprinting of these pawky old 'classics'). Nevertheless one striking feature of the movement illumined in Dr Royle's pages was its longevity and continuity. Men like E. T. Craig lived from the days of the Owenite Halls of Science to those of the Hammersmith Social Democratic Federation. George Julian Harney, a Chartist horse from a similar stable, had an even longer run. He lived to see the ILP – though not to join it; he was never at home in a chapel. *Infidelity* runs a red linking thread through populist radical thinking, particularly among those *artisans* and their spiritual kin in later generations who have been so central to British labour tradition. And of course in the insular peculiarity of British radicalism, *infidelity* makes one sector of it a recognisable member of European democracy (indeed, in the dimension it added to populism, might be said to substitute for the radical Marxisms which characterised some continental movements).

It is the essential Englishness of the movements however which emerges from Dr Royle's book (despite George Eliot's translations, the labour of the German Young Hegelians and others at 'de-Christianisation' seems to be curiously absent). Just how English they were is exemplified, even in the first militant generation, in Elijah Dixon, a milkman in Manchester whose wrongful arrest precipitated him into radicalism and, at that stage inevitably, into a quest for a new radical cosmology. Carlile's *Republican* turned him towards deism, but he could not rid himself of a belief in a trinity, at least a trinity of *something*. Readers may find his solution (reported to Carlile's journal) reassuring: 'And so, in deep perplexity, I took the Bible in one hand and D'Holbach's System of Nature in the other and went into my bedroom and kneeled me down with the books open and prayed for that divine illumination of which I was so much in need.'

When illumination came, he joined the Owenite movement as a 'free-thinking Christian'.

GWYN A. WILLIAMS

Acknowledgements

The publishers and I are grateful to the following for their hospitable assistance and for permission to reproduce manuscript materials: the Co-operative Union, Manchester (Documents 14, 15, 16, 18, 19, 32, 45, 55); the Bishopsgate Institute (Document 63); Leicester Secular Society (Documents 21, 61); and Newcastle upon Tyne Central Reference Library (Document 56). Transcripts of Crown copyright records in the Public Record Office (Document 68) appear by permission of the Controller of H.M. Stationery Office. The publishers have made every effort to trace copyright-holders but if they have inadvertently overlooked any, they will be pleased to make the necessary arrangement at the first opportunity.

I should also like to thank all the librarians who have helped me as I have ploughed my way through the obscure literature of Freethought. Those whom I have most troubled are at the Bishopsgate Institute (where all Holyoake's works are to be found), and at the Manchester Central Reference Library (where Carlile's *Republican* and Bradlaugh's *National Reformer* rest in comparative peace).

E. R.

A Note on Presentation

Treatment of the theme is both chronological and analytical. In Part One the editorial introduction to the whole book is set out chronologically in four sections, each of which contains documents illustrative of the development of the Paineite tradition. Parts Two to Five, which have only brief introductions of their own, then follow up specific aspects of the tradition. Cross-references between documents are indicated thus: (Doc. . . .).

Editorial matter within the quoted documents is placed in square brackets, and the editor's explicatory notes on each document appear immediately after that document. Spelling and punctuation have not been changed, even where an obvious printing error of no significance had occurred in the original.

Abbreviations

A.A.C.A.N.	Association of All Classes of All Nations
L.C.S.	London Corresponding Society
N.S.S.	National Secular Society
N.M.W.	*New Moral World*
U.C.S.R.R.	Universal Community Society of Rational Religionists

Preface

Richard Carlile, the infidel publisher, once unsuspectingly employed George Edwards, the notorious Home Office informer, to make a plaster cast of his hero and inspiration, Thomas Paine. The cast in turn passed to Carlile's fellow-publisher, James Watson, who in 1871 offered it to Joseph Cowen Jr, the most vocal of radical-republican leaders in mid-century Newcastle upon Tyne. So in a symbolic way one of the most influential traditions in nineteenth-century British radicalism was expressed.[1]

The aim of this book is to study in depth, by means of often unfamiliar sources, one aspect of this ultra-radical tradition. Paine's political views were rapidly diffused among the leaders of nineteenth-century radicalism and any attempt to isolate this general influence would be fruitless, but there was a much more specific Paineite tradition, and it is this which is treated here. In 1888 the writer of a libellous biography of Charles Bradlaugh touched upon the heart of the matter:

> The 'Age of Reason,' theologically, like the 'Rights of Man,' politically, was the first theological work published in the English language, which was adapted to the comprehension of the unlettered classes, as distinct from those who had enjoyed a liberal education. Paine's influence was immense. To-day it is a mere tradition, but it created in England that peculiar propaganda, uniting extreme political and theological opinions, which in their progress in the great Social Agitations of this century, has done for us what the Encyclopaedists did for France. Why those works of Thomas

Paine created such a sensation it is difficult for us to ascertain. That they inaugurated a new political and theological era is undoubted.[2]

The subject matter of this book is this 'peculiar propaganda' and the men and organisations that created it. This means that many aspects of nineteenth-century radicalism which do not bear *directly* on the tradition have been omitted. There is little, for example, on Chartism, for as G. J. Harney asserted in 1848, 'There is nothing concerning Infidelity in the Charter',[3] though for part of its life the *Northern Star* was edited by two infidels, Joshua Hobson and Harney himself.

The world 'infidel' probably needs further clarification. It was usually used as a term of abuse – although the more extreme groups of freethinkers accepted it with pride – to signify anyone who rejected orthodox Christianity and who combined such a rejection with a low social position or an appeal to those in such a position. Thus on the lips of a socially respectable Victorian Christian the word could apply to anyone from the man (or woman) who openly disliked the local parson to the widely-read critic of all things not explicable in the light of untutored reason. The latter was probably not very common and the usual characteristic of an infidel was likely to be his anti-clericalism and anti-Evangelicalism – opposition to what, in the cant of the day, was known as Priestianity or Priestcraft. The members of infidel organisations were recruited from the ranks of those holding such sentiments, though they were then expected to read their Paine for themselves and sharpen their weapons of intellectual criticism on the weekly grindstone of periodicals, lectures and debates.

In this way latent anti-clericalism could be developed into an alternative infidel culture – a culture which appears to have gripped a considerable minority (or even a majority in some places) among the artisans, tradesmen and respectable working folk of London and the industrial regions – and it is this culture which gives meaning and life to the tradition, as is testified by the Thomas Paine tea parties and *soirées* held on or around 29 January each year by local societies in Britain and the United States for much of the nineteenth century. In 1890 the West Ham branch of the National Secular Society held a children's Thomas Paine birthday tea party, with food, music and a magic-lantern show; and at the close each child was given a printed memorial card on which was fixed a photograph of the immortal Paine.[4] Whether the children realised the significance of this or not, it was of the greatest symbolic importance to their parents.

NOTES

1. *Republican*, 28 Apr 1820; James Watson to Joseph Cowen, 22 July 1871, Cowen Collection, no. B. 107.
2. C. R. Mackay, *Life of Charles Bradlaugh, M.P.* (1888) pp. 17–18.
3. *Northern Star*, 12 Feb 1848
4. *National Reformer*, 9 Feb 1890

PART ONE
The Tradition

The Impact of Paine

Criticism of the Christian religion and its institutions was not new in the 1790s. Respectable voices had been raised against the corruption of the Church and its personnel for centuries; dissenters from its teachings had existed for almost as long as there had been teachings to be questioned. Even on a popular level this had to some extent been true, though the level of such criticism had usually been insignificant. The conjunction of political and religious radicalism was also an accepted occurrence, and the two had been associated most recently in those events which had disrupted English life in the middle of the seventeenth century. The work of Paine, though, was very much an expression of the thought of his own century — the age of reason. He said little that was new, but he spoke out to the common man — he was an infidel. Polite deism had already supplied the reasoning, but few men before Paine had dared to communicate anti-Christian ideas to the world outside that of scholarship and letters. Those who had done so had been punished (Doc. 66), chief among whom was Peter Annet (1693–1769).[1] His works were re-printed by the London Corresponding Society (Doc. 4) and by Richard Carlile, and thereafter were quoted or referred to on many occasions by later freethinkers. In 1839, for example, a periodical published in Manchester by Abel Heywood, entitled The Natural Mirror, or Free Thoughts on Theology, *edited by 'an Owenian', contained extracts from, among others, Annet, Voltaire, Paine, and the French classic,* Bon Sens.[2]

The political antecedents of Paine were even more respectable than the majority of eighteenth-century deists had been — men like Major Cartwright, the Rev. Christopher Wyvill, John Wilkes, Lord Shelburne and Pitt himself had, at times with more or less frequency, suggested that the present political system was less than perfect and that some degree of reform might not be amiss. The Duke of Richmond had even suggested universal suffrage. The French Revolution did little at first to change this situation. Reformers welcomed the news, and Paine expected his acquaintance Edmund Burke to show towards the French the same friendliness which he had earlier shown the American revolutionaries. But Burke was fundamentally opposed to the idea that a social system could be reconstructed in accordance with abstract first principles, and Paine, who was already writing a book along such lines when Burke's Reflections on the Revolution in France *first appeared in 1790, redirected himself to an attack on Burke and a defence of the new French Constitution.*

Such was the purpose of Rights of Man, *part 1, published in February 1791, and followed in February 1792 by part 2 which more directly disputed the extravagant claims Burke had made on behalf of the Hanoverian constitution of England. Paine's work met with a mixed reception: 'Have you seen Mr. Paine's answer to Mr. Burke?' wrote Joseph Priestley to his fellow-member of the Birmingham Lunar Society, Josiah Wedgwood, 'it is most excellent, and the boldest publication I have seen.'[3] Christopher Wyvill, on the other hand, wrote in alarm in 1792, 'If Mr. Paine should be able to rouze up the lower classes their interference will probably be marked by wild work, and all we now possess, whether in private property or public liberty, will be at the mercy of a lawless and furious rabble.'[4]*

'Respectable' opinion seems to have settled in favour of the latter sentiments. The government may have attempted, unsuccessfully, to interfere with the publication of part 1, and almost certainly did try to prevent the appearance of part 2. Proceedings were commenced against J. S. Jordan, the publisher of part 2, who pleaded guilty, and on 21 May 1792 new proceedings were begun against Paine himself. On the same day a Royal Proclamation was issued against 'divers wicked and seditious writings'. The timing of this indicates the importance which Paine's work was beginning to assume in the official mind. Soon he was to be identified with the spread of popular societies in London, and elsewhere, at which the events in France were hailed, and renewed demands made for reforms at home to establish the rights of man (Docs. 1, 2).

Paine was not present at his trial. In September he went to France to take his seat in the Convention, to which he had been elected by the Pas de Calais. Just before his departure he had issued his parting shot, A Letter addressed to the Addressers on the late Proclamation, *his most outspoken republican work, in which he denounced the corruption of the government and its legal system, and appealed openly to the people of England to take affairs into their own hands through the calling of a National Convention based on male adult suffrage.*

Next to Rights of Man, *Paine's most influential book among his nineteenth-century British followers was the* Age of Reason, *written in Paris between 1793 and 1795. This work was originally intended to maintain the religion of pure deism in the face of materialistic atheism (part 1) and superstitious Christianity (part 2). Neither part was strikingly original, but its power, like that of* Rights of Man, *lay in its forthright, unambiguous and rather impious tone. Paine had as much respect for the Christian religion as he had for the British constitution, and the ridicule to which he exposed both proved to be popular.*

These writings were first disseminated in a rather unreal atmosphere of heady enthusiasm among some radicals, and unfounded panic among many men in positions of authority. The year 1793 brought the Terror to Paris and war between England and France. Radical societies multiplied, and grew more extreme as bread prices rose in 1795. Secret Committees of the House of Commons looked out for, and therefore saw, treasonable conspiracy about to break out everywhere, and laws were passed accordingly (Docs. 2, 3). A minority of Whigs, led by Fox and Sheridan, pointed out that there was nothing wrong which the reform of abuses would not put right and that the government was becoming the victim of its own illusions, but to no avail. Habeas Corpus *was suspended in 1794, while the London Corresponding Society, which was chiefly responsible for propagating Paine's works, went from strength to strength. Much to the government's dismay Thomas Hardy and other leading members of the L.C.S. were actually acquitted of treason by a jury in the autumn of 1794.*

The year 1795 saw the peak of radical success. Thereafter, stringent government measures, the collapse of revolutionary idealism, and a fall in the price of bread weakened the radical societies. Extremist elements (many of whom were Irish) moved in and frightened both English radicals and the government. Neither need have feared for the violent fringe of Anglo-Irish radicalism was small and uninfluential. Paine's Rights of Man *had been against the British 'constitution' only because there was no such thing. Radicals of the Paineite school wanted to be citizens – law-abiding ones – and the persistent constitutionalism of British radicalism suggests both the nature of Paine's appeal and its relative ineffectiveness. In the face of a government which at national and local levels was determined to suppress any 'treasonable conspiracy', most men put aside their views against the time when they might again be more easily held. A few lonely martyrs remained, like Daniel Isaac Eaton, the printer who in 1793–4 had issued a version of* Rights of Man, *part 2, the* Address to the Addressers, Hog's Wash *and* Thelwall's *speeches, and who returned from self-impose exile in America to publish and be pilloried for publishing the so-called* Age of Reason, *part 3, in 1812. But such men were not to lead an English revolution. Just how many copies of Paine's works had been circulated is difficult to estimate. The contemporary guess of 200,000 copies of* Rights of Man *sold by 1793 is totally unsubstantiated. If there were so many, then few survived even into the early nineteenth century. Some may have been burnt on loyalist bonfires along with effigies of Paine; some may have been disposed of by frightened radicals, aware of the threat of a prosecution or mob violence; and some may have fallen to pieces in a decade of constant usage. Some volumes, however, were preserved, and the ideas expressed in Paine's works were certainly cherished for the coming generation.*

NOTES

1. Ella Twynam, *Peter Annet, 1693–1769* (1938).
2. Manchester Central Library, Tracts 335.1 B 26.
3. Quoted in B. Simon, *Studies in the History of Education, 1780–1870* (1960) p. 64.
4. Quoted in E. P. Thompson, *The Making of the English Working Class* (1965) p. 24.

1   The polarisation of opinion, 1792*

In its summary of the History of Europe for the year 1794, the Annual Register *recalled the impact which Paine's work had made and the manner in which popular politics had thereafter developed. These events formed the background to the Common's decision to set up a Committee of Secrecy on Seditious Practices in 1794, which resulted in the Act for the suspension of Habeas Corpus.*

The publication of Mr. Burke's sentiments on the French revolution, and the subsequent answer to Mr. Paine, in his celebrated performance, styled the Rights of Man, were the first signals to the ministerial and the popular parties in this country, to engage in that violent and acrimonious contest, which is not yet terminated. These two famous performances revived, as it were, the royal and republican parties that had divided this nation in the last century, and that had lain dormant since the Revolution in 1688. They now returned to the

* From 'History of Europe', *Annual Register* (1794), pp. 266–8.

charge with a rage and animosity equal to that which charac-
terized our ancestors during the civil wars in the reign of King
Charles the First; and it remained a long time in suspense,
whether this renewed contest would not be attended with the
same calamities: so eager were the partizans of the respective
tenets contained in those performances, to assert them with
unbounded vehemence.

Among those who publicly and unequivocally maintained
the doctrines contained in the publication styled the Rights of
Man, were all the popular societies in the three kingdoms. The
book written by Mr. Burke was chiefly patronized by the upper
classes. But this, instead of intimidating the lower, served
rather to rouze them to dangerous enquiries into the nature of
that superiority claimed over them by those very classes. Thus,
the dispute between the higher and the lower orders became
every day more virulent, and threatened very serious consequences. It was not however till the middle of 1792, that government took any formal notice of those transactions. They then
issued a proclamation against seditious meetings; which,
instead of preventing the reading of that performance, against
which it was chiefly levelled, the Rights of Man, contributed to
its dissemination throughout every part of Great Britain and
Ireland, and gained it more readers and proselytes than ever. In
the course of that year, the events that had happened in France
so much alarmed government, that it was thought necessary to
counteract the societies in this country, by opposing to them
other societies, on principles wholly contradictory to theirs.
With this view were instituted the associations against republicans and levellers. But these, associations, tho' numerous, and
composed of the genteeler parties in society, did not deter their
still more numerous antagonists. These continued resolutely to
act on the plan they had primarily adopted, and to manifest a
spirit of resistance to their new opponents; which afforded sufficient ground of alarm to the friends of domestic tranquillity.
Government in the mean time kept a watchful eye on the proceedings of the popular societies. These continued to hold their
meetings as usual, and to declare their sentiments with unlimited freedom. In some of those meetings, however, they exceeded the bounds of discretion so far as to use expressions that
laid them open to the charge of sedition: but the circumstance

which principally rendered them obnoxious was, the regular correspondence they had established with the many societies in the kingdom acting on their own principles; but chiefly the intimate communication they held with the convention that assembled in Scotland, and to which they sent deputies to represent them; intending shortly to summon a convention in England on the same plan, and composed of the deputies from all the societies established in this part of the united kingdoms.

But after the trial and sentence passed on the principal leaders in the Scottish convention, government, it seems, resolved to pursue the same measures respecting the English societies. To this end the principal members of the Corresponding Society, and of that for constitutional information, were apprehended as guilty of treasonable practices, and committed to the Tower. Their names were Thomas Hardy, secretary to the Corresponding Society; Daniel Adams, secretary to the Society for Constitutional Information; the celebrated Horne Tooke; Jeremiah Joyce, domestic tutor to Lord Mahon, son to Lord Stanhope; and John Thelwall, well known as a political lecturer.

On the 12th of May, a message from the King was delivered to the House Commons by Mr. Dundas, informing them that seditious practices had been carried on by societies in London, in correspondence with other societies, to the intent of assembling a convention to represent the people of England, in defiance and opposition to Parliament; and on principles subversive of the laws and constitution of the kingdom, and introductory of the anarchy prevailing in France. Their papers had been seized, and would be laid before Parliament; to which it was recommended to examine them, and to adopt such measures as might appear necessary. They were produced accordingly on the next day; when Mr. Pitt moved an address of thanks to the King, for the communication received, and proposed that the papers should be referred to a committee of secrecy, consisting of twenty-one members, chosen by ballot. The report of this committee was produced to the House by Mr. Pitt on the 16th of May. It contained the proceedings of the two societies, from the year 1791: most of which, however, had been already published in the newspapers by the societies themselves.

2 The Committee of Secrecy, 1794.*

The Committee was in no doubt of the close connection between the popular societies and the ideas of Paine's Rights of Man *which, having already been proved seditious, was held to demonstrate the truly seditious purpose of the popular societies.*

In this pamphlet, published in the year 1791, the National Assembly of France was represented as occupied in establishing a constitution founded on the rights of man, and the authority of the people, the only authority on which (it was stated) government had a right to exist in any country; monarchy and hereditary succession were treated as absurdities; the revolution of 1688, and the succession of the House of Hanover, were also made the subject of ridicule; and a distinction was drawn between two modes of government, which were stated to prevail in the world: first, government by election and representation; and, secondly, government by hereditary succession. The former generally known by the name of republic, the latter by that of monarchy and aristocracy. On the 23rd March 1791, the society resolved, 'That the thanks of the society should be given to Mr. Thomas Paine, in the terms expressed in the copy of their resolution of this day,' inserted in the Appendix. A continuation of Paine's book, entitled 'Rights of Man, Part the Second, combining Principles and Practice,' was published early in 1792, in which the principles of the British constitution were again attacked; the principles on which the French constitution, accepted by the king in 1791, had been established, were approved, with an exception of the hereditary succession of the crown: this pamphlet, recommending the overthrow of the British constitution and the establishment of a democratic senate, as the sole legislative and executive power of the state, was also circulated with great industry: and the Society for Constitutional Information, on the 16th of March 1792, expressed their approbation of the work, in answer to a letter from the Manchester Constitutional Society,

* From the Second Report from the Committee of the House of Commons respecting Seditious Practices, 6 June 1794; from *Cobbett's Parliamentary History*, vol. XXXI, cols 709–10, 716–17.

containing the thanks of that society to Mr. Paine. On the 23rd of March, 1792, the Constitutional Society at Sheffield applied to the London Society, that twelve of their members might be admitted as associated members of the London Society; and there appears in the books of the London Society a printed paper of the Sheffield Society, in which that society declares, that the practice as well as the principle of government was laid down in the works intituled, 'Rights of Man, Part the First and Second,' in a manner so clear and irresistibly convincing, that the society resolved to give their thanks to Mr. Paine for those publications.

Other entries, expressive of approbation of the same works, and of other seditious publications, frequently appear in the same books during the course of the year 1792. . . .

The London Corresponding Society was instituted in January 1792. A general account of the plan according to which it was formed and distributed into different divisions has already been given in the last report; and a list of the number of divisions, which had been gradually established, has been found among the papers in the possession of the secretary.

In one of the first communications from the London Corresponding Society to the society for Constitutional Information they state that 'The delegates of the Corresponding Society think it their duty to acquaint the Constitutional Society without delay, of the subscription begun amongst several of their divisions for the defence of the prosecution said to be commenced against that worthy member of the Constitutional Society, Mr. Thomas Paine, in consequence of his valuable publication, intituled, "The Rights of Man," and that they had no doubt that a numerous body would be found to follow an example, so just in itself, and so essential to the support of that small portion of liberty which the people of England are still supposed to enjoy.'

3 Another view of the conspiracy*

Not all politicians were willing to accept this report, though, and a min-

* Sheridan's speech in the resumed debate on the suspension of Habeas Corpus, 'History of Europe', *Annual Register* (1795) p. 156.

*ority of Whigs continued to fight the policies of the government. Early in
1795 R. B. Sheridan moved that the Act suspending Habeas Corpus be
repealed. He lost his motion by 41 votes to 185, but his arguments served to
cut the government's fears down to size.*

On the 5th of January, the discussion on the suspension of
the habeas corpus act was resumed by Mr. Sheridan. The
preamble to that suspension stated that a dangerous and treasonable conspiracy existed in this country; but a verdict in
court had shewn this conspiracy to be a mere fabrication of
ministers, who had exercised an illegal influence over the grand
jury, that found the indictment against the parties accused. He
severely animadverted on the expression of acquitted felons,
used by Mr. Windham, in the preceeding debate, as scandal-
ously misapplied. The parties had undergone the strictest trial,
and no pains had been spared to criminate them. Eight thousand pounds had been paid to the crown-lawyers, and no less
than two hundred witnesses had been procured against one
alone, at a vast expence. He strongly ridiculed the epithet of formidable, bestowed on the supposed conspiracy; the strength
and preparations made by which, he jocularly stated, as consisting of an arsenal furnished with one pike and nine rusty
muskets, and an exchequer containing nine pounds and one
bad shilling. These were the ways and means with which the
conspirators proposed to overturn the government of Great
Britain.

4 The infidel metropolis *

*A similar impact was observed of Paine's Age of Reason, which was
prosecuted for blasphemy in 1797. Although infidelity was probably never
so widely popular as political radicalism, it certainly seems to have been
endemic among the anti-clerical members of the popular societies. The
exposure of this was the aim of W. H. Reid who, writing in 1800 when he
thought the worst was over, gave this colourfully biased version of the
events of the 1790s.*

* From W. H. Reid, *The Rise and Dissolution of the Infidel Societies* . . . (1800) pp.
5–7, 8–9, 15–16.

It is still fair to admit, that the adoption of Paine's Age of Reason was not agreed, to in the London Corresponding Society, without considerable opposition, especially in the general committee; but as zeal superseded judgment, in their discussions upon the subject, the epithets of d–m–d fool, and d–m–d Christian, ultimately prevailed; and a bookseller was soon persuaded, by the heads of the party, to undertake a cheap edition of the Age of Reason, for its more ready dissemination through the divisions, at that time rapidly increasing in number every week: but after Williams, the bookseller just alluded to, was imprisoned for this publication, his family received much less assistance from the society, than from mere strangers.

In the hour of its admiration, this rhapsody was ridiculously termed the *New Holy Bible*; a circumstance which fully evinced the intentions of Mr. Paine's partizans: in fine, the attachment of the party was carried so far, that the bare circumstance of having the Age of Reason in a house, was deemed a collateral proof of the *civism* of the possessor.

It may be urged, that this conduct of the society was never justified by any act of the body at large: this is granted; but when it is considered, that their inclination for deism was sufficiently powerful to occasion a schism, which produced a *new society*, under the denomination of the *Civil* and *Religious*; it follows, that the preponderance of a party, in the original body, was equal to a decision of the whole, and fixes the charge of a partiality to infidelity, beyond the possibility of a doubt.

If farther proofs were wanting, I might urge the circumstance of the establishment of a test, by the newly formed body, in which, each member acknowledged the *belief of the Holy Scriptures, and that Christ is the Son of God*; and this as a necessary qualification for their admission. This fact alone, I presume, would be sufficient for my purpose; to which may be added, that Bone and Lee, two seceding members, and booksellers by profession, were *proscribed* for refusing to sell Volney's Ruins, and Paine's Age of Reason; and that refusal construed into a censure upon the weakness of their intellects. Still, nothing like a miraculous conversion of the London Corresponding Society is to be imputed to Mr. Paine's Anti-theological Work. On the contrary, their minds were prepared for this more popular performance, by the more learned and elaborate productions of

Mirabaud's System of Nature, and Volney's Ruins of Empires: the latter, in point of style, is looked upon as the Hervey of the Deists; the former, as the Newton of the Atheists: and, as the System of Nature was translated by a person confined in Newgate as a patriot, and published in weekly numbers, its sale was pushed, from the joint motive of serving the Author, and the cause in which the London Corresponding Society were engaged.

Northcote's Life of David was also reprinted in a very small edition; and if this vehicle for degrading the Bible had been better received, it was in agitation to biographize all the leading characters in the Old and New Testaments, as the most certain means of bringing the Christian religion into contempt.

Proposals were circulated for reprinting the whole works of Peter Annet; much being expected from the plainness of his style, and his mode of reasoning against revelation by scriptural quotations; but, owing to the dread of a prosecution, not more than three weekly numbers, at three-halfpence each, made their appearance. The Rights and Duties of Citizenship, most remarkable for copying the blunders of Voltaire, was one of the last things, of this kind, ushered into public view; but being prosecuted, and the publishers sentenced to two years solitary imprisonment, a final stop was put to this mode of promoting scepticism and infidelity.

The Beauties of Deism; A Moral Dictionary; Julian against Christianity; and, lastly, that paragon of French Atheism, LE BON SENS, *Ou Idées Naturelles opposes aux Idées Surnaturelles*, were in agitation to have followed. The latter, for its audacity and virulence, has possibly never been surpassed, . . .

Impregnated with the principal objections of all the infidel writers, and big with the fancied importance of being instrumental in a general reform, almost every division-room could now boast its advocate for the new philosophy. In fact, such a torrent of abuse and declamation appeared to burst from all quarters at once, that as the idea of a *Deist* and a good *Democrat* seemed to have been universally compounded, very few had the courage to oppose the general current. On the other hand, several persons really sacrificed their private sentiments to the public opinion, merely to avoid the contempt every where bestowed upon those who dared to open their mouths in defence of principles and opinions, till then held sacred.

Next to songs, in which the clergy were a standing subject of abuse; in conjunction with pipes and tobacco, the tables of the club-rooms were frequently strewed with penny, two-penny, and three-penny publications, as it were so many swivels against established opinions; while, to enable the members to furnish themselves with the heavy artillery of Voltaire, Godwin, &c. reading-clubs were formed. But still, so it happened, that those who despised the labour of reading, took their creeds implicitly, from the extemporaneous effusions of others, whose talents were comparatively above their own. And yet these people were invariably in the habit of ridiculing Christians, in concert with the orators, for being blindly led by priests.

After these notions of infidelity were in a manner established in the divisions, it is natural to suppose, that in choosing their delegates, those persons were preferred who were doubly recommended by *their religion*, and their politics; in fact, this was so prevalent, that in the recommendation of any person to an office among them, it was common to distinguish him as '*A good Democrat and a Deist.*' Or, to fix the character more strongly, to add, '*That he is no Christian.*' . . .

Still as the reins were then held by government, very little was to be feared from any overt-acts among these descriptions; though, if their temporary ebullitions of zeal could be deemed a fair criterion, this negative obedience might be imputed more to a want of power than of will. Vain glory, and a blind resentment, as silly as it is savage, often hurry men into the wildest extremes. – I am an Atheist! exclaimed one of those persons, and, jumping upon a club-room table; here, said he, holding up an infant, here is a young Atheist! Another, to shew how little he regarded the Bible, observed, at another meeting, 'That just before he came from home, he kicked something before him, and, picking it up, what should it be but an old Bible; that, till then, he did not know he had any such thing in his house!' A third philosopher, censuring the present mode of education, observed, 'There would never be any good done, till towns and cities were built without a single church, chapel, or any place of worship, in them!' Another member, being weary of the deliberations at which he was present, exclaimed, '*What signifies our sitting here? let us go and kill all the bl—dy priests!*'

I mention these instances, only as the effects of a party spirit, breathing sentiments by no means natural, but merely forced from the hot-beds of the clubs.

It should be observed, that as apprentices were admitted into these assemblies; and, according to the modern notions of equality, eligible to the chair; so sudden a transition, from domestic inferiority to professional importance, often turned a weak head: and, if the same extremities had been proceeded to as the religious fanatics of the last age were engaged in, the London apprentices might again have distinguished themselves, and the cry of *no king* followed that of *no bishop*, as a natural consequence.

But in hinting at a parallel between modern democratic zeal and the fanaticism of the sixteenth century; of the latter I ought to beg pardon. – A degree of monstrosity, sufficient to make any humanized being shudder, seems to have been reserved for the English Clubbists and *Anti-Religionists* of later times. – I allude to a common toast, which used to be received among them with acclamation, *viz.*

'May the last King be strangled in the bowels of the last Priest ! ! !'

Richard Carlile and the Zetetics

The revival of Paineite radicalism after the conclusion of the French wars in 1815 was initially the work of two men who had been too young to appreciate the events of the 1790s – W. T. Sherwin and Richard Carlile. Sherwin was still a teenager when, having been dismissed from the keepership of the Southwell bridewell for being a follower of Paine, he came to London and set up as a publisher at 183 Fleet Street. Here he issued a Paineite periodical, the Republican *(soon renamed with caution, and an eye on the success of Cobbett's* Weekly Political Register, Sherwin's Weekly Political Register.*) Carlile (1790–1843), a young tinsmith from Devon who had turned to hawking the* Black Dwarf *when unemployed in London, was attracted to Sherwin and on the latter's marriage he took over the publishing business together with legal responsibility for what was sold in the shop.*[1]

Carlile was a bold publisher, and also a shrewd one. When William Hone, an antiquarian bookseller, published a number of witty parodies on the Catechism, Creed and other religious and political themes, Carlile exploited the market by continuing to sell the works while Hone was in prison awaiting trial for blasphemy. As a result, Carlile himself was put in gaol for eighteen weeks until Hone's acquittal removed the cause of his imprisonment. During these weeks Carlile completed his conversion to Paineite views by reading the Age of Reason. *His purpose was now clear, and with Sherwin he began to reprint and reissue the works of his hero.* Common Sense *and* Rights of Man *were published in weekly parts, and the* Age of Reason *appeared in a half-guinea volume in December 1818. The Society for the Supression of Vice (the 'Vice Society'), a private body and successor to the Proclamation Society which had been responsible for the original prosecution of the* Age of Reason *in 1797, grew alarmed and laid charges. These were not, however, taken up until Carlile made himself unpopular with the government after he had published an eye-witness account of the 'Peterloo massacre' in* Sherwin's Weekly Political Register.[2] *Carlile's reaction to these events in the autumn of 1819 was typical: he immediately reverted to the original title of* Republican *for his weekly periodical (Doc. 5), and when subsequently tried on the blasphemy charge he read aloud the whole of the* Age of Reason, *which thereby appeared in the* Proceedings of the Mock Trial *of which 10,000 twopenny numbers were sold. The prosecution had been no more successful than earlier attempts to suppress Paine's works. Carlile was found guilty on several counts, but his works were well-publicised and their circulation increased dramatically (Doc. 10).*

Carlile spent the next six years in Dorchester gaol, but he by no means languished there. The authorities closed his shop in Fleet Street, and when his wife Jane and sister Mary Ann successively reopened it they too were sent to join him in prison. The Republican *continued, despite a rise in price from 2d to 6d following the Blasphemous and Seditious Libels Act (1 January 1820), but in 1821 it too was effectively silenced. Nevertheless the victories of repression were short-lived. Between 1822 and 1824 the agitation was given new life by numerous volunteer shopmen dedicated to keeping open Carlile's 'Temple of Reason' in Fleet Street and publishing his works (including the* Republican *which was recommenced in 1822), and those of Paine, Elihu Palmer (the American deist) and other freethought pioneers (Docs. 6,7). Through the* Republican, *which he edited from his cell, Carlile was able to maintain his control over his followers, to inspire them to emulate his martyrdom, and to encourage little groups of them to form local Zetetic (i.e. free enquiry) societies, the main purpose of which was to encourage the faithful, spread the gospel of infidelity, and collect subscriptions to maintain the cause and its victims (Docs. 8,9).*

These zetetic societies were the first avowedly freethought societies organised on a national scale. Most did not last long. They were linked only by their reports in the Republican, *and possibly by some local hero who had gone to Fleet Street (and thence to Newgate prison) as a worker in Carlile's cause. But a few survived into the 1830s, and the one at Glasgow had direct linear descendants in the eclectic and secularist societies of the 1860s.[3]*

While in prison, Carlile's religious views became more extreme, and his deism gave way to the atheistic materialism of Mirabaud's (d'Holbach's) System of Nature. *Atheism had been, and was long to continue to be, a less important part of infidelity than anti-clericalism or opposition to orthodox Christian dogmas, but the leaders of the various*

*freethought movements of nineteenth-century Britain were henceforward
to emphasise materialism and atheism. In this respect they were not true
Paineites, though no one seems to have been unduly worried by this. The*
Age of Reason *continued to be a classic of anti-Christian propaganda.*
*Carlile's own atheism did not long survive his release from prison in
November 1825. The end of martyrdom saw a collapse of his cause, and
freedom achieved what prosecution had failed to: the* Republican *closed
at the end of 1826, and Carlile's other publishing plans of that year met
with equally little success.*

*At this point in his fortunes he became aware of the Reverend Robert
Taylor (1784–1844), a clergyman who had been converted to deism by a
reading of Voltaire.*[4] *Carlile began to publish items by Taylor in the*
Republican *in 1824, and he also gave notices of Taylor's deistical
'Christian Evidence Society', though he deplored the ban on materialism at
the society's meetings. Taylor was a pure deist, and Carlile viewed his
proceedings with mixed feelings: 'Such trash as this new liturgy,' he wrote
in 1826, 'is not instructive, is hypocritical, must be read without emphasis
and effect in such a place, and is a disgrace to the other pretensions of Mr.
Taylor and his flock. . . . But Mr. Taylor, in the pulpit of his chapel,
becomes a very different man. Here he was listened to with delight. Here he
said nothing about Almighty God; nothing about Sun, Moon, or stars.'*[5]
*But soon these religious trappings were to begin to appeal to Carlile him-
self.*

*The imprisonment of Taylor for blasphemy in 1828 convinced Carlile
that he and Taylor were working in the same cause, and the two men became close friends and allies. Carlile's latest journal, the* Lion, *gave
Taylor a mouthpiece, and through it they sought to revive the zetetic movement (Doc. 11). In 1827 Carlile had made a provincial lecture tour on
which he had met the Lancashire infidel, Rowland Detrosier, who
'breathes and preaches the doctrines of the immortal Paine', according to a*
Republican *correspondent from Stockport.*[6] *Detrosier was a deist like
Taylor, who had been converted to zeteticism in a debate with his local society in Stockport. He had allowed Carlile the use of the Brinksway
Chapel, which belonged to the Swedenborgians and of which he held the
pulpit. For this he lost his tenancy, and was released for a brief but
influential life of activity among zetetic and radical societies in the Manchester area. In 1829 Carlile and Taylor resolved to go on a new 'infidel
mission' to these faithful followers. The latter proved to be less numerous
than had been hoped, but the new towns of the textile districts provided
some good audiences: 'In Leeds and Manchester,' wrote Carlile, 'we have*

been but ill supported in the project', but of Stockport he reported, 'There is much more Infidelity here than either at Leeds or Manchester', and the reception at Huddersfield was similarly gratifying.[7]

The centre of gravity of popular radicalism had begun to move. Although London continued to be important as the political centre and main source of finance for popular movements, the provinces had begun to undergo dramatic social changes between the days of Paine and his revival by Carlile. Industrial villages had grown into thriving towns; workshops were giving way to factories; handloom weavers were losing their living, and skilled factory spinners were finding a new one. New communities, thriving with chapels, clubs and mutual improvement societies were coming into being (Doc. 28). 'Without disparagement to the London working men, who have qualities of their own,' wrote the Owenite socialist, Lloyd Jones, in 1867, 'it is certain that almost, if not quite all, great movements affecting the [working] class have had their origin in the provinces.'[8]

Nevertheless the political importance of London brought Carlile back to base during the reform crisis of the early 1830s. He took out a lease on the Rotunda lecture theatre in Blackfriars, making it a centre for his own and Taylor's infidelity, and also hiring it out to other radical groups such as the National Union of the Working Classes. Here Taylor set up as the 'Devil's Chaplain' (as Henry Hunt called him), expounding his weekly astrologico-theologico theories of comparative religion, and roundly denouncing Christianity to the great amusement and entertainment of his audiences. He was soon back in prison, for two years, in July 1831.[9]

By this time Carlile too was in detention, this time for the political offence of issuing an address to the insurgent agricultural labourers during the 'Swing' riots. With the two leaders out of the way, the mission at the Rotunda passed to John Gale Jones, a veteran of the London Corresponding Society who had returned to radical activity after 'Peterloo' in 1819. He was assisted by 'a lady from the country' who had been attracted to Carlile and Taylor on their visit to Bolton in 1829 (Doc. 11). This lady was Eliza Sharples, known as 'Isis', and Carlile took her as his common law wife on his release in 1833. Taylor also married on release from gaol, and retired to France.

This ought to have been the end of the affair. Taylor had passed from the scene and, although Carlile continued to be active and was again imprisoned in 1834, he too was ceasing to be important. He had managed to quarrel with most other radical leaders and he was opposed to the mainstream of contemporary radical thought. Increasingly mystical in his religious views, he even managed to think of himself as a Christian, despite his unrelenting anti-clericalism and opposition to orthodoxy. Yet the tradition of Paine and its association with the name of Carlile survived, and indeed entered on a new phase in the hands of London artisans, radical newspaper vendors, and one-time members of northern zetetic societies.

NOTES

1. *Republican*, 3 Mar 1820, 14 July 1826.
2. 'Horrid Massacre at Manchester', *Sherwin's Weekly Political Register*, 21 Aug 1819.
3. *National Reformer*, 12 July 1862.
4. For Taylor, see entry in the forthcoming *Biographical Dictionary of British Labour Movements*, ed. J. O. Baylen and N. J. Gossman
5. *Republican*, 11 Aug 1826.
6. Ibid., 14 July 1826; for Detrosier, see G. A. Williams, *Rowland Detrosier, a working class infidel, 1800–34* (York, 1965).
7. The full mission is reported in *Lion*, 29 May–25 Aug 1829.
8. J. M. Ludlow and Lloyd Jones, *Progress of the Working Class, 1832–67* (1867) p. 7.
9. Extracts from the two 'sermons' for which Taylor was imprisoned are in E. Royle, *Radical Politics, 1790–1900* (1971) pp. 107–8.

5 A call to action, 1819*

Carlile was stirred to action in 1819 by the 'Peterloo' massacre which he witnessed and for reporting which he was charged with sedition. Immediately he ended Sherwin's Weekly Political Register *and recommenced under the title of the* Republican. *The first article in the first number was this call to action.*

TO THE PUBLIC

As this cannot be altogether considered a new publication, but merely a continuation of that entitled *"Sherwin's Weekly Political Register*, which has been invariably the bold advocate of the only rational system of Government, namely, the REPUBLICAN; the Editor presumes that he need not make any apology for, or issue a new prospectus of this work, as its title needs no explanation, nor shall its object be disguised. As the honest avowal of sentiment, is becoming daily more danger-

* From *Republican*, 27 Aug 1819.

ous to the Englishman, and the advocates of a full, fair, and equal representation, must inevitably be subject to frequent arrests and imprisonments, whilst the present deficient representation exists, the Editor humbly stands forward to fill the post of danger, ambitious of incurring, (if martyrs must be found) even *martyrdom*, in the cause of liberty. The question of reform is at this moment to be looked at in two points of view, the first is whether there is sufficient virtue to be found in the aristocracy and landed interest of the country to enforce it; or whether the unrepresented, and consequently, the injured part of the community, must rouse and bring into action their strength to bring about that which *must* finally be enforced. I am of opinion that every opportunity has been afforded the former, had they possessed the virtue; and having neglected the opportunity, or rather having shewn a want of feeling altogether in the cause, the latter are imperatively called upon immediately to unite, to rally their strength; and I have no doubt but they will be found sufficiently formidable to carry the measure, with very little obstruction.

In the words of our famous countryman, our great and only prototype, THOMAS PAINE, we might say, "these are the times that try men's souls." The editor, impressed with the importance of the moment, has resolved, that no correspondence or essays be admitted into the pages of the *Republican*, unless accompanied, with the real name and address of the author. In doing this, he is aware that he will exclude much talent, but the necessity of every man making a frank and candid avowal of his principles and sentiments at the present moment, far exceeds any other feelings that may be put in competition with it. He hopes that there are to be found in the country, men, not only of talent, but with sufficient property and virtue to render them men of importance and weight in society, who dare openly avow what they think necessary to be done. Most periodical publications of the day, are filled with anonymous essays, correspondence and information on various subjects, which are as many proofs of a degree of talent existing in the country, equal, or superior, to any former period; but, it cannot be denied, that those essays, &c. would produce more effect and conviction, were they signed by some individual, whose motives and moral character are unimpeachable. In noticing the talent of the age, a painful reflection occurs, that it has invariably happened in those countries which have been brought to the verge of destruction by misrule, that the greatest talents and virtues have been produced. It is the misery, which ignorant, imbecile, and wicked rulers, bring on a country, that draws forth the natural energies of the virtuous mind. It was the conduct of Cæsar, which became so fatal to the liberties of Rome, that produced a CATO. It was the miseries experienced in this country, by the incursions and ravages of the Danes, that produced an ALFRED. It was the tyrannical caprice of Charles the 1st, that produced a HAMPDEN, a LILBURNE, and a CROMWELL; and that of the Second Charles, that produced a RUSSELL, and a SIDNEY. It was the cruel and oppressive conduct of the British Cabinet towards the colonists of North America, that produced a PAINE, a FRANKLIN, and a WASHINGTON. It was the accursed despotism of the ancient regime of France, that produced the talent so very conspicuous during the revolution, which often shone as brilliant as the stars in a clear atmosphere, and was as often buried in the black clouds of anarchy and misrule, until by the efficacy of its superior virtue, it became the sun of Europe, and could never have been clouded, but by the intrigues of the British Cabinet, destroying the resources and happiness of its nation, to goad a Bonaparte to become the victim of his own ambition, and his country's ruin. It is to be hoped, that the germ of revolution is not rooted out of France, but that she will again shake off her fetters, and rescue her character. Indeed it is apparent and evident, that the tree of liberty, which was planted, and which grew and bloomed in France, although its blossom was blasted, yet it has taken a root deep and wide, spreading over the Continent of Europe, a root that will baffle the despot, who attempts to eradicate it. By dwelling on, and illustrating subjects like these, the editor hopes to rouse a unanimous and corresponding feeling among his countrymen, by endeavouring to subvert on the one hand, the evils of anarchy, and on the other, those of despotism. He will studiously point them to that state of society, which produces the greatest benefit to the greatest portion of the community—an equal representation in the legislature. The editor pledges himself that in this publication there shall be found nothing that has a tendency to create dissension among the advocates of a change in the present state of things: to those gentlemen who call themselves moderate in their claims, he would say, I have taken my stand on the rock of republicanism; I will advocate its principles, without looking back to those who do not go so far; and should the breath of calumny be raised, I shall leave it to be dispersed by the passing breeze, conscious that a rectitude of intention will sooner or later find its reward.

R. CARLILE.

Giltspur Street Compter, August, 22, 1819.

6 Carlile's appeal for volunteers*

Following further attacks on Carlile's publishing shop in Fleet Street, and the arrest and imprisonment of his wife, Carlile issued an appeal for volunteer shopmen to continue the war of attrition against the government.

TO THE PUBLIC.

In consequence of the verdict of Guilty given against Mrs. Carlile for selling Sherwin's Life of Paine, and No. 9, Vol. I. of the Republican. She is now liable to banishment by serving in the shop according to our glorious constitution. The business will therefore be managed by Mary Ann Carlile, the sister of R. Carlile, on the behalf of the infant children, or rather on the behalf of the whole family. In case the house—Fleet-street, should again be exposed to the violence of the legal thieves, the business will be opened as near the spot as possible immediately, of which due notice will be given. As this kind of business might be said to be renewed every week, at least, it depends on the periodical publications, we can begin any where with half an hour's preparation, and laugh at the Vice Society, and all the influence they can use against it. If one web be destroyed, a few hours' work will spin another stronger and better than before: This is the only way of meeting the persecuting thieves, and I hope and trust that Mrs. Davison[1] will follow the steps of Mrs. Carlile. If half a dozen persons were resolved successively to oppose the Vice Society, their prosecutions would become of the greatest advantage to the propagation of good principles. I

* From *Republican*, 27 Oct 1820.

will expose every branch of my family, that will listen to my advice, to the venom of this society, with the confidence, that in a few months we shall triumph over them. I have to add, that Mrs. Carlile is quite as composed and unconcerned as I was last year, and I now call upon my sister to perform her part in the same manner. The thieves have the power to shut up 55, but they cannot prevent the opening of 56, so let them go on.[2] Their prosecutions are my joy and comfort, particularly whilst I can see one of my family opposed to them. For my own part, I am resolved never to cease, in consequence of any laws that come short of putting to death, in the open avowal and promulgation of such opinions as I conceive to be founded in truth, and the practice of which appear to me to be conducive to the interest of society. It matters nothing to me what another man thinks. I claim the same right to think and speak, and to write what I think, and to publish what I write as he does. I will never truckle to opinions propagated by force and violence because it is *prima facie* acknowledgment that they are founded in falsehood and cannot bear the scrutiny of a rational criticism. I contend that there is no necessity for laws to regulate opinions in society; a diversity of opinion with mutual toleration will form the most stable base of its well being. But when we see men crushing the propagation of certain opinions, because the opposite are productive of profit to them, it is no longer society, but a nest of robbers who prey upon the weaker part. However I shall hope to see the imprisonment of Mrs. Carlile and Mr. Davison produce half a dozen new shops in the same line.

R. CARLILE.

Dorchester Gaol, Oct. 18, 1820.

NOTES

1. Thomas Davison (or Davidson), editor of the *Medusa, Cap of Liberty* and several popular translations from the French classics (see Doc. 48). He was indicted in 1820 for selling the *Deist* and the *Republican* and imprisoned for two years.
2. Carlile had moved from 183 to 55 Fleet Street in January 1819.

7 The response*

The response to this appeal, which was renewed in 1822, was considerable. Volunteers came to work in the Fleet Street shop and, despite numerous arrests, kept the business open. The following account is not entirely accurate in detail, but it conveys the spirit of the campaign.

THE PEOPLE'S FIRST STRUGGLE FOR FREE SPEECH AND WRITING.

LED BY RICHARD CARLILE. IN WHICH THEY WERE COMPLETELY SUCCESSFUL.

THE writer hereof was one of those who took a prominent part in the struggle, and he writes because no one has given any account who were the individuals that took the responsible part in keeping open the House in Fleet Street; and by that means assisted Mr. Carlile in his arduous task against despotism.

I will give as correct an account as memory will enable me to do. There may be several things that have escaped me. I shall commence at the time when Miss Mary Ann Carlile was imprisoned. Calling, as I usually did, on a Saturday evening, I found her in great trouble, when I inquired 'what was the cause of her trouble?' Her answer was, that 'next week she was to surrender, to receive sentence of the Court, and be imprisoned. Then the House in Fleet Street would be closed, and they would be starved in prison.' It struck me forcibly that this would most probably be their fate, knowing the apathy that generally follows after a person gets into prison. It completely staggered me for the moment, that I hardly knew how to answer, for I saw that what she anticipated would inevitably be the case. After considering for a minute or two, I asked her if she knew any one that she thought would meet me, at 55, Fleet Street, on the next Monday evening? Her answer was, she thought she knew one. I told her to get him to come, and I would be sure to be there at eight o'clock precisely.

At this time I used to have on a Sunday afternoon a few Atheistical friends to meet at my house, and have tea; and after

* From *Reasoner*, 5 June 1859.

tea we used to read and discuss—in this way we used to amuse ourselves for the evening.

When my friends arrived on the Sunday evening, after I had seen Miss M. A. Carlile, and our tea was over, I informed them in what predicament Mr. Carlile and family stood; and that I thought we ought not to let that be the case; that we should endeavour to keep the House open at all hazards, and do our best towards finding funds for the maintenance of Mr. Carlile and family. After canvassing what would be the best method to proceed, we came to an agreement that we should go to 55, Fleet Street, and four of my friends agreed to call on me on the Monday evening for the furtherance of our object.

On the Monday evening we met according to promise. These are the names of those who met: B. B. Jones, John Hawes, Joseph Trust, Thomas Evans, and William Ethel, when we proceeded to 55, Fleet Street, where we met three more—thus making eight. We then formed ourselves into a committee, for the purpose of aiding Mr. Carlile. The following are the names of the persons we met at 55, Fleet Street—W. Henman, P. Phillips, the other name I have forgotten; the only thing I recollect is, he had a wooden leg. Our first act was to get two books—one for the purpose of entering any rules that we might think requisite; and the other to enter the subscriptions in. After we settled our rules, the next thing was the person that should take charge of the House and business.

Mrs. Susannah Wright volunteered to take charge of the House, and attend to the business at all risk, and we, on our part, agreed to support her; and this finished our first meeting.

On the next Monday evening we met again. This evening we agreed to call a public meeting, to have some placards printed for that purpose, and to get John Gale Jones to be our spokesman. I being acquainted with him, undertook to see him, and get him to attend: I saw him, and he met our views.

Our first meeting was held at the Paul's Head, Cateaton Street, City, which was very well attended. J. G. Jones at that time was a first-rate orator, and he made the building ring in pointing out the barbarity and cruelty of the Carlile sentence of imprisonment and fine, which amounted to imprisonment for life, showing that the Government robbed him of his property, and thereby left him no means to pay the unjust fine. Mr.

Henman followed; he was one that had got a good deal to say. These two took up the whole evening. The rest of the committee were busy collecting the money. There was a good collection, considering the shortness of the notice.

The next week we met as usual, then it was canvassed what was to be done with the money. One of our party proposed that we should take all monies collected, and allow Mr. Carlile what we thought would be a sufficiency for him to live on. This I opposed, and proposed that we should hand over all monies to Mr. Carlile, or to any person he might think proper to appoint. This was agreed to. (After this we did not see anything more of our wooden-leg friend.) Our friend Henman was deputed to write to Mr. C., and inform him what we had done, and to know what he would have done with the money. We got for answer that we should hand it over to his printer, and his signature should be our acquittal.

Thus we went on meeting every Monday evening, without much interruption—excepting a stone coming through the window at us now and then, till there was but few squares of glass left whole; and, as they were not repaired, they found that the throwers were no annoyance to us, so they left that off.

One evening when we were assembled, in walked the parish beadle in his full dress of office, followed by several gentlemen. One of the party wished to know what we were doing there? This was left to our friend Henman to answer, which was simply that we were collecting subscriptions for Mr. Carlile and family, incarcerated. After examining our books, they took their leave, and we had no further molestation from the authorities for some time.

Mr. Carlile had formed a plan to sell the books down a spout, so that the person purchasing the books could not see the person that sold them. In this way it was accomplished:—There was a little door on the counter, which the person wanting a book had to rap at, when the door opened, and the purchaser asked for the book which he wanted. Then a small bag was lowered down for the money. When it was drawn up, the book with the change—if any was required—was lowered down to the purchaser. By this system the informers were baffled; and Mr. C. was enabled to carry on his business, and also to collect subscriptions from the different parts of the

country direct, without passing through the hands of the committee, which was of essential service to him, in case of his shop
being closed. In this way his business was carried on for some
time; and the Government, with the 'Bridge Street Gang,' as
they were called, were thus foiled, till at length the Government
made a seizure; and by that means closed the House, 55, Fleet
Street. But this was but of short duration, for we found another
house not far from the other, which I took in my name. I saw the
landlord, and agreed to take the house. I gave him reference to
the landlord that I was then living under, which was so far satisfactory that he accepted me as his tenant. When I had got possession, I let the first floor to Mr. Carlile, when Mrs. S. Wright
took her abode there, and Mr. Carlile's business was carried on
as usual.

While I retained possession of this house, I was summoned as
a juryman on the petty sessions at Guildhall. Of course I
attended, and went through the regular routine, and made one
of the twelve to hear, and give verdicts with what seemed to give
the Judge satisfaction; for he thanked us for the way we had
given them, little knowing that one was an Atheist.

Mrs. S. Wright, the first victim after Miss Mary Ann Carlile,
was taken, and was for several weeks confined in Newgate,
where I used to visit her three or four times a week;[1] and I took
care she should have a hot dinner every Sunday. This was done
by getting a joint of meat, and putting it down to a brisk fire,
and scorching the outside, so that it had the appearance of
being well done, when she cut the outside off, and had it roasted
over again, which a shilling or two would always accomplish.
This I managed till she was liberated.

When Mr. Carlile got possession of the house in Fleet Street,
then commenced a regular struggle, for no sooner did a person
stand behind the counter in the shop, than he was taken to
Newgate. We had one week seven taken, and lodged in Newgate. I had to get them some blankets. This was on a Saturday.
At this time I was in Newgate every other day. Sometimes the
man at the door would refuse me entrance: I had then to go to
Mr. Wontner's office. I used to stand no parley with the men,
but go directly to the office, and knock at the door, when it used
to be, 'Come in,' and I opened the door and went in. 'Well,
Jones, what is the matter now?' 'Your man at the door, sir,

won't let me pass to see such a person (mentioning his name).'
'Oh, he won't,' he used to say; then Mr. Wontner used to write
on a slip of paper. 'Give him that.' I used to be often stopped,
but that was of little consequence, as I was sure to get an order
to pass from the Governor. At this time I was in Newgate three
and four times a week, so that I was well known there.

When any of the shopmen were taken, I was generally sent
for to communicate with them, and to get them anything that
they wanted.

The Society for the Suppression of Vice[2] (or, more properly,
the upholders of vice) found that their funds would not support
the number of prosecutions which Mr. Carlile gave them to do,
that they were obliged to give over taking up any more of his
shopmen, although there were such men as Wellington, Lord
Kenyon, and others, included in the Vice Society. Powerful and
wealthy individuals, even their purses would not put down one
man, because he had the thinking men on his side; and then
there was a stop put to the taking up any more of the shopmen.

After several delays from one cause or another, the trial of the
first victim after Miss M. A. Carlile, was the heroic Mrs. Susannah Wright.

On the morning of the trial, Mrs. S. Wright, myself, Mrs.
Jones, and Mrs. W.'s children, went from my house, and
entered the Court, together with some more friends. When
called upon, Mrs. W. answered, and I attended her to the dock;
and I had permission to enter with Mrs. W. for her assistance.
When the witness had sworn to the purchase of the pamphlets,
I wrote the questions that Mrs. W. put to the informer. When
this was over, and the usual indictment gone through, Mrs. W.
was then called on for her defence. She commenced in a clear
distinct tone of voice, and went through it with that ease
peculiar to herself.

We had two boys in the dock, seemingly about fourteen
years of age. These boys annoyed Mrs. W. by making wry
faces at her, and when she complained of them, they were not
removed. When Mrs. W. arrived at some parts of her defence,
the Judge would mildly stop her, with 'Really, Mrs. Wright,
we cannot sit here, and let you go on.' After the Judge had
done, I used to point out to her where to commence again, so as
not to be stopped in her defence, as our object was to get as

much of the defence delivered as possible, and by this means we accomplished it. In one of these stoppages by the Judge, I was standing rather too near to Mrs. W., when the Judge called out, 'Who was that interrupting him?' I directly saw my position, and stepped a yard or so back. There was a bustle in the court by the officers coming forward to take me off, but the Judge put up his hand, and I was allowed to remain. After that, when he stopped her, I took care to be a little distance from Mrs. W., that I might not get into trouble.

When Mrs. W. had read about two-thirds of her defence, I reminded her that it was time she should ask permission of the Court to be allowed time to suckle her infant; and having got permission, we left the Court for a tavern, and got some refreshment; there were about twenty of us. We took half an hour, and then returned into Court to finish the remainder of the defence, which Mrs. W. did in very good spirits.

Now, our next care was to see that she should not be locked up. I gave our friends in the Court a nod, which they understood, and so soon as she had finished her defence, I took up the papers, and Mrs. W. and myself left the dock, and our friends in the Court joined us, and we made the best of our way over Blackfriars Bridge into Surrey, and to my house, where we congratulated Mrs. W. on the bold and clear manner in which she had delivered her defence.

In a few days after her trial, we put in bail for her appearance when called for, to receive the judgment of the Court, which was some time after, when we had notice to produce her in Court; I and other friends attended Mrs. W. to the Court at Westminster, where she received the judgment of the Court. When this was over she then was given over to one of the officers, to be taken to Clerkenwell Prison, to be there confined. I attended her there, and was permitted to see the governor, and made arrangements that I should see Mrs. W. once a week; and that Mrs. Jones should also have the same liberty, as also to bring her children with her, which was granted. Mr. Wright and children found a home at my house, so long as Mrs. W. was in prison, and was taken care of by Mrs. Jones, till Mrs. W. came out of prison. When that time arrived, she then lived with her husband so long as he lived.

B. B. JONES.

NOTES

1. Jones seems here to have been mistaken. Mary Ann Carlile was tried on 24 July 1821, and Susannah Wright was not tried until 8 July 1822. In the meantime four shopmen had been convicted, starting with W. V. Holmes on 1 March and John Barkley on 4 March. Mrs Wright was a Nottingham lace-mender.
2. This is an error for the 'Constitutional Association for opposing the Progress of Disloyal and Seditious Principles' (the 'Bridge Street Gang'), founded in December 1820.

8 The Edinburgh Zetetic Society*

Freethinking or Zetetic societies were formed to support Carlile and to propagate his views – the first of them at Edinburgh, founded in December 1821 – and the Republican *each week contained letters of support and subscription lists. On one occasion Sheffield also sent some local produce.*

TO MR. R. CARLILE, DORCHESTER GAOL.

Edinburgh, Dec. 12, 1821.

DEAR SIR,

To prevent any approach to sectarianism, we have denominated ourselves the Edinburgh Freethinkers' Zetetick Society, and we are resolved to support you as far as our abilities will admit. We have also adopted a new and regular plan of conducting our meetings on Sunday, which I think bids fair to succeed. As many of our members as choose, and who consider themselves qualified, produce an essay or a lecture in succession each Sunday, on any subject they think proper, and we have already had some excellent discourses delivered before us; then, as soon as the essay or lecture is over, the member that delivered it comes from the chair, which is immediately taken by the persons who read the Sunday before, and who acts as president for that day, then all the members of the Society have liberty to address the president and comment upon what was delivered, and after they have made their observations; the person that read the essay or lecture makes his reply, after which the president offers his observations, and closes the proceedings of that day. As I mentioned to you before we have a library of good books; and intend to purchase a pair of globes

* From *Republican*, 18 Jan 1822.

and an orrery as soon as our funds will admit, and probably at no very distant period, we may become a large scientific society; and I am persuaded, that if people of our opinions would form themselves into societies of the same kind throughout the country, it would be a proper means of uniting them, and be attended with the most happy results; as both women and children might attend as well as men.

[James Affleck]

9 Presents from Sheffield*

TO MR. R. CARLILE, DORCHESTER GAOL.

DEAR SIR,   Sheffield, Oct. 8, 1823.
Be pleased to accept the inclosed presents as tokens of our respect for you and your family, and
I remain yours, &c.,
T. TURTON.

A Reticule from W. Lindley, for M. A. Carlile.
A Penknife with sixteen blades* for R. Carlile from Adam Renwick.
One Case of Razors and Ivory Folder for R. Carlile, from T. Turton.
And a double blade Stag Penknife for W. Campion, from T. Turton.
One Pair of Scissors for Jane Carlile, from Charles Ward.

* Each of these blades has a name on it—and are as follows:—Copernicus—Galilei—Newton and Herschell—Mirabaud—Palmer—Stewart and Lawrence—T. Paine—C. I. Volney—W. Cobbett and R. Carlile—Mrs. Wright—Jane Carlile—M. A. Carlile and Hypatia[1].

NOTE

1. Hypatia was a pagan philosopher of Alexandria who was torn to pieces by Christians in A.D. 415 – *Mosheim's Institutes of Ecclesiastical History* (revised ed. 1860) p. 126. (*Mosheim* was first published in 1737–41 and was a favourite source book for freethinkers.) Carlile and Eliza Sharples named their elder daughter, born 1830, after her, and Charles Bradlaugh named his elder daughter after Carlile's.

* From *Republican*, 24 Oct 1823.

10 The power of the press *

Carlile's power lay in the printing press. By this means he was able, even from prison, to maintain his cause and publicise the ideas associated with the name of Paine. His own assessment of his work, though a little exaggerated, is not far from the truth.

TO MR. JOHN HEYES, BOLTON, LANCASHIRE.

Dorchester Gaol, October 26th, 1822,
CITIZEN,   of the fabled Carpenter's Wife's Son.
AFTER returning my thanks to the Republicans of Bolton for this their third subscription, I wish to enliven you a little upon the certain power and progress of the Printing Press. You observe justly, that it has been established for centuries, and that it has done but little yet towards rooting out all constrained idolatry. This is true, but recollect, the little that has been done, has been done within the last thirty years; and within the last four years in this country more has been done than during the whole period of the establishment of the Printing Press before that time. Thomas Paine's "Age of Reason" was the first serious and honest attack ever made upon the Christian Idolatry in this country. Many sneers and jeers were passed upon it, from the time of what is called the glorious Revolution of this country, down to the close of the last century; but nothing like a serious attack until the first part of the "Age of Reason" appeared. The works of Annett, Chubb, Morgan, Gordon, Collins, Tindal, Toland, Bolingbroke, and all the half measured Deists of the last century, had left little or no impression in the country; so that when the "Age of Reason" appeared, it was received as a perfect novelty by the great body of the people. There have been a number of Atheists and Deists in this country among the educated part of the people ever since the reign of Elizabeth, but their opinions were never avowed through the Printing Press, until the Revolution of 1688 had taken place, and after that, but in a very ambiguous manner.

The impressions of the Printing Press when made applicable to the progress of truth can never be erased from the public

* From *Republican*, 1 Nov 1822.

mind. Sophistry and falsehood will be sure, sooner or later, to find refutation and rejection, but truth, when once spoken, will stand for ever, and is alike in all ages and to all persons. Every repetition becomes an addition to its force, and every impression of the Printing Press adds to its former power when rightly applied. There is much of sophistry and falsehood yet to be brushed away, but I feel satisfied, that the Press is competent, when worked by the arm of courage, and devoted to the cause of truth and liberty. Just calculate how many persons may read one copy of the "Age of Reason," if it be taken care of. I know several persons, who have kept copies, which they purchased of me in 1819, in constant use, in the way of lending them up to this time, and instances where a single copy has gone through fifty families, all approving as they read. This is the way to calculate the power of the Printing Press. Had the "Age of Reason" kept circulating from its first appearance, as it has within these last four years, it would ere this, have undermined the Christian Idolatry of this country; but it is notorious that it was spell bound for twenty years, with the exception of a few copies put forth by Daniel Isaac Eaton. From December 1818, to December 1822 near twenty thousand copies will have gone into circulation. "Let Corruption rub out that if she can," as Mr Cobbett said of his forty thousand Registers.

The power of the Printing Press progresses arithmetically, it is continually doubling itself, and a free press for a very short period would annihilate all corruption if it was honestly conducted. Be of good cheer, my good friend John Heys, you I hope, will live to see the commencement of a bright era in Europe, and every chain that keeps down human liberty burst asunder.

[Richard Carlile]

11 The 'Infidel Mission'*

After release from gaol, Carlile gradually came to be associated with a renegade clergyman, the Rev. Robert Taylor, and between Taylor's release from Oakham gaol, where he had served a year's imprisonment for blasphemy, in 1829 and Carlile's and then Taylor's next imprisonments in

* From *Devil's Pulpit* (1832).

1831, they worked together on their 'Infidel Mission'. First they toured the provinces, and then leased the Blackfriars Rotunda in London where Taylor established his 'devil's pulpit'. This account is from the preface to the second volume in which Taylor's 'sermons' were published after his imprisonment.

On his return to town, in February, 1829, the Rev. Gentleman officiated a little in the large room of Mr. Carlile's house, in Fleet-street, and occasionally at the Universalist's Chapel, in Windmill-street, Finsbury-square, preparatory to an infidel mission, through the North of England, with Mr. Carlile. This mission was entered upon in May, and begun at Cambridge[1], by a general challenge to that University, in the most formal and most complete way in which it could be made, to the public defence of the Christian religion. The only answer given to this challenge was, in the persecution of Mr. Smith, of Rose Crescent, the printseller and lodging-house keeper, for lodging the infidel missionaries.

Waiting near a week at Cambridge to no purpose, but with some threats of personal violence from the members of the University, the mission proceeded to Wisbeach, to Stamford, and to Nottingham, without being able to get standing room under a roof for an audience; but not without formally challenging the priests by a printed circular. From Nottingham, a movement was made to Leeds; and here the fine Music Hall was obtained for one night; but the Mayor interfering, in the least possible offensive way, the use of the hall for the purpose of their discussions could not be continued. Another place was obtained; but it was inconvenient; and on finding that it was to be used on the Sunday, a magisterial interference again took place, and Leeds was left to its superlative bigotry and native darkness, a complete specimen of the prostration of mind to large masses of wealth. From Leeds a movement was made to Bradford and to Manchester, in neither of which places was there any success worthy of mention. Ashton-under-Line and Bolton afforded more game; but at Liverpool the mission was crowned with success and glory, by the Rev. Mr. Thom stepping forward to accept the challenge of the missionaries. Here Christianity, as it is in common practice, was completely put to trial and as completely failed. The mayor (Robinson) blustered forth his magisterial authority, and hunted the engagement for a theatre from place to place, and when the fine room of the shipwrights was at last secured, the Rev. Mr. Thom, after one night's attempt, refused all further invitation to keep his ground. A Unitarian printer of the name of Wright, made a similar attempt, and came on twice, but to little purpose. The agitation of Liverpool has done a deal of good; for it has been the means of bringing forth the 'LADY FROM THE COUNTRY,' who is now about to lecture at the Rotunda. It was the general shrinking of the Christians there that first raised a doubt in her most sincerely religious mind.

From Liverpool the mission proceeded to Wigan, Blackburn, Bury, Hyde, and to Huddersfield, in Yorkshire, having profitably spent some days in Stockport, before going to Liverpool. At Huddersfield a powerful effect was produced, and, after four months' absence from London, and the approach of winter, a return was made to town.

NOTE

1. Taylor was a graduate of St John's College, Cambridge.

12 The tradition continued*

Carlile's achievement had been to establish the tradition of Thomas Paine, and Paine's birthday was to be celebrated among radicals of this school throughout the nineteenth century. In 1823 Allen Davenport contributed this sonnet to the Republican *to mark the occasion.*

POSTSCRIPT.

Britons, hail the bright auspicious day
On which the great immortal Paine was born,
Whose works all future ages shall adorn,
For he has written for eternity!—
When he exhorted nations to be free,
Columbia hailed him with a loud "huzza!"
She cried, "to arms!" her heroes march'd away,
They fought, they bled, they conquered! so must we.[1]

* From *Republican*, 24 Jan 1823.

No more shall kings, Columbia's sons command,
No more oppression there shall be obey'd,
'Tis England now, that feels her iron hand;
But Hope still lives for Paine is not yet dead:—
His voice is heard through all this hapless Isle,
He lives, he breathes, he speaks in R. Carlile.

A. D.

NOTE

1. A reference to the American War of Independence inspired by Paine's *Common Sense* (1776) and *Crisis* papers (1776–83).

Owenism

The most important new development in radical thinking in the 1820s came from the disciples of Robert Owen. His contribution to the shaping of British ultra-radicalism is as important as that of Paine, and in one respect their views were the same: both were hostile to the dangers of superstition; both men were infidels. Richard Carlile, who was otherwise opposed to Owenite socialism, recognised this common ground. He wrote in his Lion *in 1828, 'We cannot see the practical utility of his cooperative system; but we admire the honesty and the general usefulness of the man, on the subject of religion. Mr. Owen has promised to make a very bold attack upon religion, as a universal evil, in this country, on his return. We shall hail that return as a sign of good.'*[1]

This was written while Owen was in America attempting to create a working model of his new moral world at New Harmony. When he returned he held a series of public meetings in London, which confirmed his hold over a section of the artisans of the metropolis. The merits of Owenism were debated in the Lion *and in local zetetic societies. Carlile thought Owenism was a futile example of sectarianism, but others saw it as the positive creed of the new order which would be needed when the old Christian order had been swept away.*[2] *James Simpson of Glasgow had defended Owenism in a paper read to his local zetetic society as early as 1823, and in the personality of Alexander Campbell of Glasgow the two strands of Owenism and zeteticism were to be wedded. Campbell was a leading local Owenite, champion of freethought and a free press, active trade unionist, and radical reformer from the 1820s until his death as a revered father of reform in 1870.*[3]

The primary concern of the Owenites was to demonstrate the great environmentalist truths revealed to them by the Social Father. This was to be done through the creation of communities on the land. Owen himself looked to the government to finance such communities as alternatives to the Poor Law, and the refusal of those in authority to take heed had led him to conclude that they were blinded by their religious superstitions. But while Owen was attempting to create his new social order at New Harmony, working men in London and Brighton, and then in a multiplicity of localities throughout the industrial districts, began to set up co-operative trading stores to raise funds for their own communities. Owen had nothing to do with all this, and indeed despised the co-operators who soon came to sacrifice his great ideal to their own immediate financial ends. In the early 1830s, however, he did begin to think that the trade union movement, especially strong in Manchester, the Potteries and Birmingham, might enable the workers to control sufficient productive and consumptive power, organised through Labour Exchanges, to enable them to by-pass the capitalist system and to introduce the new social system by direct economic action.

This was naturally very appealing, especially to men like the builders who felt threatened by capitalist organisation, but Owen's emphasis on economic as opposed to political action lost him some support. It is doubtful how widespread was the direct appeal of Owen: the Grand National Consolidated Trades Union, which he attempted to impose on the trade unions, was neither long-lasting nor effective.[4]

Far more radicals sympathised with Owen, though, than were prepared to follow him as avowed disciples, only they found other outlets for their views. Leaders of the National Union of the Working Classes, like James Watson, Henry Hetherington and William Lovett, were Owenite co-operators, and these men also took the lead in the radical 'war of the unstamped' in the early 1830s.[5] This campaign for the freedom of the press centred not on Carlile, like that of the 1820s, but on the Owenite Henry Hetherington whose **Poor Man's Guardian** *took the lead in a war of attrition waged against the newspaper stamp. Although Carlile's* **Prompter** *was one of the many unstamped papers issued at this time, he took little part in the general struggle (and he was kept out of the way in prison for two years between 1831 and 1833). The techniques of the campaign, though, were the same: the law was challenged; prison was boldly faced; volunteers kept the work going; and further volunteers stepped forward when they were imprisoned. A number of those involved had previously supported Carlile and Taylor, and some had learned the tricks of their trade in the Carlile battle of the early 1820s. Chief among these was James Watson (Doc. 30).*

With the failure of the trades union and labour exchange movements after 1834, Owen turned to promote a community on English soil with the establishment of his Association of All Classes of All Nations (1835) and National Community Friendly Society (1837 – the two were amalgamated in 1839 to form the Universal Community Society of Rational Religionists, renamed the Rational Society in 1842). The Association of All Classes was not, at first, a great success. In London it made little headway, but from 1837, when a congress was held at the Salford Social Institution at which missionaries were appointed, the movement spread rapidly. Though it at no time matched Chartism in the scale of its activities or the scope of its membership, by 1839 there were sixty branches throughout the country, six of which had over 150 members (London John Street, Salford–Manchester, Huddersfield, Leeds, Birmingham and Stockport).[6] *The audiences at lectures far outnumbered this committed hard-core of members.*

What these members, still less what the wider lecture audiences, wanted from Owenism is difficult to determine. Some undoubtedly looked to the community which was begun at Queenwood Farm, East Tytherley in Hampshire in 1839 as a refuge from the harsh realities of industrial capitalism. But many more seem to have been attracted simply by the community life of the local social institution or hall of science. Here respectable working people, small tradesmen and shopkeepers could find social relaxation in congenial surroundings. The religious could go to their chapels and the non-respectable to their public houses, but it was the Owenites with their tea parties, soirées, *mutual improvement classes and Sunday lectures who provided a sociable and rational alternative to both.*[7]

One of the main attractions of these local Owenite activities was their anti-clerical appeal. Owen had, in 1837, begun the practice in Manchester of debating his views with Christians, and these public gladiatorial contests proved to be very popular. Local Owenites, some of them lacking Owen's self-restraint and boring moderation, responded further to meet this need for public lectures and debates on theological issues (Doc. 15). Partly in response to this, and partly provoking it, a few self-appointed champions of Christianity – most notably John Brindley of Birmingham – appeared to do battle with Owen's social missionaries and local stationed lecturers. The word 'infidel', which in the 1820s had meant a supporter of Carlile, now became synonymous with a follower of Robert Owen (Doc. 71). Clergymen viewed the spread of the new infidel socialism with alarm as halls of science appeared to rival their chapels and churches, particularly in the Manchester area and in parts of the industrial West Riding. Rumours of sexual immorality in socialist communities were circulated and believed.[8] *Seeking an apt phrase to describe Owen at a Church missionary meeting in Manchester, the Reverend Hugh Stowell called him 'the modern apostle of infidelity, the Tom Paine of this day'.*[9]

This was hardly what Owen had intended when he had denounced religion. He was no democrat, and still looked to 'all classes', especially those with political or social influence, or money. Indeed Stowell's attack on him was provoked by the action of the Prime Minister, Lord Melbourne, who had permitted Owen personally to present a petition on socialism to the young Queen. This action also gave the Tory parliamentary opposition its opportunity, and an attack on infidel socialism was mounted in the Lords by Bishop Phillpotts of Exeter in January 1840.[10]

Phillpotts' action was politically motivated, and in so far as it was intended to suppress Owenism it was a failure, but it did give heart to some other local clergymen and their champions. The test case came in Manchester, where Hugh Stowell helped the Reverend J. W. Kidd when the latter found the Owenites building their magnificent new hall of science almost next door to his own church in Campfield.[11] *The consequent legal actions resulted in the local missionary, Robert Buchanan, taking the oath of a dissenting preacher, much to the fury of those Owenites who were unwilling to regard themselves as belonging to a Christian sect.*

The unfavourable turn which public opinion was taking caused a number of leading Owenites, including Owen himself, to regret the more extremist behaviour of some of their lecturers. Christian bigotry was to be defeated by reason, not by anti-Christian bigotry.[12] *Moreover, the Queenwood community was in financial difficulties and if Owen were to have a chance of attracting capital investment he would have to improve the public image of his movement.*

Not all the lecturers were willing to accept either this moderate trend in official policy or Buchanan's decision to take an oath. To some, notably Charles Southwell, this policy seemed like hypocrisy, and to judge by the loss in morale among the branches after 1842, when the missionary structure of the Universal Community Society was dismantled, he was not alone in this opinion. For many the community was secondary to the weekly life of the hall of science, and central to this weekly life was the lecture. In the twelve months ending May 1841, nearly half the 1500 lectures delivered were on religious or ethical subjects. 'Thus we find that much of the time of lecturers and audiences is taken up with the clearing away of errors in religious matters,' noted the editor of the weekly New Moral World. *'These may be attractive according to the past education of the people; but it is to be hoped that the next year's returns will exhibit an increase in the more useful and practical departments.*[13]

Charles Southwell (1812–60)[14] *was not prepared to see the anti-theological side of Owenism played down by hypocrites on the Universal Community Society central board. He had entered the Owenite movement through the Lambeth branch after he had made a reputation for himself as an anti-theological lecturer on Kennington Common. He firmly believed, and many Owenites shared his view, that religion must be destroyed if truth were to prevail: freethought was therefore the necessary prerequisite for socialism, and neutrality on religious issues was impossible.*

Southwell made his break with the Owenites in the autumn of 1841 when he was social missionary in Bristol. With the help of a local member, William Chilton (1815–55), who was a compositor, he started his own weekly paper, the **Oracle of Reason**, in which to advocate downright atheism. *In spirit and in content the* **Oracle** *was a return to the days of Carlile's* **Republican**, *and for an article in number 4 on 'The Jew Book' Southwell was imprisoned for twelve months.*[15] *Officially the Owenites had little sympathy for him, but a number of individual lecturers and members who agreed with him on the necessity of attacking Christianity responded to the lead he had given them (Docs. 14,17). The young stationed lecturer in Sheffield, George Jacob Holyoake (1817–1906), spoke up on Southwell's behalf in a lecture on 'The Spirit of Bonner in the Disciples of Jesus' (December 1841) and, despite the rebuke which this earned him from the central board, he agreed to take over the editorship of the* **Oracle**. *Six months later Holyoake was accused of blasphemy following comments made at a lecture on Home Colonisation which he delivered in Cheltenham, and he was committed at the assizes to six months in Gloucester gaol.*[16] *Another Owenite, Thomas Paterson, filled the editorial breach until he too was imprisoned – for one month in January 1843 for displaying obscene and blasphemous literature in the window of the* **Oracle** *office in Holywell Street; and for fifteen months in November 1843 for selling blasphemous publications in Edinburgh. The masthead of the* **Oracle** *began to look like a police gazette.*

The tactics employed by these men were very much in the tradition of Carlile. Indeed Carlile relived the 1820s in a long correspondence with Holyoake both before and after the latter's trial (Doc. 16). The law was challenged, martyrs were made, subscriptions were sent to aid the victims, and volunteers came forward to keep the work going. The **Oracle** *continued until November 1843, thanks mainly to the efforts of William Chilton and a member of the Lambeth branch, Maltus Ryall. Paterson had originally gone to Scotland along with Southwell after the police had* *threatened two Edinburgh booksellers – one of whom, Thomas Finlay, was an old zetetic; the other, Henry Robinson, had sold Hetherington's unstamped at Derby, assisted by young G. J. Harney.[17] Paterson's place was, in turn, taken by other volunteers, including, as in Carlile's case, a woman – Matilda Roalfe (Doc. 67).*

The Owenite organisation gave these people an ideal public platform. Though some Chartist groups, most notably Harney's in Sheffield, showed support, most of the encouragement for the infidels came from the Owenites. All the leaders had been involved in Owenism; the Anti-Persecution Union, which organised the victim fund, drew largely on Owenite support; and those leaders who were free to do so lectured in the Owenite halls and to Owenite audiences. Indeed the decision of the central board not to employ any missionaries after May 1842, taken partly because of their cost and partly because of the damage some missionaries were doing, played into the hands of the infidels, for those local Owenites who had built large halls on large mortgages needed popular lecturers to attract numerous fee-paying audiences. So, as long as the Owenite movement was able to maintain some momentum, freethought lecturers like Southwell, Holyoake and others – the most important of whom were Robert Cooper of Manchester[18] and Mrs Emma Martin – were able to find a useful, if not very remunerative, employment.

When the Owenite community at Queenwood collapsed in 1845, and as local societies sold off their halls to pay their debts, these lecturers found themselves redundant (Doc. 18). Of the leaders, Southwell's histrionic abilities ensured his survival as a freelance lecturer and actor, and Holyoake turned to journalism. He had followed the Oracle *with a more moderate weekly periodical called the* Movement, *but in 1846, when the last Owenite papers were collapsing, he was without any employment or outlet for his views. So at the suggestion of James Watson (Doc. 19) he began a new weekly, the* Reasoner, *in which to continue the causes of freethought, socialism and republicanism.*

NOTES

1. *Lion*, 16 May 1828.
2. Ibid., 22, 29 Feb 1828, 1 May 1829.
3. For Campbell see entry in *Dictionary of Labour Biography*, vol. 1, ed. J. Bellamy and J. Saville (1972).
4. G. D. H. Cole, *The Life of Robert Owen* (1925, 3rd ed. 1965) pp. 252–92.
5. See J. H. Wiener, *The War of the Unstamped* (1969) and P. Hollis, *The Pauper Press* (Oxford, 1970).
6. Congress Reports, *New Moral World*, 21 May 1836, 3, 10 June 1837, 28

May 1838, 8 June 1839; Central Board Minutes, 8 Apr 1839, International Institute of Social History, Amsterdam.

7. See E. Yeo, 'Robert Owen and Radical Culture', in S. Pollard and J. Salt (eds), *Robert Owen, prophet of the poor* (1971) pp. 84–114.

8. For an example, see the extract from J. Barker, *The Abominations of Socialism Exposed* (1840) in E. Royle, *Radical Politics*, pp. 112–13.

9. *N.M.W.*, 20 July 1839.

10. *Hansard*, vol. LI (1840) cols 237–8, 510–46, 566–72, 928–34, 1175–1217.

11. *N.M.W.*, 20 June, 4, 11 July 1840. For a description of the Manchester hall see L. Faucher, *Manchester in 1844* (1844, reprinted 1969) p. 25, reproduced in E. Royle, *Radical Politics*, pp. 114–15. There is a photograph of the hall in J. F. C. Harrison, *Robert Owen and the Owenites in Britain and America* (1969) p. 197.

12. E.g. Address of the Central Board, 28 Jan 1840, Owen Correspondence, no. 1235.

13. *N.M.W.*, 29 May 1841.

14. For Southwell, see entry in *Biographical Dictionary of British Labour Movements*.

15. *Oracle*, 27 Nov 1841. Part of the article is reprinted in E. Royle, *Radical Politics*, pp. 116–17.

16. G. J. Holyoake, *The History of the Last Trial by Jury for Atheism in England* (1850).

17. *Oracle*, 1 July, 16 Sep 1843.

18. For Cooper, see *Dictionary of Labour Biography*, vol. 2 (1974).

13 The Association of All Classes*

The freethinkers found one of their most effective forms of organisation in the Owenite socialist movement which, from 1837, began to make its impact on major centres of population throughout the country. The basis of Owenism was Enlightenment rationalism: a belief in the innate goodness of man, the overwhelming importance of the environment in the formation of character, and the natural harmony of a rational and well-ordered social system. The object of the A.A.C.A.N., founded in 1835, was to bring about this latter state of affairs.

ASSOCIATION OF ALL CLASSES OF ALL NATIONS, ESTABLISHED 1st MAY, 1835, REVISED BY THE CONGRESS, HELD IN THE RATIONAL SOCIAL INSTITUTION, ON THE 10th MAY, 1837.

---

* From *New Moral World*, 10 June 1837.

SECTION I.

1. *Object.* – The object of this association is to effect, peace-
ably, and by reason alone, an entire change in the character
and condition of mankind, by establishing over the world, in
principle and practice, the religion of charity for the convictions, feelings, and conduct of all individuals, without distinction of sex, class, sect, party, country, or colour, combined with
a well-devised, equitable, and natural system of united property; which united property is to be created by the members of
the association, without infringing upon the rights of any private property now in existence. And this great change is to be
introduced and accomplished by devising and adopting new arrangements, of a much higher order than any now in existence,
for forming a superior character for the human race; for producing and distributing in the best manner the best qualities of
all kinds of wealth abundantly for all; and for governing mankind without *artificial* rewards or punishments, most bene-
ficially for each individual.

2. *Means.*—These objects are to be attained, first by the establishment of a central association, with branches extending
to every part of the world. Secondly, by the central association
and its branches, creating a new public opinion in favour of this
entire change in the character and condition of man, by public
meetings, lectures, discussions, missionaries, cheap publications, mutual exchanges of productions upon equitable principles, without individual competition; and finally, by
founding, as soon as possible, COMMUNITIES OF UNITED
INTEREST, in which for ever to well educate and advantageously employ all the members of the association, under such
superior arrangement as will ensure their health, permanent
prosperity, intelligence, union, and happiness.

3. *Principles.*—That man is a being, formed by that Power
which "directs the atom, and controls the aggregate of nature,"
to have a two-fold compound character; first, as he is formed at
birth, before he receives any direct ideas or impressions from
external objects; and second, as he is subsequently made to
become, by the influence of external objects upon his natural
organisation, and by the action of man on man, and especially
of experienced man, or society on infant and inexperienced
man. That all man's *convictions* are formed *for* him, by external

objects acting upon his natural organisation and its reaction. That all his *feelings* are formed *for* him, by the action of external objects upon his natural organisation and its reaction. That his *will* is formed *for* him by the convictions *or* feelings separately, or the convictions *and* feelings united, which have been formed *for* him, by the action of external circumstances upon his organisation. That man is organised to *act* in accordance with his *convictions* or his *feelings*, whichever may be the strongest at the moment of action, or to act in obedience to these *convictions* and *feelings* when united, and which nature and society combined, have compelled him to receive. That man has been so organised that he *cannot act* in opposition to his *convictions* and his *feelings*, both of which he is by his nature compelled to have, and which separately or unitedly create his *will*—and thus is the whole character of man, physical, intellectual, and moral formed *for* him. That it is therefore evident that man has NOT been created to be a responsible being, otherwise than as he is left to experience the *certain effects* of his conduct which are nature's *rewards* and *punishments*, teaching all in the best possible manner, through the sensations of pain and pleasure, the means of increasing happiness, by avoiding the one and seeking the other, and that through this knowledge, adult man or society may effect the greatest improvement in the character and condition of infant man and of the human race.

That from these unerring and unchanging laws of human nature, the religion of charity for the convictions, feelings, and conduct of all men is derived, and discovered to be the only TRUE RELIGION, and the only one which man can adopt without becoming irrational in his thoughts, feelings, and conduct.

That this association therefore discards the fundamental errors by which the past and present character of man, and the past and present deplorable condition of the human race have been produced. These fundamental errors are: That man is bad by nature, and that he can believe or disbelieve, feel or not feel, as he pleases; that he forms his own character, and that, consequently, he ought to be rewarded or punished for it, both in this world and in the world to come.

14 Reaction to persecution*

When the principles of Owenism brought the Owenites into conflict with orthodox Christianity, a number of public debates and discussions were held on the merits of each system. For many of the rank and file this method of attacking Christianity became the most immediate and engaging aspect of the Owenite movement, and anti-Christian propaganda seemed in danger of pushing the community schemes of Robert Owen into the background. Owen himself, followed by some of his closest associates, began to urge a more moderate policy, but some of the lecturers were not inclined to pay much attention to this. When one of the latter, Charles Southwell, started his own periodical, the Oracle of Reason, *in November 1841 and then was arrested in December, the infidel Owenites were thrown into a flurry of activity. Maltus Ryall of the Lambeth Socialist branch, of which Southwell had once been a member and lecturer, took the lead in organising a defence fund for Southwell, and he sought the help of G. J. Holyoake, the Owenite lecturer in Sheffield, who was about to become the second editor of the* Oracle *and who had just issued an Address on Southwell's behalf. Out of their combined efforts was formed the first of the new infidel organisations, the Anti-Persecution Union.*

Huggett's Coffee House,
3 North Place, Lambeth.
4 Jan[u]ary 1842

Dear Sir,

Though unknown personally your 'sayings & doings' are sufficiently familiar to afford me peculiar pleasure in adding your name to the list of auxiliaries.

I have so much to do for the London agitation that I can barely refer to main features.

We have issued subscription books. Collections in other ways have been made. Many private friends have been rallied round us who have furnished money and other assistance. Every step has been taken with the advice of able counsel. Public meetings take place this and ensuing week to which will be as extensively reported as circumstances will permit [sic]. We shall shortly advertise an account of our stewardship. Hetherington is to accompany Southwell. Mr. Carpenter[1] is expected to report.

* M. Q. Ryall to G. J. Holyoake, 4 Jan 1842, Holyoake Collection, Manchester, no. 24.

Counsel is retained for the trial – for watching and advising not pleading. All has been hitherto done quietly but efficiently.

If you think similar measures advisable, you can co-operate with us; or act independently. Your own judgment I think will serve you best in deciding on your course. We shall have addresses out shortly to be either sold or distributed gratuitously. We will send some.

On the Defence business address as above to yours truly

M. Ryall. Secry. to Committee

for assisting in Mr. Southwell's defence.

Mr. Holyoake

With reference to the Oracle, I meet you entirely in your own spirit which is after my own heart, I will take any position for which I may be deemed qualified or in which I can be most useful. How very desirable for us to meet as well as Chilton. Would your branch & contiguous classes pay or help to pay expences [sic] for lectures. I am one of the volunteers here and though of no great mark or likelihood in manner might serve to be stared at in the Country.

What I here say has
no reference to the Com-
mittee business which
is sedulously kept from
all identification with the Oracle, or Southwell's opinions.

Fraternally Yours

M Ryall

Direct to me (apart from Committee business) –

29 Gibraltar Row,

West Square, Lambeth.

Funds are wanted incontinently to support Oracle &
we can't touch the subscriptions for the purpose.
Can any thing be done – £5. to £10 would to [?do] a great
deal. We must get the O[racle] to London.

Mr. Holyoake.

NOTE

1. William Carpenter (1797–1874); a radical journalist and founder member of the National Union of the Working Classes. His *Political Letters* (Oct

1830–May 1831) began the 'war of the unstamped'. See P. Hollis, *Pauper Press*, pp. 308–9.

15 The views of an infidel lecturer*

In an attempt to reach a compromise with the orthodox Owenites, Holyoake proposed that separate discussion classes should be set up for theological matters, so that opposition to Christianity would not turn public opinion against the more practical aspects of Owenism — the Queenwood Community at East Tytherley. The response of Henry Jeffery, the lecturer in Edinburgh, to this suggestion was typical of the ultra-radical infidels.

21 Canal St. Edinburgh
7 April 1842

My dear Sir

I have given your proposal of an anti superstition class further consideration, but still think it not advisable to press the subject of your document on the attention of our members at present. I am yet of opinion that the publication of the document, especially as it is worded, would be an admission on the part of those whose signatures were appended that the missionaries as agents of the society ought to "leave religion alone." In my opinion also very few of the Branches would form a class of the kind. For instance in Edinburgh, any increase in the number of classes would weaken those already formed, and for this there is no occasion, as the members almost without exception and I as their missionary, do most vigorously combat the follies & falsehood of theology. The same I believe is the situation of Glasgow. A Sunday morning's lecture constantly delivered not for the Branch but a class, I am persuaded would not work. Thus you perceive that the few individuals who object to religion being touched upon by the missionaries of a *"Rational Religionists'"* Society would in consequence of the failure of your plan fancy themselves to be in the majority.

The desirability of letting Congress know the feelings of the lecturers & branches upon the subject of opposition to superstition is evident; but an express declaration on our part would be

* H. Jeffery to G. J. Holyoake, 7 Apr 1842, Holyoake Collection, Manchester, no. 37.

giving by far too much importance to the crotchets of a few timid demi Socialists & expediency mongers. However, if in your correspondence you have found the missionaries generally favourable to your plan and willing to append their names, then, to avoid the appearance of want of unanimity, put down mine. Pray do not imagine that I should be afraid of standing with a protesting party however small, or even of standing alone, when principle or the interests of truth require it. Such a course would be the very thing we are condemning. I have not pursued it in Edinburgh. Twelve months since, when I arrived here, the branch was a hybrid, unitarian kind of concern.[1] The members were fond of hearing the nonsense sometimes spoken about "Socialism being genuine, primitive, practical, or some other sort of Christianity." A word against religion nearly frightened them from their seats. A few withdrew their names, but we had a much larger accession, and now they take strong meat like men. From our rostrum things are now said which were never spoken publicly in Edinburgh before. I have been engaged by this Branch at their last meeting till May 1843, with an understanding between them and the Glasgow friends that I exchange with their missionary six months out of the time.

If at the ensuing congress measures be taken for preventing the missionaries from removing the obstacles which religion presents to the progress of truth & an improved state of society; if an attempt be made to remove those laws by which persons are required to assent to certain views of human nature before becoming members of our society; if we are to become the waiters & hangers on of public opinion instead of its leaders; then we must take decided steps to counteract such suicidal proceedings. You have favored me with an extract from a letter of Mr. Galpin's;[2] but the sentence is as indefinite and incomprehensible as an Old Testament Prophesy. I look with much anxiety to next congress. It will decide whether we are to become a mighty instrument of mental, moral & Social progress; or to degenerate into an insignificant association of hucksterers. Withdraw all great principles, because some people who are no doubt vastly practical[3] call them abstract & speculative; flatter the prejudices of the world; temporise with error; discountenance discussion upon all subjects except more bread & cheese questions; and we shall instead of raising a New Moral World, add fully & dishonestly to the present superabundant supply of both, and in a short time pass through the paths of absurdity into the vale of oblivion. All the bright anticipations which we had associated with the Social body are doomed to disappointment if it become nothing more than a Joint stock connection of men whose only principle in the movement is the princip*al* they may advance for the sake of profit; and whose main interest in the affair is the 5 or 10 per cent. We ought not, certainly, to be lost in speculating upon metaphysics or theology so as to neglect the practical; at the same time it ought to be borne in mind, that the people will not be prepared to create or to enter a better state of things, unless they be mentally & morally elevated. This cannot take place while religion continues to cramp the intellect & blight the best feelings of our nature. I do not overlook the importance of our proceedings at Tytherly. On the contrary let us strain every nerve to make it succeed. But let us not forget that we have to operate upon the public opinion of society at large; and that if we wish to be something different from the Shakers & Rappites; if we wish to be the agents for effecting a glorious purpose in the destiny of mankind; we must connect great principles & efforts for a mental emancipation & expansion, with our wealth producing operations.

It appears by the N[ew] M[oral] W[orl]d that the Central Board addresses will till the meeting of congress contain a statement of the changes they intend to propose in the organisation of the society.[4] We must look well at these. If anything be proposed perversive of what you & I, and those who think with us consider the proper objects of our association, let us correspond immediately and consult as to the steps which should be taken. On Saturday I go to Glasgow & stay there for a month. Letters addressed to the care of Mr. Nockles will reach me.

I am happy to say that my health is considerably improved, though I am still weak. I presume you are in no want of matter for the "Oracle", and consequently I have sent nothing.

Sincerely yours
H. Jeffery.

Mr. G. J. Holyoake,
    Sheffield.

NOTES

1. The Edinburgh branch had been founded in 1839 when the local Unitarians split. The Owenites hoped to capture the radical Unitarians and were exceedingly cautious when applying to the Central Board for a branch charter. James Lindsay to Robert Owen, 11 Aug 1839, Owen Collection no. 1140; L. Jones, *Life, Times and Labours of Robert Owen* (1890, reprinted 1919) pp. 331–2.

2. William Galpin, a banker, was one of Owen's closest associates and a leading member of the Home Colonisation Society which provided the capital for the building of Harmony Hall at Tytherley. He also became general secretary of the U.C.S.R.R. in September 1841 and in this capacity sent a circular, dated 22 March 1842, to all lecturers giving them three months' notice unless they were reappointed by the May Congress (which they were not). W. Galpin to G. J. Holyoake, 22 Mar 1842, Holyoake Collection, Manchester, no. 31.

3. Robert Owen was always insisting that he was a *practical* man.

4. The Central Board was proposing to change the rules so as to put the Community in trust for the shareholders, not the members, and also to modify the democratic structure of the society by introducing the so-called 'elective paternal' system of government. See *N.M.W.* 21, 28 May 1842.

16 Support from Carlile*

When Holyoake himself fell foul of the law, at Cheltenham in May 1842, Richard Carlile rushed to his aid. Though Carlile had by this time adopted a mystical and totally unorthodox brand of Christianity, he still felt that Holyoake was the latest victim in what he regarded as his cause.

21 Regent Street, Cheltenham Augst. 16
1842

My Dear Holyoake,

I had not made a proper estimate of your worth to society until I heard your defence yesterday.[1] It was certainly the most splendid of the kind ever delivered in this country. More power, as physical power, in delivery, might have been found; but more moral power, more sweetness, more beauty, more persuasion, could not be found. I could scarcely restrain myself from jumping into the dock to embrace you on several occasions. I envy not the man his earthy, clod like, vicious religion, that, after that defence, could condemn you. It is not my

* R. Carlile to G. J. Holyoake, 10 Aug 1842, Holyoake Collection, Manchester, no. 65.

Christianity; nor that of the Bible, nor that of the Natural and the Spiritual Worlds, that could so condemn you; but the same Pharisaical "righteousness," that crucified the Saviour, gave the poison cup to Socrates; and that has destroyed, banished or persecuted the wise and good of all nations.

I shall not be idle: will fill the Oracle of Reason weekly, if that help be wanted. The moral world shall lose nothing in progress through your imprisonment. I will either join you or shame the authorities of your imprisonment.

At a moment of leisure, I shall write to the Judge and to Peel.[2] I know nothing of the character of Sir James Graham, to write with effect to him.

I advocate all your principles; but my dearly purchased experience has put them beyond the reach of indictment. It is not that I fear imprisonment, but that I have grown wiser and stronger. I have as much resolution now to suffer for the battle of free discussion as in 1817 when I began.

I have a second letter today pressing me to come on to Bristol. I purpose being there on the 29th; but I have a great taste for three nights in the Theatre of Gloucester. On Sunday, I visit Stroud, to preach on Rodborough Common.

> Let your imprisonment
> be like a rod in pickle for
> your enemies. This was my
> sustaining resolution through

nine years. I feel, as if I had been well pickled, and will lay it on those who now need tickling with it. Take care of your health. Six months imprisonment would have been felt by me as a joke. I have taken as much voluntarily, rather than yield an asking for liberation.

Adieu and strengthen

Richd. Carlile

Respect to Adams; have just sent Mrs. A. a large bundle of books.[3]

NOTES

1. Holyoake was tried at Gloucester Assizes on 15 August. His defence speech lasted nine and one-half hours. Carlile had been put in touch with Holyoake by Thomas Turton of Sheffield (for whom, sec Doc. 9). R. Carlile to M. Q. Ryall, 11 July 1842, Holyoake Collection, Manchester, no. 56.

2. Peel, now Prime Minister, had been the Home Secretary who had released Carlile in 1825. Peel sent Carlile's letter on to Sir James Graham, the Home Secretary, with the note 'The enclosed – which I have not answered – is from the notorious Richard Carlyle [sic]'. Peel to Graham, 19 Sep 1842, Graham Papers. Carlile's opinion of Peel was 'I never knew Peel yield any thing on complaint. There is nothing noble or generous in his nature. He is a small meddler with small things and the necessary minister of small minded men.' Carlile to Holyoake, 25 Oct 1842, Holyoake Collection, Manchester, no. 82.
3. George Adams: a Cheltenham cabinet-maker and, with his wife Harriet, a bookseller; he was tried at the same time as Holyoake for selling *Oracle* no. 25 and sentenced to a month. Harriet was arrested for selling number 4 (the 'Jew Book' issue) but was not brought to trial.

17 The Anti-Persecution Union*

While Southwell and Holyoake were in prison, their friends rallied to the Oracle and the Anti-Persecution Union, which was formally constituted in June 1842 while Holyoake was in London on bail.

CIRCULAR OF THE ANTI-PERSECUTION UNION:
TO ASSERT AND MAINTAIN THE RIGHT OF FREE DISCUSSION, AND TO PROTECT AND DEFEND THE VICTIMS OF INTOLERANCE AND BIGOTRY.

TREASURER: J. Watson, 5, Paul's Alley, Paternoster Row, London.
SECRETARY: M. Ryall, 8, Holywell Street, Strand.

8, *Holywell-Street, Strand, London, July* 19, 1842.

It is now forced on the attention of all parties, that "Liberty of Speech," the Briton's boast, and "Freedom of the Press," his supposed palladium, are mere chimeras or fancy pictures, which the admirers of the "glorious constitution" delight to eulogise, but which the continued acts of authority and power show to be naught but fictions. The real liberty of speech is the liberty to speak as allowed by the dignitaries of the state church, and the liberty of the press is the limits prescribed by the attorney-general. Recognizances, securities, judge-made and parson-justice-administered law, police and private espionage, meet at every step the free-thinker and the free-

* From an *Oracle of Reason* supplement (1842) pp. 1–3.

writer. The "right of private judgment" is a hollow pretence put forth by one sect to exalt themselves at the expense of another, instead of a great principle inclusive of all opinions without reference to time or place. High and noble efforts have been made by bold enthusiastic men to resist the tyranny of power, and who, in winning for others a nearer approach to justice, have fallen sacrifices themselves. Not only so, but numerous as have been the supporters of such arduous struggles, and large the assistance rendered in proportion to the numbers and the means, the fight has still to be fought again—the full and complete triumph has yet to be achieved.

It has become necessary to adopt for the protection of Free Discussion, the plan so effectual for the furtherance of the narrower purposes of party or faction. 'Union is strength." It has been strength to partizans; it shall be strength to the lovers of liberty. A union is now evoked, not for the promulgation of dogma religions or new religions, but for the protection of all who may be disposed to publish their speculations on all subjects, being assured that the only legitimate correction for erroneous doctrine is free public investigation and discussion. With such views the Anti-Persecution Union has been formed.

Its *principle*, that of the right to the free publication of opinion.

Its *objects*, the promulgation of such principle, and the attainment and maintenance of that right.

Its *means*, the organisation of an association for the periodical collection of funds, to be managed by a committee selected by subscribers.

The promulgation of the principle will be at first necessarily confined to occasional addresses by the committee, with every other information calculated to benefit the cause. It is in contemplation, when the resources are adequately strengthened, to publish a periodical organ, and issue tracts. Public and friendly meetings have already taken place, and will be convened from time to time to rally the friends of freedom, diffuse more correct information and assist the movement generally. The obtainment and maintenance of the right to freedom of expression will be comprised in the defence and support of the victims of persecution, until the iniquitous laws are either virtually or constitutionally abrogated. The union will recognise *all* as having claims on their assistance, who may be interfered with by the law in the publication of speculative opinions. No money qualification, by subscription or otherwise, will be required as a title to the society's support. This support will have no reference whatever to the kind of opinion, whether religious or anti-religious, orthodox or heterodox, nor to the style or manner of the language, which is understood to be a mere matter of taste, to be decided by the individual and the public. Thus, Christian, Jew, Turk, Theist, Pantheist, or Atheist, all of every sect or no sect at all, are embraced in the scope of the society's operations.

The actual business of the organisation will be the collection, receipt, and disbursement of the funds for the defence of the prosecuted, the alleviation of their condition, if subject to prison discipline, and the support of those dependent on them, and the arousing of the public to a sense of the iniquity of all measures to shackle the mind; the collection of a body of information for the service of all sufferers for conscience-sake, is also occupying the attention of the union. These proceedings include operations of a varied and complicated description. A rapid outline of past proceedings will serve to show what may be expected with extended means.

In the case of Charles Southwell, the best legal assistance was secured, as far as required, and the most eminent counsel were consulted at every step; large and sympathising public meetings were called, and contributed to the objects; the assistance of Henry Hetherington and William Carpenter was obtained at his trial; a full and accurate report was extensively circulated; an ample allowance has been supplied daily at the prison; memorials and petitions have been presented to the houses of parliament and the queen, and other important aid has been afforded, not only to Southwell but all future sufferers. Finally, a nucleus, now principally occupied with the affairs of Holyoake and the two Adams's, has been formed for the "Anti-Persecution Union."

A Public Account will be rendered, at the end of the quarter, of the proceedings of the union, when auditors, a committee, treasurer, and secretary will be appointed by the subscribers.

The warm responses that have already succeeded our appeals, and the increasing contributions from various parts of the country, as well as the metropolis, afford grounds for hope greatly exceeding previous anticipations. It will be best for each to act as though the success of the great and noble movement depended on his individual exertion, and a speedy defeat of all the mind-restrictive laws must be the result.

The Machinery of the Union is as follows:— The number of collectors in London now exceeds eighty; we calculate on one hundred. Each has a book: dated, numbered, and signed, and having printed instructions. The book is to enter periodical subscriptions, and any sum, however small, and at any period, however short (as little as a penny per week), to suit the circumstances of the subscribers. Circles of collectors are being organised in the provinces; the books to be issued by the liberal publishers and their known friends. Penny subscription cards will be substituted for books for the use of those who collect under a shilling weekly.

Subscription sheets for casual donations or subscriptions are issued to the liberal institutions or places of resort, where they may be advantageously located. These may be obtained by known friends, or those who can give known references, by applying to the Secretary. Drafts of petitions, and all other information, furnished on application. Donations, &c. to be transmitted to the Treasurer, Mr. WATSON, St. Paul's Alley, London. Returns will be periodically published of the result of the collections; no names will be printed of collectors or subscribers without permission. Names and addresses are requested both in London and the country of either active or passive friends; such, for instance, as could collect or subscribe; who can advantageously dispose of subscription sheets or otherwise assist the cause. It is requested that all those who still hold books and subscriptions for Mr. Southwell will hand them over to the committee. There are arrears of subscriptions in Whitechapel, London, and in Bolton, Lancashire.

M. RYALL, SECRETARY.

18 The threat of redundancy*

The atheistic lecturers also continued to lecture in the Owenite branches and remained one of the most popular features of grassroots Owenism

* R. Cooper to G. J. Holyoake, 21 Mar 1846, Holyoake Collection, Manchester, no. 162.

despite official disapproval, but as the Queenwood Community began to fail in the mid-1840s the branches dwindled and the lecturers found themselves without regular employment. Robert Cooper of Manchester, who had been an infidel lecturer since his teens in the early 1830s, was employed in Edinburgh in 1846 when the Socialists there closed their hall. He wrote despondently to Holyoake, who was currently at Glasgow. He begins by recalling Maltus Ryall who had just died and after whom Holyoake had named his latest child.

5, Parkside Street,
Edinburgh,
March 21st, 1846.

My dear Friend,

I have this moment received your kind letter, which I have read with no small emotion. Though hard at work at my "sermon" for to-morrow, I cannot deny myself the gratification of forwarding an immediate acknowledgment [sic]. The spirit of your communication is noble, generous, confiding, which I reciprocate with all my heart. But before I speak of self allow me to express the real pleasure I feel on learning that Mrs. Holyoake and Master Maltus Questell are doing well. Mrs. Cooper joins me in this congratulation. Your naming your infant son after your late amiable and talented friend does honor to your heart.[1] I perused the memoir in the "Herald" with painful interest. Another victim, I apprehend, to the merciless selfishness of the world! Such noble spirits are like so many bright stars in the midst of darkness – a green spot in a desert. Peace to his ashes! I hope you are quite convalescent. I presume so, as you do not complain. Our friends here have been most anxious about you, I shall be happy to tell them I have heard from you. I will now reply to your favour frankly. Friend Thriepland did right in saying I was unsettled. Indeed, I am. I have endeavoured, perhaps injudiciously, to dissipate all thoughts of the future, as the prospect was so gloomy that I felt the frequent contemplation of it would entirely unfit me for my duties. But I *must* look before me now. There is but a short distance between me and a precipice. I have no plan for the future, nor can I form one. I have no means of settling in any way. As respects our present profession I think we may truly say with Othello our "occupation's gone." The only opening *at all* probable is either at Glasgow or London. I have written to Nockles,[2] inquiring what they think of doing in May next, and stating I shall be open to an engagement. But the Board can give me no definite answer. I am afraid their worst fears will be realized – *they must sell the Hall.* So there will be an end to *that* chapter. With respect to the *South* I have no hope. Certainly not of a *permanent* engagement, and it is *that* which I require with my family. There is a "surplus population" in our line in that quarter already – Martin, Southwell, Ellis.[3] If I can find no refuge in either of these places, I must wander through the wilderness of the "Old World". And what a wilderness to *me.* But *I* would not care for that, were it not that beings dear to me must bear me company. *That* is the source of my uneasiness. Mr. Waed of this city is the only one connected with our branch in competent circumstances, and I *know* he *cannot* assist me. His capital is entirely absorbed in his business, and it is not sufficiently extensive to find me employment. If he *could* he *would* befriend me. There is, therefore, no chance here, as it is now certain Mr. Trevelyan[4] will sell the Hall in May or June. My impression is he came to Edinbro' *for that express purpose.* His determination has much disheartened our friends. I answered an advertisement last week in one of the city papers for a *bookeeper and correspondent,* with Mr. Waed's recommendation. Dr. Goulden of Stockport would also have been security to any amount – but they have not even answered my application. My name, I have no doubt, would *alarm* them. *That* would be sufficient to damn me, especially in this emporium of piety and cant. I do not see any means of returning to the Old World except by the interposition of a friend who would not care for my *opinions.* Do you know such an one? Or could you advise me? Any council or information you can render I shall receive in the spirit in which I know you would wish me to receive it. Believe me, my dear friend, I am delighted to hear that an opportunity for settlement on your return to England occurs to you. May you prosper![5]

Pray remember me most kindly to Mrs. Holyoake. Salute the young stranger for me, and the other dears. If you should see Mr. Thriepland tender him my thanks and my esteem. I await his letter with impatience.

Presenting my warmest acknowledgements for the brotherly interest you have taken in my welfare, and anxiously awaiting

any further favours, I beg to remain
My dear Friend,
Most truly yours,
Rob. Cooper.

NOTES

1. Ryall died in poverty, aged 37, on 11 February 1846. *Herald of Progress*, 14 Mar 1846.
2. James Nockles, secretary of the Glasgow branch of the Rational Society.
3. Mrs Emma Martin (1812–51): a former Baptist; popular lecturer on free-thought and women's rights. *Reasoner* 15, 22 Oct 1851. Like Southwell, John Ellis was a former social missionary.
4. Arthur Trevelyan (1802–78): 2nd son of Sir John Trevelyan, 5th baronet and brother of Walter Trevelyan; a longstanding patron of freethought and total abstinence advocate; president of the National Secular Society in 1871.
5. Holyoake's engagement at Glasgow had ended on 26 February 1846, the day before his son (originally called Prospero) was born. He had secured a temporary post at Paisley on 1 March and then went back to London to start the *Reasoner* for Watson – Holyoake Collection, Bishopsgate Institute, Log Book no. 2. Cooper eventually went to Huddersfield where he lectured part-time for the branch and worked for Messrs Holliday (manufacturing chemists and forerunners of I.C.I.) before going to London as a commercial traveller and Robert Owen's personal assistant. R. Cooper to R. Owen, 10 July 1847, Owen Collection, no. 1480.

19   The need for a new infidel periodical*

Holyoake also needed to find new employment, but James Watson had already written to him suggesting a new freethought periodical. This was to result in the Reasoner *which Holyoake edited and Watson published from June 1846.*

5 Pauls Alley, P[aternoster] Row
London Jan[uar]y 27th 1846
My Dear Sir,
I will write to Mr. Love today to request him to pay you four pounds on my account:[1] When I tell you I am preparing to re-move to another shop you will not wonder at my not sending

* J. Watson to G. J. Holyoake, 27 Jan 1846, Holyoake Collection, Manchester, no. 154.

you even a rough account. I have taken a house at no 3 Queen's Head Passage, which runs into Paternoster Row and Newgate Street. I hope to be in my new place on Saturday or Monday next.

I do not know what may be doing in Scotland, but here everything is a[s] dull as the worst enemy could wish it. The infidel works were never so dull since I have been in the Trade, and their increase in number just now is only an increase of debt and outlay to those who embark on it. The [New] Moral World before the split was useful as an Advertising medium.[2] Now we have none, and the want of a weekly periodical devoted to theological investigation was never so much wanted as at present. Is not this want felt in your quarter? All the pamphlets issued against superstition or religion for years past lay on the shelves like so much waste paper. The readers are scattered for want of some such connecting link, and though all complain of it yet nothing in the way of remedy is applied by anyone. What think you? I write this to you in perfect confidence and not for publicity, or to be communicated to any one else. I am about to see if I cannot move the large heap of paper I have got about me by Advertising in the Dispatch &c, with what success a little time will show. If this fails I must ask counsel of friends as to what is the next best step to be taken, to keep unfettered investigation before the public. I occasionally see a religious periodical, and I never do so without regretting that we have no vehicle of intelligence to show up the debasing trash these idiots inculcate as acceptable to God. At your leisure let me have a few lines from you on the topics embraced in this scrawl. And excuse my pressing on your notice matters that may savour too much of selfishness. I have only one wish in the matter, and that is to see all connected with mental freedom and progress, have some claims to the respect of men of morals and character.

Yours Resp[ect]f[ull]y
J. Watson

NOTES

1. William Love was the leading radical publisher and bookseller in Glasgow and handled Watson's business there. Watson had already published four works for Holyoake and was to become his regular publisher until 1853.

2. The Owenites split, roughly between pro- and anti-Owen factions, at the 1844 May Congress. The N.M.W., which was pro-Owen, closed on 23 August 1845. The working-class Central Board continued with a fortnightly *Herald of Progress* (25 Oct 1845–23 May 1846), which was merged with Holyoake's *Reasoner* when it commenced on 3 June 1846.

Secularism

After the failure of the main Owenite Rational Society in 1846, Holyoake attempted to rally the remnants of the movement with the help of South-well, Cooper and other infidel lecturers. The venture was not very success-ful. One gets the impression that many local radicals were weary of failure and disillusioned with both Chartism and socialism. Such revival of inter-est as there was went almost entirely to the Chartists. Holyoake's 'Society for the Promulgation of Naturalism' or 'Society of Theological Utilita-rians', which he tried to push through the Reasoner in 1846, made little impression outside London, where a headquarters was established at the City Road Hall of Science. The Theological Utilitarians were no more than a remnant, and the circulation of the Reasoner was scarcely a thou-sand, but they were faithful to their heritage: on 30 January 1848 the Uti-litarian Society organised a Thomas Paine birthday tea party at the Hall of Science; and on the same day in South London, Southwell was organis-ing a similar party, to be followed by a lecture and discussion on the immortal Paine.[1]

Revival came to freethought in the early 1850s. With the collapse of Chartism after 1848 local radical groups were in disarray, and a variety of campaigns appeared to pick up the pieces. Some men joined David Urquhart's Foreign Affairs Committees which studied the Blue Books and persuaded themselves that Lord Palmerston was a Russian spy.[2] Others were attracted to the freethinking infidels, who were organised nationally through Holyoake's Reasoner, and the new name coined by Holyoake to describe his followers was Secularism.

The new movement was launched at a meeting at the City Road Hall of Science in December 1851, and was taken to the provinces the following spring by Robert Cooper. He had been a public lecturer since his early teens, first in his native Manchester and then at various Owenite branches *in the north of England and in Scotland. Everywhere he went on his tour of 1852 he saw the need and demand for a new radical organisation, especially a revival of Owenism. The men he had known in his youth were clamouring for a renewal of the old Social Cause, and, inspired by Cooper's work, they again began to organise themselves. In Lancashire and Yorkshire, where the Owenites had been particularly strong, local conferences were called, local societies revived, and even regional boards established again as in the early days of Owenism (Docs. 20,22).*

Such activity did not long go unnoticed, and a Congregational clergyman, the Reverend Brewin Grant, took upon himself the task of countering this latest heresy. Grant had, as a young student, taken part in the Brindley campaign against the Owenites and now he prepared to do battle again with the infidel. Twice he challenged Holyoake to debate for six nights on the relative merits of Secularism and Christianity – in London, January and February 1853; and in Glasgow, October 1854. Between these two debates Secularism reached its first peak of influence. As local groups met to discuss the debate, and as local champions repeated their own version of it, Grant toured the country, pursued by Cooper, Southwell and Holyoake. Secularism became a national concern, infidelity again became an issue of the day, and the circulation of the Reasoner *soared to 5000.*[3]

This situation could not last long. The Crimean War soon replaced Secularism as the topic for conversation in clubs and coffee houses. Although local organisations, especially in the West Riding, made some headway in the mid-1850s, Holyoake was scarcely equipped to give the necessary strong national lead. His weakness was threefold: personal, financial and intellectual. On the personal level he was neither physically robust nor a powerful orator. Financially his position was very weak: his Reasoner *rarely made a profit, and an ambitious venture he commenced with his brother Austin in 1853 to bring James Watson's radical publishing business and their own printing work together in a grand Fleet Street House, which would also provide a national headquarters and facilities for international and national republicanism and freethought, proved to be over-ambitious. Business worries sapped Holyoake's spirit and made him more and more dependent on a few wealthier radical allies, such as J. S. Mill, Arthur Trevelyan, W. H. Ashurst and William Shaen. Holyoake's intellectual problem was interpreted by his enemies to be a natural consequence of this lack of financial independence. He had deliberately framed the concept of Secularism to avoid the implications of such labels as 'atheism' and 'infidelity'. In an age such as the 1850s, when working-class movements were in disarray and when middle-class reform was also in decline, he hoped to build bridges between infidelity and honest doubt, Chartism and Manchester School radicalism, Christian socialist and secular reformers. Although he himself remained an atheist, he was becoming convinced that insistence upon such personal party labels was likely to hinder much of the good which an entirely neutral platform might be able to achieve. In other words, Holyoake was moving round to the Owenite position which he had rejected in 1841. Secularism, like socialism, failed partly because Christians like Grant were convinced, and convinced others, that the new name still signified the old infidelity, and partly because many Secularists themselves believed that this ought to be so (Doc. 23). In sociological terms, Holyoake may be regarded as a 'denominationalist' — open, non-dogmatic, and emphasising similarities with rather than differences from the outside world. On the contrary, those who viewed his Secularism with dismay may be regarded as sectarian in their approach — stressing their atheism, their separation from the standards and values of the world, and emphasising their own tradition. The feelings of such men, who included with varying degrees of extremism both Southwell and Cooper, were summed up by one of the Glasgow leaders, J. H. McGuire, when he welcomed the* London Investigator, *a new monthly periodical edited by Cooper:'Oh, for an hour of such critics of clerical men and things as Thomas Paine! Oh for such a leader for a week as Richard Carlile! We should once more feel that pride and satisfaction which takes its rise in a sense of duty well done.'*[4]

In the face of such opposition, Holyoake was able to maintain his position only so long as no comparable rival appeared on the scene to lead the militant traditionalists. Southwell, who was too much of an individualist to lead any movement for long, emigrated in 1855; Cooper, who was in ill-health, handed his Investigator *over to an erratic Yorkshire militant, W. H. Johnson, in 1857 and retired to his native Manchester in 1858. Local London leaders, J. P. Adams and John Maughan, caused some trouble, but not until Charles Bradlaugh began to make his mark in the late 1850s were the infidel militants to find a leader strong enough to overtake Holyoake.*

Bradlaugh came from Hoxton. As a youth he had lodged for a while with Mrs Eliza Sharples Carlile and her family. His world was one of back-streets radicalism in dismal halls, and outdoor missions in the fresh air of Victoria Park on Sundays. Strongly built, eloquent, committed to the cause of Paine and Carlile, he was just the man to rally the societies of the provinces, to awaken the radicalism of London, and to stamp Secularism with its true image of infidelity. By 1860, when the Sheffield Secularists

asked him to share in the editorship of their new paper, the National Reformer, *his prestige was approaching that of Holyoake, and when the*
Reasoner *closed the following year he was on the way to becoming the
most important man in the movement.*

*Bradlaugh cannot have been an easy man to work with. He was im-
mensely able, fully convinced of the rightness of his own approach and —
what was often most infuriating of all — usually right. He soon quarrelled
with his co-editor on the* National Reformer, *Joseph Barker — the
Methodist–Chartist–freethinker of many persuasions[5] — and in 1862 an
effort to work closely with G. J. Holyoake similarly failed. These quarrels
were, in the short term, disastrous for any efforts to create national organisation out of the now-thriving local and regional societies, and not until
1866 was this achieved. Then Bradlaugh, with the help of Charles Watts,
announced in the* National Reformer *the formation of the National
Secular Society.[6]*

*Unlike most previous freethought organisations, the N.S.S. was fully
centralised. At first only individuals could join, on payment of a shilling a
quarter, thus making the society a nucleus of committed infidels dependent
upon Bradlaugh, but this was soon altered to admit local societies and
branches of the Reform League on a reduced (4d) subscription. This was
to be important for the future development of the N.S.S., firstly because
Bradlaugh was thereby able to associate his own organisation with that of
the Reform League, so that when the latter declined after 1868 he was able
to make a number of its branches his own; and secondly because the reduced
society subscription gave individuals a financial incentive to form an
organisation. So local political or Secularist societies were encouraged to
join the N.S.S., and wherever seven or more individual members of the
N.S.S. were met together they were encouraged to form a branch. By this
means the N.S.S. was gradually able to take over most independent Secularist societies, and Secularist organisation was extended into rural parts
of the country which had scarcely been touched by previous radical efforts.[7]*

*Bradlaugh's personal position as a prominent member of the Reform
League greatly enhanced his position in the N.S.S., though much of the
actual grassroots work was done by Charles Watts, who was appointed
official lecturer and secretary to the N.S.S. The London Hall of Science
became the base for the Bradlaugh brand of radicalism, and its capacity
had to be doubled to 1400 in 1869. Audiences of 2000 were often crammed
into the large lecture hall during the next twenty years. From this base, and
other smaller ones provided by local London societies, the work was spread
throughout London by means of open air meetings; and notable advances*

continued to be made in the provinces. There was however in the late 1860s the first hint that Bradlaugh's Secularism was to be much more of a London-based movement than it had been earlier under Holyoake. Many of the topics on which Bradlaugh lectured were specifically political and fitted well the mood of London radicalism in the late 1860s – the Irish Church, the Land Question, the Monarchy, Education – and he seems to have picked up a great deal of artisan ultra-radicalism which had been dis-appointed with the Reform League and George Howell's acceptance of Gladstonian Liberalism. This trend became clear in 1870 when Brad-laugh decided to devote himself full-time to propagandist work. He emerged rapidly as leader of the English republicans. In Bradlaugh and the N.S.S. at this time the dual legacy of Paine – freethought and repub-lican internationalism – was more clearly expressed than perhaps at any time since the 1790s. But the moderate constitutionalism was also there, and for the first time Bradlaugh found himself under attack from the Left – violent republicans and members of the International Working Men's As-sociation under the influence of Karl Marx.[8]

These political interests, however, gradually began to push Secularism into the background, and at the N.S.S. annual conference in September 1871 Bradlaugh and Watts decided to stand down.[9] Arthur Trevelyan was elected ppesident, and D. K. Fraser secretary, but neither man had the force of character to maintain the momentum which had now raised the af-filiated membership of the society to over a thousand. Bradlaugh continued to run the movement in effect, through the pages of his National Re-former, *but he needed more time in which to recoup his own health and personal finances. By September 1872 the N.S.S. was defunct and no at-tempt was made to revive it. Bradlaugh went off to America in 1873 in the hope of making enough money on a winter lecture tour to pay off his debts. He rushed back early in 1874 to contest the Northampton seat in the gen-eral election, and then, having failed there, he once more put his energies into Secularism. By means of lecture tours and mass meetings, all reported in the* National Reformer, *he again breathed life into his organisation. Without doubt he was becoming the leading ultra-radical orator in the country.*

The extent to which the future of Secularism was now dependent upon the personal exertions of Bradlaugh is illustrated by the events of the next decade. In 1877 he plunged Secularism into a long and difficult legal battle over the freedom to publish neo-Malthusian birth control propa-ganda; and in the early 1880s he was involved in one of the major civil rights contests of the nineteenth century – the Bradlaugh case.

The neo-Malthusian issue broke in January 1877 when Charles Watts pleaded guilty to being the publisher of the American birth control pamphlet, Dr Charles Knowlton's Fruits of Philosophy *(Doc. 65). This work had, in fact, been on James Watson's lists since the 1830s and had been sold for him by the Holyoake brothers, but on Watson's death in 1874 the original publisher's plates had passed to Watts, and Watts was now not particularly anxious to associate himself with this portion of his radical inheritance. Bradlaugh and his new associate, Annie Besant, immediately broke with Watts and republished the work. They were prosecuted and found guilty, but Bradlaugh found a legal loophole and had the sentences quashed.*[10] *Meanwhile a purge had begun, and the venerable Owenite publisher (who had actually lived in the Queenwood Community), Edward Truelove,*[11] *was gaoled for four months for publishing another birth control work by Robert Dale Owen.*

Bradlaugh had taken a gamble. The advocacy of birth control was not universally popular among Secularists, and his action splintered the N.S.S., which had in 1876 at last begun to recover from the setbacks of the mid-1870s. Several other prominent Secularists, led by Holyoake, Watts and G. W. Foote, withdrew from the N.S.S. to form their own British Secular Union, but Bradlaugh succeeded in projecting the issue not as birth control but as freedom of publication. He was thus able to set up all the old cries of bigotry and persecution, which brought renewed support to his movement. His own legal victory in 1878 added further to the prestige of his name and that of all associated with him (Doc. 25).

In 1880 Bradlaugh fought the parliamentary constituency of Northampton, as he had in 1868 and 1874 (twice); only this time he was elected. In parliament he applied to make a civil affirmation instead of the customary oath, on the grounds that he was an atheist. This was refused him, but he was also prevented from taking the oath because he had already owned it to be meaningless to him. This seemed to Bradlaugh to be an unconstitutional act, for he was a legally elected representative. The Tory opposition, egged on by Lord Randolph Churchill, took advantage of a weak Speaker to use the Bradlaugh case to waste the time of Gladstone's government. Other Tories perhaps more sincerely felt that a notorious and avowed atheist should be prevented from joining the governors of a Christian country. The technique used by Bradlaugh's opponents was to try to bankrupt him in order to disqualify him from parliament, and to do this one Tory M.P., Charles Newdigate Newdegate, pursuaded a common informer named Clarke to sue in the courts for the £500 penalty payable for each parliamentary division in which Bradlaugh had voted without having first taken the oath. Bradlaugh fought this case through all the courts, by all the legal twists he knew, right to the House of Lords. The more his costs and those of his opponent mounted, the more vital it was that he should win. Finally after three years he obtained a ruling that a common informer could not sue for the penalty. Then, in triumph, he successfully prosecuted Newdegate for the antique offence of maintenance[12] (Doc. 70).

During this constitutional crisis, in which Bradlaugh was repeatedly re-elected by Northampton and repeatedly rejected by the House of Commons, and during which the drama of several tense legal battles was never far from the headlines, Bradlaugh became a national figure, and his instrument, the N.S.S., became a campaigning organisation with a strong moral conviction and sense of purpose. More new branches were founded and over a thousand new members were added every year during the campaign. By 1884 there were over a hundred branches and membership must have exceeded 10,000. Those attracted to Bradlaugh himself, though, far exceeded this number. Wherever he held meetings, particularly in his London Hall of Science, the audiences were packed and overflowing (Doc. 25).

The year 1885, though, probably represents the turning point in the history of Secularism. References to decline and setbacks begin to occur, problems usually being attributed to the trade depression.[13] New forms of political activity began to emerge in the shape of the Social Democratic Federation. The violent socialists with no respect for property, whom Bradlaugh had condemned since the late 1860s, were beginning to make their marks on English radicalism. However small the early socialist groups were, they began to draw off some support, and in so far as Secularism had had a mass appeal because it was associated with the political Left, this outflanking movement was to have serious consequences for future growth (Doc. 61). Further, the admittance of Bradlaugh to parliament in 1886 took his name from the headlines. Whether he liked it or not, he had joined the Establishment.

Bradlaugh had no real successor. After his retirement in 1890 and premature death early in 1891 the N.S.S. continued under the presidency of G. W. Foote, and although the National Reformer *failed in 1893 Foote's* Freethinker *(founded 1881) continued the tradition, as it still does. But though the N.S.S. carried on with its work and still, at least until the Boer War, attracted much support, it no longer appealed in the same way to the same sorts of people who had earlier joined it. Thinking working men were finding new outlets for their energies in the growing numbers of socialist*

*societies, and although some of the most attractive of the new leaders (such
as Robert Blatchford) were infidels, their freethought was no longer central to their radicalism. Paine was no longer the founding father – he had
been displaced by Marx – and when the Fabians resurrected the reputation
of Robert Owen it was to present him as the father of English socialism,
not as a pioneer of English freethought. The sort of doctrines propounded
by Paine – individualism, rationalism, freethought, republicanism – wore
an old-fashioned look by the end of the nineteenth century. Charles Bradlaugh was really the last of the old-style radicals to make any real impact
on the national scene, and with him the Paineite tradition as a separate and
potent force in British ultra-radicalism can be said to have come to an end.*

NOTES

1. *Utilitarian Record* (issued with *Reasoner*, vol. IV) 26 Jan 1848; *Reasoner*, 16 Feb 1848.
2. See R. T. Shannon, 'David Urquhart and the Foreign Affairs Com- mittees', pp. 250–2, in P. Hollis (ed.), *Pressure from Without* (1974) pp. 239–61.
3. For further details, see E. Royle, *Victorian Infidels* (1974) pp. 203–7.
4. *London Investigator*, May 1854.
5. For Barker, see entry in *Biographical Dictionary of British Labour Movements*. He broke with Bradlaugh over the latter's praise of a birth control book, *The Elements of Social Science*, which he thought immoral.
6. *National Reformer*, 2, 9 Sep 1866. A list of 'Objects' of the National Secular Society is reprinted in E. Royle, *Radical Politics*, p. 124.
7. *National Reformer*, 14 Apr 1867.
8. The International claimed that Bradlaugh had sold himself to the Tories – *National Reformer*, 12 Nov 1871; Bradlaugh had already attacked the Inter- national as foreign and unrepresentative. Ibid., 8 Oct 1871.
9. Ibid., 1 Oct. 1871.
10. D. Tribe, *President Charles Bradlaugh, M.P.* (1971) pp. 173–82.
11. Edward Truelove (1809–99): secretary and bookseller at the Owenite John Street Institution; went to Harmony Hall; opened a shop in the Strand, 1852; prosecuted for publishing sedition, 1858. *Reformer*, 15 May 1899.
12. W. L. Arnstein, *The Bradlaugh Case* (Oxford, 1965).
13. E.g. *National Reformer*, 31 May 1885, 2 Dec 1888.

20 Secular societies in 1852*

Secularist organisation was slow to develop, but the report of the first Secular Conference, held in the hall of the Manchester society in 1852, gives some idea of the extent to which local remnants of radicalism (of zetetic, Owenite and Chartist varieties) had survived.

THE FIRST SECULAR CONFERENCE FOR THE ORGANISATION OF FREETHINKERS.

REPORT.—II.

Bolton Secular Society.—Twenty-seven members. Place of meeting, Bowker's Row, Gt. Bolton. Secretary, Stephen Bulmer, Union Buildings, Bradshawgate, Bolton. Bolton members conceded to be sober and intelligent.

Blackburn Secular Society.—Fifty members—increase probable. Meet in the Mutual Instruction Association Rooms, Ainsworth Street. Secretary, Thomas Stevenson, jun., 33, Lyon Street, Blackburn. Estimation of the society by the public open to improvement. 300 persons are known to hold views similar to the seculars in Blackburn.

Burnley Branch of the Secular Society.—Twenty-eight members. Meet in Hammerton Street. Secretary, J. Catton, St. James Street. The seculars considered, in a moral point of view, quite equal to Christians.

Bury.—Mr. Meadows gave hopes of the activity of this place, where many friends exist. A new society is being formed here, upon the plan laid down at the Conference. Secretary, Christopher Meadows, Princess Street, Bury.

Bradford Branch of the Secular Society.—Forty-nine members. Meet in Mitchell's Temperance Hotel, Union Street. Secretary, Thomas Wilcox, 32, Adelaide Street, Manchester Road, Bradford. The society has lately lost position by the engagement of Mr. W. W. Broom. The council paid Mr. Broom according to agreement, and suspended his lectures, being such for which they felt they could not be responsible.

Glasgow Eclectic Hall.—The members are about fifty in number. Meet at 14, Garthland Street, opposite the Trades' Hall, Glasford Street. Secretary, John Wright, 160, High Street,

* From *Reasoner*, 27 Oct 1852.

Glasgow.

Keighley Secular Society.—Twelve members. Hold lectures in the Working Man's Hall, where they have established a school. Secretary of the society, Joseph Firth, care of Mr. D. Weatherhead, Keighley. The report from this place had the following passage worth quoting in the first person:— 'There are many freethinkers in Keighley, but for different reasons they do not appear to be free to associate. In any neutral place, say the market, we believe we could obtain a show of hands in favour of our principles. Hoping that your deliberations will be guided by sound discretion, and that you will aim at little but do much, is the sincere wish of yours, on behalf of the members of the Keighley Secular Society, JOSEPH FIRTH.'

Leigh Secular Society.—Sixteen members. Assemble at James Cook's, Bookseller, Sugar Street. Secretary, John Cook, Sugar Street. Public estimations favourable—good prospect of wider union of freethinkers.

Manchester Secular Society.—Seventy members—the society recast. Meets at the Secular Institution, Old Garratt. Corresponding Secretary, Wilkinson Burslam, 43, Brook Street, Old Garratt, Manchester. The members of this branch have been associated two years. They have engaged as lecturers Messrs. G. J. Holyoake, George Hooper, Thornton Hunt, R. Cooper, George Edwards, &c., during which time they have paid upwards of £100 for lectures, and £50 for advertising. 'The delegates do not claim to represent the very large number of secularists resident in Manchester, but simply those who choose to avail themselves of the opportunity afforded them of meeting for mutual improvement and the hearing of lectures at the Secular Institution. The number enrolled for this purpose will be about seventy, while the actual number of freethinkers in Manchester must be over two thousand. We could not expect, for various reasons, that all this number would attend to our appeal for organisation. To some we were too insignificant, to others our place of meeting was rather obscure. But we intend to make an effort to remedy these defects. We are taking steps to erect a new Hall, in which we are promised Mr. Holyoake's aid.

Miles Platting.—No special society was reported from in this district. Correspondent, Mr. Thomas Hayes, Failsworth, near

Manchester.

Newcastle-on-Tyne Secular Society.—The report of this society was as follows:—One of those Christians who think it useful to come up to the battle of the Lord, recently described Newcastle-on-Tyne as 'swarming with atheists.' Although this, like the Bible, is not to be understood literally, yet is so far true that there are some 'Complete Dissenters'—what is more, they appear to have a desire to 'swarm' into one hive, from whence they think they can sally forth in a compact body to do battle with the 'common enemy' somewhat more effectually than by the isolated, *guerilla* kind of warfare they have practised in the past. They have therefore formed themselves into a society, which at present numbers twenty members, and which has taken the name of the Newcastle Secular Society. They hold weekly meetings in the Committee Room of the Nun Street Reading Rooms, which they occupy free of charge. The Lecture Room in Nelson Street, capable of containing 1000 persons, is open to them on the same conditions as to other bodies. Freethinking lecturers attract large audiences in this town, and, notwithstanding the silence of the local press respecting us, our principles have made, and are making, hopeful progress. Reverend gentlemen are beginning to find that they must do something, and we have accordingly from time to time a running fire of lectures and tracts. . .

The society has issued a neat card of membership.—JAMES CHARLTON, Corresponding Secretary.

Nottingham Secular Society.—The number of paying members are thirty-one, and the attendance of non-members very encouraging. The place of meeting is capable of holding 250 persons. The society can obtain the use of the Assembly Room, holding 1200 or 1300, which has been refused to other parties very recently—a proof that the society is held in higher estimation than some sections of the Christians. Secretary, Joseph Place, Chancery Court, Broad Marsh, Nottingham.

Over Darwen.—Four members. No place of meeting at present—no public credit, unless discredit in religious opinion may be called credit. Secretary, George Adcroft, Green Street, Over Darwen.

Paisley Society of Social Friends.—Numbers fifty members. Meets in Wilson Hall, 40, High Street. The Hall holds 150 persons. The society can command a large hall capable of holding 800. Secretary, James Motherwell, Bookseller, Cross, Paisley. As to character, 'Detested by the rigidly religious, tolerated by the mass, and held as honest and honourable by a few.' 'Pursuant to request in No. 329 of the *Reasoner*, the Paisley Society of Social Friends beg leave to report further, that their society has maintained an existence for the last fourteen years, originally and for some years in connection with the Rational Society; lately—when, in our opinion, the connection served no useful purpose—as an independent body, holding the same views as before, seeking to promote their progress by weekly meetings for lectures, discussions, social parties, schools, &c. Like all bodies of a similar kind, our teachings have never been strictly secular; more anti-theological than socialistic. Because, when we attempted to demonstrate the possibility of an improvement in temporal matters, opponents called upon us to think upon things unseen, so we were compelled to demonstrate the futility of such attention. We consequently hail with satisfaction the meeting of the Conference, and trust its deliberation will result in establishing an extensive organisation. Next Sunday our society discusses the propositions of the Secular Society as given in the *Reasoner*.—JAMES MOTHERWELL.'

Preston.—The number of freethinkers associated here is about twenty, but 300 might be organised under the name of the Secular Society. We have a small room for meeting in, but a hall capable of holding 700 is available. We have no secretary permanently, but I shall always feel happy in acting as such myself. Freethinkers as a body are looked upon with Christian abhorrence, which meaneth much in this town.—JAMES LENNON, Bookseller, Newton Street.

Rochdale.—The number of persons associated here are fifteen, under the denomination of the Rochdale Secular Society. They have no regular meeting place yet, but one can be commanded capable of holding 1000 persons. Secretary, Abraham Greenwood, Mooss, near the Ship Inn, Rochdale. Public estimation for practical capacity favourable—that is, of freethinkers generally in this place.

Stafford.—A few persons only are professedly associated, but they are likely to confederate with the Conference societies. Distinctive action is much needed here.—WILLIAM TUNSTALL.

Stockport Rational Society.—Twenty-four members. Hall, the Lyceum, Wellington Street. Secretary, Martin Birch, Thomas Street, Stockport. 'The estimation in which freethinkers are held in Stockport rather low by the religious, but by the general public is pretty good.'

Sheffield.—The Rational Society of Sheffield numbers thirty-two members, having for meetings a large Hall ('Hall of Science') at their command. Sheffield has a large population of freethinkers, who, though unorganised, exercise great influence in the public affairs of the town. The well-known convictions of several men of considerable mental attainments, tend much to soften down the expressions of discourtesy and rudeness too commonly used by the Christian public regarding those who differ in principle with them upon theology. Indeed, the class of secularists are acknowledged (grudgingly) to be of 'service' to the well-being of the community, and the activity of more than one challenges respect from all quarters. Secretary, William Lawton, Pea Croft, Sheffield.

Todmorden.—A society is in progress here. The Court House can be had for lectures, and many friendly parties exist. Secretary, William Mallalieu, Todmorden.

After these reports were delivered, the chairman read the draft of a constitution, which closed the morning sitting.

At the conclusion of the afternoon sitting (which we hope to report next week) a meeting, numerously attended, was held in the Secular Institution, which was addressed by Mr. James R. Cooper, of Manchester, Mr. John D. Hague, jun., of Sheffield, and Mr. G. J. Holyoake, who spoke to the following resolution, which closed the business of the day:—'That this meeting is of opinion that the conduct of Christian preachers, the tone of Christian literature towards freethinkers, and the disabilities imposed by Christian laws upon the freedom of theological conviction, warrant the organisation of secularists, both for the defence of themselves and the dissemination of their views.'

21 The Leicester Secular Society*

One such local society, that at Leicester, was recommenced in 1852, and its
* From the Minutes of the Leicester Secular Society, Leicester Museum.

progress was typical. The initial impetus came from former local Owen-
ites, but the occasion for the revival was a visit from one of the national lea-
ders, Holyoake. His lectures led to public controversy, a set debate, and
renewed interest as in the days of Owenism.

Leicester Secular Society　　　　　　　　　　　　Officers
　　　　President　　　　　　　　　　Mr. James Plant
　　　　Treasurer　　　　　　　　　　Mr. Josiah Gimson[1]
　　　　Corresponding Secy.　　　　　Mr. Thomas Emery
　　　　Financial Secy.　　　　　　　Mr. William Holyoak[2]
　　　　General Secretary　　　　　　Mr. James Plant

　　　　　　　　　Committee
　　　　Mr. Wm. Bilson
　　　　Mr. Wm. Cooke
　　　　Mr. Wm. Glover

Rules. Meetings, held by summons, or otherwise as deemed
　　　　necessary. Subscriptions, made at such times as
　　　　required, not to be less at one time than Sixpence
　　　　each member

　　　　　　　Objects of the Society
First,　To Register in a book provided for the purpose a List of
　　　　all Persons in Leicester or Leicestershire favour-
　　　　able to Freedom of Thought & Speech
Second,　To superintend & extend the Sale of The "Reasoner"
Third,　To prepare & manage all discussions upon the Prin-
　　　　ciples of 'Secularism'
Fourth,　To aid in abolishing all Laws limiting the fullest free-
　　　　dom of Thought & Speech, & to procure that
　　　　respect & freedom for the Principles of Secularists
　　　　accorded to all other Sects & Parties

　　1852, Lectures by Mr. George Jacob Holyoake delivered at
the Assembly Rooms Granby Street on Evenings of May 19th
& 25th.

　　Subject of the Lectures "Roman Catholicism the type of the
Churches around us" 1st night "On a New Developement [sic]
of the Principles of Free Enquirers" 2d night. Admission 3d &
1d Total Receipts 1st night £1-9s-11d 2nd £1-6s-9d

Total Expenditure £6-14s-0d Loss £3-17s-4d
Collected by Voluntary Subscriptions among friends of free
thought 5-9-5½ Average attendance each night 250

Receipts	2–16–8
Collected	5– 9–5½
	8–6–1½
Expenses	6–14–0
Balance	1–12–1½

A Mr. Cecil offered some remarks at the above Lectures which
brought on the following Discussion

Days. – Wednesday and Thursday June 9th & 10th.
Time. – ½ past 7. half an hour to each at opening and ¼ of an
hour afterwards, close at ½ past 10.
Wednesday – Cecil opens. Holyoake concludes
Thursday – Holyoake opens. Cecil concludes
Terms of Admission. 6d. Front. 3d. Orchestra and back seats.
1d Hall
Expenses. Each Party pays its own Advocate's expenses and
the Committee pay out of receipts all other
expenses, of hiring Hall, Police, Printing, Adver-
tising &c. in Journal Mercury & Chronicle.
25 Posters 500 small bills after expenses paid the
overplus to be divided between the two Committees. Mr. Anderson Treasurer
Doors. Mr. Brown & Mr. Emery at bottom
Mr. Cox and Mr.   at top
Mr. Plant engaged two Police
100 Tickets for Front 400 back 500 Hall. If any loss
the Committee of each party to pay an equal share.
On behalf of Mr. Cecil's Committee J. F. Winks[3]
On behalf of Mr. Holyoake's Committee James Plant
June 3rd 1852.

June 13th at a meeting of the joint committees. present Mr. J. F.
Winks, Cox, Preston, Plant, Bilson, Emery, Holyoak the following was read

Receipts, First night	£4–11–10
Receipts, Second night	4– 9– 7
Total	9– 1– 5

Expenses, Hire of Hall   2–11– 0
  Advertising, Journal Chronicle Mercury   0–17– 6
  Police 2/6, Bill dis[tributin]g   0– 8– 0
  Printing   0–19–11
  Cash dividend   4– 5– 0
                               £9– 1– 5

Attendance, June 9th Hall 352. Back Seats & Orchestra 156.
Front 47   – Total 555
June 10th Hall 345. Back Seats & Orchestra 150. Front 47
     – Total 542
at the close of the Second Nights Discussion Mr. J. F. Winks
challenged Mr. Holyoake to discussion, which was accepted
Received for above discussion   2– 0– 0
Money collected for loss per balance   1–12– $1\frac{1}{2}$
     Total received   3–12– $1\frac{1}{2}$
Mr. Holyoakes Fee & paid, to allow 2/-   4– 6– 0
Loss on di[scu]ss[io]n   0–13–$10\frac{1}{2}$[4]

NOTES

1. Josiah Gimson (1818–83): head of a Leicester engineering firm; follower of
   Robert Owen and secretary of the local Owenite branch; later president of
   the Leicester Secular Society, and a town councillor.
2. William Holyoak (1818–1907): tailor and draper; bookseller at the Leicester Secular Hall; behind every move to set up freethought organisations in
   Leicester for fifty years.
3. Joseph Foulkes Winks (1792–1866): a Baptist printer and editor; friend of
   Thomas Cooper, the Chartist; pioneer of Adult Schools; leading member
   of the Leicester Complete Suffrage Association in 1842; prominent advocate of disestablishment; unpaid minister at Carley Street Church, Leicester, 1839–60. *Baptist Handbook* (1867) p. 139. I am grateful to Dr D. M.
   Thompson for this source.
4. This loss was more than covered by the debate arranged next between
   Holyoake and Winks.

22 West Riding district organisation*

Attempts at national organisation did not make much progress in the

* Leaflet in Holyoake Collection, Manchester, no. 882

1850s, but there was more success at the regional level, especially in Lancashire and Yorkshire which had been at the heart of Owenite strength.

PRINCIPLES, CONSTITUTION AND OBJECTS OF THE WEST RIDING SECULAR UNION.

PREAMBLE.

This being the second year of the Union's existence, the friends of secularism desire to extend its operations.[1] For this purpose, they invite other persons to come forward and organize for the attainment of the objects here specified. A selection of earnest men will suffice! The invitation is to ALL those who agree with us as to what is to be done, and who will do it, with moderate speed, in labour, and in good faith. These ARE the persons indispensable for the work we have to do. The time is come when we must seek that unity which gives strength and means. While we have restricted ourselves to individual exertion, the believers in Popular Theology, have treat us with contempt, ignored our existence, – and have refused to believe our word as to our opinions. The purpose of this Alliance is to render secular service to mankind; and the PROTECTION of its members against the PRACTICAL consequences of speculative errors. This Alliance endorses the right of free discussion on all subjects; and pledges its support to the secular movement, by extending its literature, and by promoting its efficient organization throughout the country. The principle upon which the union is founded is SECULARISM.

Secularism is the practical philosophy of life. And a secularist is one who believes that his duties pertain to this life, and who gives primary attention to those subjects, the issues of which can be tested by human experience! Secularism teaches that SCIENCE is the providence of man, and warns them that absolute spiritual dependance in human affairs will inevitably involve them in material destruction! Secularism inculcates MORALS, independent of religion, by basing them upon secular considerations more immediate, more demonstrative and universal than those furnished by scriptural theology! These are a few of the fundamental principles of secularism.

OBJECTS OF THE ALLIANCE.

1st. The inculcation of Positive Philosophy, corrective of Popular Theology.

2nd. Devising of secular plans for the improvement of human kind.

3rd. Defence of secular truth, against whatever contradicts it, or whatever impedes its progress.

4th. Where a special error requires to be combated, or some erroneous impression to be corrected, a paper upon it will be prepared in this manner. The subject being stated, each person will give his opinion upon it. After this suggestive discussion, papers will be prepared by the several members and read at the next meeting, and the best chosen. The other papers will be placed at the service of the successful writer, and the writer remunerated for its production. Such paper or tract to be the property of the union.

OPERATIONS OF THE UNION,

Will consist of CAMP MEETINGS, LECTURES, DISTRIBUTIONS OF TRACTS, THE ESTABLISHING OF SECULAR SUNDAY SCHOOLS, rendering help to those that are in existence in the shape of Donations of Books, Delivery of Lectures, &c.; also the formation of Freethought Libraries in most towns and villages in the riding.

For this purpose they invite the co-operation of all friends of secularism. They would also suggest to the Secular Societies the propriety of contributing one penny per month per member to the funds of the union. And to those friends who are not members of any society, they invite to come forward and join the union. "Union is strength." Our efforts to be successful must be in concert one with another. If you think your principles worth propagating – organize! If you desire to free the land from superstition, priestcraft, and ignorance, under whatever name, come forward and render your support! If you wish to see the benign principles of secularism spread o'er the land, come forward and assist! If you wish your children to be educated – to be taught truths of democracy and of secularism – and to be taught apart from an immoral and vicious system of theology – give us your support! If you wish to be a friend of your country and your kind, come and help to spread the glorious gospel of social advancement, of education, of progress, and of freedom, "and the work will go on and bravely too."

Annual subscriptions One Shilling and upwards. Parties wishing to join the union may do so on application to the Secretary, or to any member of the Committee.

Donations of Money, Books, Tracts, &c., will be thankfully received, and duly acknowledged. Meetings are held on the 2nd Sunday in each month.

The place of meeting will be announced in the *Reasoner, Investigator,* and *Tribune,* prior to the time.

SIGNED,

JEREMIAH OLIVE, *President*

SAMUEL FIRTH, *Vice President*

UNION COMMITTEE.

ALBERT THORNTON,	DAN BOTTOMLEY,
THOMAS WILCOCK,	JOHN HALSTEAD,
JOSEPH WILKS,	JONATHAN HINCHLIFFE,
J. PEARSON,	ROBERT WILSON,
ABRAHAM DRAKE,	SAMUEL HALSTEAD,
HENRY HARTLEY,	FRANK FIELD,
SAMUEL HODGSON,	THOMAS BENTLEY,
JOSHUA WOMERSLEY,	THOMAS TAYLOR,
WILLIAM PICKLES,	J. WOFFENDEN,
WATTS BALMFORTH,	MOSES CLAYTON,
JOSEPH BAMFORD,	WILLIAM MITCHELL.
URIAH LANGLEY,	

CHARLES BARRACLOUGH, *Treasurer.*

THOMAS OATES, *Secretary*

To whom all communications must be addressed, at SHIBDEN, NEAR HALIFAX.

NOTE

1. The West Riding Secular Union (or Alliance) was founded at a meeting at Mitchell's Temperance Hotel, Bradford, on 13 June 1852. *Reasoner,* 7 July 1852.

23 Robert Cooper's militancy*

Differences in policy began to emerge in the 1850s between Holyoake, who

* From *London Investigator* (Apr 1854).

increasingly wished to compromise his militant views when secular progress seemed to demand it, and Robert Cooper, who wished to maintain the traditional outspokenness of ultra-radical freethought. This latter position was the one subsequently adopted also by Charles Bradlaugh. In 1854 Cooper began his own monthly periodical, the London Investigator, *in which to advocate his own policies against the expediency of Holyoake's* Reasoner.

OUR POLICY

Reason has never two faces. Let us show but one front to the enemy.

The age of expediency in theology, as in politics, is past. We aim to be a Reasoner but not a Trimmer. Aspiring enough we may be as a Leader, but not weak enough to be a Feeler. A true Reasoner is one who has the courage to follow reason *wherever* it leads him. A legitimate Leader[1] is one who is in *advance* of his contemporaries, labours to develope the *full* object of his mission, and bring the world to it. He who only follows reason as far as it is fashionable, or, as it is now the fashion to designate it, "useful," is only a hanger-on of progress. If truth is only to be spoken so far as it is "useful," or, in other words, convenient, we are necessarily led to the conclusion it is sometimes "useful" to allow error to remain unchallenged. This is only the old doctrine of the Christian Fathers recast—the *end* justifies the *means.* Such a policy throughout our public life we have uniformly repudiated, and to its rules we can never subscribe. Popular advocacy, to be honourable or healthy, must be based on *principle*— not "art." The warmth of honesty, rather than the coolness of expediency, can alone give life and vigour to a great movement. Temporizing till error seems in the humour to give way, will always keep truth in the rear, and enable oppression and superstition to ride in pomp and pride through the world. No delusion could be more fatal than supposing that despotism, political or religious, will concede one inch, except by force, moral or physical. The spirit of domination will never voluntarily relinquish her throne.

History teaches the great lesson that no epoch in progress has been developed and consummated by expediency. The Reformation was not the work of expediency. The English Revolution was not the result of expediency. American Independence was not the reward of expediency. A Free Press, and a Cheap Press, in Great Britain, was not achieved by expediency. Had Luther been a trimmer he would never have shook Papacy. Had Cromwell been a trimmer he would never have dethroned Kingcraft. Had Paine been a trimmer, he would never have set our aristocracy at defiance. Had Richard Carlile and Henry Hetherington been trimmers, a Free and Cheap Literature would have been strangled at their birth.

Neither do we eschew antagonism, for, if "opposition is our opportunity," antagonism is a duty. By antagonism we do not mean personality or recrimination, but a bold, a manly, a straightforward, an unmistakeable attack on error, and an unflinching and undisguised development of the truth. It is to place a cause in a false position to see Right and Wrong standing at a respectful distance, tendering reciprocal blandishments, or, which is more equivocal, walking arm and arm so closely that neither party appear to know at what point they met, or to what destination they are tending.

We have been led into these observations from the growing conviction that a crisis has approached when the nature and policy of Secularism must be distinctly defined. We must understand whether it is to be a laboured iteration of unmeaning homilies on some vague principle—so large in its character as to include anything, so indefinite in its object as to explain nothing—or whether it is to consist in a well-disciplined and openly-avowed organization against the theological fallacies of the age, with the direct view of calmly leading mankind to the rational conviction that it is our duty to secure that happiness, freedom, and virtue *here*, so long promised us *"hereafter."* We are Secularists, not as having a right to give preference to the duties of this life "over another," but because we know of no other— believe in no other. We are Secularists, not because we esteem the theory of a First Cause a "problem," but a fallacy. We are Secularists, not as considering science "the providence of life," but the *only* providence of life. We are Secularists, not as accepting the good and rejecting the offensive in the Bible, but because we are sincerely of opinion its claims to divine origin are an assumption. The objectionable in Scripture no enlightened mind will defend,—the useful can be found elsewhere. This policy is intelligible, candid, and consistent. The Christian understands what he has to prove,—the Secularist what he has to answer. We need not take a crooked and tortuous route, when a broad and glorious path is before us. So far from conciliating, such a course excites only the secret derision of enemies, and the open distrust of friends.

The working classes need something more than that refinement of eclecticism which leads the people into a maze of ambiguity and incertitude. Bewildered they have been too long. With such regimen they are nauseated. Their want now is *sound instruction and organization*. The former can be best imparted by plainness. The latter will only be effected and maintained by consistency. Our path, therefore, is chosen.[2]

NOTES

1. An oblique reference to the *Leader*, a weekly middle-class radical paper edited by Thornton Hunt, to which Holyoake contributed political items over the pseudonym 'Ion'. The tone of these items was moderate and compromising.
2. Compare this denunciation of expediency by Cooper with the argument *for* expediency written by him eight years later (Doc. 56).

24 The progress of freethought *

In the early 1860s, under the influence of Charles Bradlaugh and his weekly periodical the National Reformer, *Secularism expanded rapidly both in London and the industrial north. The following is a description of 'Freethought in England' given by John Watts, editor of the* National Reformer, *in an open letter 'To the Editor of the "Boston Investigator"'.*

From what I have already stated you will see that the cause of truth is in the ascendant. The labours of those who have "gone before" have not been in vain; but much remains yet to be done. You will be glad, therefore, to learn that Secularistic Freethought is in a healthy condition with us. In London we have several places of meeting, where lectures and discussions regularly take place every Sunday. The Hall of Science, the place

* From *National Reformer*, 5 Nov 1864.

which we, and those most intimately connected with us, frequent, is capable of accommodating at least six hundred persons, and it is always well attended, very often crowded to inconvenience. It is a respectable looking and exceedingly well-conducted Hall. The proprietor, Mr. Bendall, is a long-tried and staunch friend of Freethought, and one in whose hands the cause would never suffer. He is, I believe, without one enemy, and he certainly deserves to be. He is assisted in the management by Mr. J. P. Adams[1], an energetic and untiring advocate, one who is seldom weary and never defeated. The lecturers at this Hall you doubtless see advertised from time to time. The most popular platform advocate is Mr. Bradlaugh, who lectures under the pseudonym of Iconoclast. He is well read in the various books in and about the Bible, possesses a good memory, with more than the average amount of wit, is very ready in reply, and has a voice that would render it a difficult task for any one in the neighbourhood where he may happen to be lecturing to escape its sound. We have also a very energetic and talented lady advocate in the person of Mrs. Law,[2] who, in addition to her many anti-theological lectures, is a persistent advocate, as you may suppose, of the rights of women, a subject that has received a good deal of attention in England during the past few years. Mr. G. J. Holyoake has recently devoted most of his time to neutral journalism, and has not, of late, often appeared on our platform, but he is, I am sure, as firmly attached to Freethought principles as ever he was. His brother, Mr. Austin Holyoake[3], who has been connected with the Freethought movement many years, has only recently appeared as a public lecturer, and has achieved a success that induced a very prevalent inquiry as to why he remained silent so long. The last addition to our lecturing staff is one to whom I am not altogether unknown—Mr. Charles Watts[4]. This is his first session, and I am informed that his last lecture was not only a success, but a great triumph. There are many others, whose names and abilities space will not permit me to enlarge upon. They are occupied at Cleveland Street Hall[5], which is a very fine one, and in various other parts of London, as you may see by a reference to our "guide to the lecture room," and by reports of their meetings. Not only in London, but also in the provinces, is the same activity apparent. In almost every large town in the North of

England are Freethinkers to be found and Freethought lecturers to be heard. At no previous period has there been so many good local lecturers and writers throughout the country as at the present time, and this, you will readily understand, is a source of great strength, for when the more prominent advocates are not "on circuit," their place is ably filled by local friends, who are always ready to expose Christian misrepresentation, and to defend those truths that are yet destined to set men free.

NOTES

1. J. P. Adams: brought into politics by the Anti-Corn Law League and had his Christian faith shaken by W. J. Fox; secretary and bookseller at the London Hall of Science.
2. Mrs Harriet Law (1832–97): a convert from the Baptists; began free-thought lecturing in 1859.
3. Charles Watts (1836–1906): son of a Wesleyan minister and younger brother of John Watts (1834–66; a printer and editor of the *National Reformer* 1863–6); secretary of the National Secular Society, 1866–71; sub-editor of the *National Reformer*, 1864–77; broke with Bradlaugh over the Knowlton Pamphlet, 1877; emigrated to Canada, 1886, and returned, 1891. Father of Charles Albert Watts, the publisher.
4. Austin Holyoake (1827–74): fourth brother of G. J. Holyoake; printer for and later publisher with his brother at 147 Fleet Street, and on his own from 1864 at 17 Johnson's Court.
5. The Cleveland Street Hall was opened in 1861 to replace the old John Street Institution.

25 The National Secular Society*

In 1866 Charles Bradlaugh gave Secularism its most enduring structure when he launched the National Secular Society. The work and activities of this society were numerous and embraced all aspects of ultra-radicalism, but all was centred on the activities of Charles Bradlaugh. One of the leading London members, George Standring, set down his recollections in a monthly paper which Bradlaugh's daughter edited in the later 1890s.

It was in 1873 that I first came into contact with Secularists. Having left the theological fold in consequence of an unreasoned but abiding conviction of the emptiness of "religion", I attended several lectures given by the Christian Evidence So-

* From *Reformer*, 15 July, 15 Aug 1898.

ciety at the Hall of Science[1], partly, no doubt, in the hope that
my faith might be rehabilitated. The trained Christian advocates, however, gave me a definite impulse towards disbelief,
and a few months of constant reading, together with the influence of many lectures by Mr. Bradlaugh, resulted in a determination to seek active communion with the Secular party.

My first efforts were devoted to a small local society called
the Hackney Secular Association, which met every Sunday for
lectures and discussion in a squalid hall in Goldsmith's Row[2].
In the conduct of this I became associated with other young
men, many of whom have long since disappeared or become
absorbed in other pursuits. As secretary, chairman, and occasional "lecturer" I worked vigorously and incessantly. My
connection with this group led, in 1874, to an introduction to
Mr. Bradlaugh, and shortly afterwards I became a member of
the executive of the National Secular Society[3] (hereinafter
called the N.S.S.).

As time went on the N.S.S. waxed stronger. Many new
branches were established in the provinces; and the re-opening
of the Hall of Science Club and Institute led to greatly increased
activity in the metropolis. The Central London Branch, for
example, had a very large number of members on its books, and
carried on out-door propaganda simultaneously at Gibraltar
Walk, Clerkenwell Green, and Victoria Park every Sunday
during the summer. At Claremont Hall and St. Pancras Arches
the North London Branch did effective work. In South London,
at Blackfriars Road and York Street, Walworth, lectures were
given every Sunday by local organisations; and at Deptford Mr.
W. H. Reynolds established an efficient and prosperous society. In East London, Mr. J. F. Haines was the centre of successful propaganda. Mr. T. E. Green kept the flag flying at
Kingston-on-Thames; he printed a penny Secular Hymn-book
on his amateur-press, from type set up by his own hands. Thus
the work of the N.S.S. went merrily on . . .

In the work of such a society as the N.S.S. there must necessarily have been large tracts of routine-desert, the crossing of
which would leave no distinct memories. The first oasis—and it
was a very fertile one—that I can recall resulted from the prosecution of the Knowlton pamphlet in 1877. It is unnecessary

here to repeat the oft-told story of that famous struggle, which ended in so signal a victory for the cause of freedom. I am now only concerned with its influence upon the fortunes of the N.S.S. The impetus which it gave to the society was enormous. In all parts of the country members flocked into our ranks; for, though the advocacy of Malthusianism was no part of our duty as Secularists, yet the right of free publication was one for which many Freethinkers had suffered. I well remember the executive meeting at which Mr. Bradlaugh and Mrs. Besant, having made themselves responsible as publishers of the Knowlton pamphlet, tendered their resignations so that it might not be said that they had dragged the N.S.S. into the conflict. Mr. Bradlaugh explained to us, with his usual clearness and straightforwardness, the issues involved and the possible results of his action. The resignations of himself and of Mrs. Besant (as his partner in the publishing business) were then formally tendered and formally declined. The action of the executive in thus associating itself publicly with the defence of free publication was endorsed with practical unanimity by the party, and throughout that long and exciting struggle Mr. Bradlaugh had the satisfaction of knowing that the Secularists of Great Britain were at his back.

THE year 1880 deeply impressed itself upon my mind, for it was marked by events of importance alike to the Freethought party and to myself as a member thereof. On April 2nd Mr. Bradlaugh was elected member for Northampton, after twelve years of persistent effort. Thereupon followed that Titanic struggle on the "Oath Question", in which one man, almost single-handed, stood against the House of Commons, pleading and fighting for the right. At the Bar of the House his eloquence and dignified bearing extorted the admiration of his bitterest foes; in the course of long and harassing litigation he worsted by his legal skill and acumen the foremost lawyers of the day; and to all this was added the frequent strain of contested elections at Northampton. Those years of storm and stress gave the death-wound to the one great leader of the Freethought party.

The reflex action of the Oath agitation upon the Secular movement was prodigious. In the metropolis and provinces eighty branches of the N.S.S. were in active operation; Mr.

Bradlaugh's lectures throughout the country attracted crowds of recuits to local societies, and the enthusiasm of new members was sustained by the courage and resolution displayed by their leader. The Hall of Science was always crowded to excess on the Sunday evenings when Mr. Bradlaugh occupied the platform; and I have known scores of people on those occasions to pay a shilling for the privilege of standing in the passage, where, by bending low, they could catch a glimpse of the speaker, although it was impossible to hear a word of his lecture.

As time went on, the strain of Mr. Bradlaugh's parliamentary work began to tell upon even his exceptional powers. One day, in 1890, Mr. Forder[4] showed me at Stonecutter Street a letter that he had just received from Mr. Bradlaugh, instructing him as secretary to convene an Extraordinary General Meeting of the N.S.S. to receive the resignation of its President. My heart sank as I read the fateful lines, for I saw only too clearly that it was the "beginning of the end" in more than one sense. In due course the meeting took place at the Hall of Science; Mr. Bradlaugh, speaking with emotion painful to witness, gave back to the members the trust which they had reposed in him for so many years, and handed to his successor, whom he himself nominated, the symbol of office—a gavel that once belonged to Richard Carlile—expressing a hope that he would prove himself worthy of the position to which he had been elected. On that day it was felt by many that the glory of the N.S.S. had departed.

NOTES

1. The Christian Evidence Society (not to be confused with Robert Taylor's earlier deistical society of the same name) was an Evangelical organisation which hired the Hall of Science on Tuesday evenings.
2. For a description of a meeting at Goldsmith's Row, see C. M. Davies, *Heterodox London*, 2 vols (1874, reprinted 1969) vol. I, pp. 351–63, partly reproduced in E. Royle, *Radical Politics*, pp. 119–20.
3. Standring became assistant secretary when Bradlaugh revived the National Secular Society in August 1874, and was secretary from June 1876 to May 1877.
4. Robert Forder was secretary of the National Secular Society from May 1877 to June 1892.

PART TWO
The Movement

This section is intended to fill out the picture sketched above and to provide some glimpse of the people who were involved, and what being infidels meant to them. Radicalism in general — and infidelity in particular — was part of a way of life, the product of a set of assumptions and attitudes shared in the common experience of weekly meetings and social activities. The historical record often underestimates this essential characteristic of any movement. The direction taken by an organisation and the reporting of events in the published sources is usually a reflection of the interests, abilities and ideas of the leaders, but without a potential following who might respond to their call the orators and editors would have been condemned to frustrating failure.

The infidels, unlike the Chartists, never really attracted large numbers of followers — the 10,000 membership of the National Secular Society in the 1880s may well represent the peak of committed followers, but a single camp meeting in the north of England or one Sunday's audiences at Bradlaugh's Hall of Science could well approach that number. This breakthrough from paid-up membership to the wider support of a popular audience and the sharing of a common cultural heritage is what marks the movement off from the mere sect. Any working-class movement had to appeal to the prejudices and attract the sympathies of at least some ordinary men and women.

From Below

26 The raw materials (1)*

Impressions of what 'ordinary people' thought can be glimpsed through the eyes of those whose duty it was to visit them in their homes — the religious missionaries. The tone of the first extract, written at the height of Owenite activity, is typically Evangelical; while the second, in its more restrained approach, is equally typical of the Unitarian mission.

No. 19 DISTRICT.

"When your Missionary first entered his district, he was received with suspicion by some, with coldness or indifference by others, and not a few absolutely declined his instructions. The great majority of the people were living in sin, 'having no hope, and without God in the world,' and very few were in the habit of attending a place of worship. Only a limited portion of the people were supplied with religious tracts; about three-fourths of them possessed a copy of the Bible or the New Testament, but alas! few of them were regularly read. The number within the district of decided Socialists, strictly speaking, was very small, but their blasphemies on the Bible, and the Christian religion, had been widely disseminated, and had taken root. Your Missionary was repeatedly assailed with assertions of the following character, 'Poor people have no time to attend to religion!' 'We have so much to think about this world we cannot think about another.' 'Poor people suffer so much in this world they ought to go to heaven when they leave it.' 'We can

* From the Third Annual Report of the Manchester and Salford Town Mission (1840) pp. 14–15, 17, 18.

get to heaven without going to church or chapel.' 'The Bible is a
bad book.' 'The Bible cannot be God's book, it is so full of
inconsistencies.' 'If we love our neighbour as ourselves, we shall
get to heaven if there is one.' 'If we do the best we can for ourselves and families, we shall stand as good a chance as another
of getting to heaven.' A notion generally prevailed that religion
was only an instrument in the hands of the tyrant, for binding
more securely the yoke of oppression, on the neck of the people;
and that professors of religion of every sect assumed its garb
from sinister motives. Your Missionary cannot refrain from
drawing a parallel here, between the period of the first French
revolution, and that of the introduction of Owenism into this
country. At the former period, when the noxious principles of
infidelity were wafted o'er the British Channel from France, a
counteracting influence was presented in England, by the good
providence of God, in the institution of sabbath schools; at the
latter, when the pestilential and soul-destroying principles of
Owenism, were spreading from city to city, and from town to
town, a fitting antidote was found in the establishment of those
heaven-born institutions, City and Town Missions.

"One man, who had worked in company with men who belonged to the schools of Carlile and Owen, declared to your
Missionary, that he had done nothing worthy of hell, and that
he did not believe God would send him there. On a subsequent
occasion, he declared to a person standing by, 'I told my wife to
shut the door upon the Missionary when he came, and we often
had words about him, but he kept coming, and kept reading to
me in the Bible, and talking to me about Jesus.' Bursting into
tears, he said, 'if it had not been for this gentleman, I should
have gone to hell.' Your Missionary requested him to give the
praise to the Lord Jesus, as none but he could save, when the
dying man promptly replied, 'I am not giving the praise to you,
I mean you was the instrument; I was ignorant and you instructed me; you told me about Christ, that He said, *him that cometh to
me I will in no wise cast out;* and I have come to him, and I believe
he will not cast me out.'

.   .   .

"Another poor man had been drawn into the vortex of infidelity by the vile trash which came from the pen of Carlile. On

visiting him in his cellar of the most abject wretchedness, on the evening of his death, he was lying on a few rags, and his head raised up by the introduction of an old box. After reading the Gospel to him, your Missionary questioned him as to the foundation on which he was building, when he calmly replied, 'I believe in Jesus Christ, and have done ever since you visited me in the fever ward.' (A few months prior to this.) He thanked me with much feeling for my instructions, and bade me an affectionate farewell. Other cases of equal interest could be given, but time forbids."

27 The raw materials (2)*

Vast numbers of our adult population share with their children, this want of a wholesome religious influence. They never enter a house of prayer, or join in the public worship of God. This, very often, arises more from indifference, and the force of habit, than from any positive repugnance. I have heard many say that they intended to have gone to some religious service, at such and such a time, but were prevented by friends calling to see them; and it is a fact that they often do visit each other on Sundays. Some are prevented by the charge of young children, and other household cares, but most, perhaps, by apathy. The number of those who reject religion on principle, or from conviction, is, I believe, not very large. But there is another and a worse class, who are enemies, practically speaking, to Christianity, because it is the enemy of their vices. They know that it requires them to "cease from doing evil, and to learn to do well;" and not having the disposition to comply with this, they banish it, as much as possible, from their thoughts. The ignorance and poor clothing of others, indispose and unfit them for attendance at places of worship. If they do go occasionally, they can scarcely understand or feel much interest in what is said, and are ashamed of the shabby appearance they make amongst well-dressed people. Owing to these and other causes, many of the poor seldom, if ever, join in public devotion. It does not, however, necessarily follow that they are all without religious

* From the Twentieth Report of the Ministry to the Poor (Manchester, 1854) pp. 13–14.

feeling, and, in fact, this is far from being the case. Some of them are very worthy people, and would appear to great advantage, in comparison with many zealous frequenters of church and chapel.

That there are avowed unbelievers among the working classes I need not testify, but whether their number is much increasing, is with me a matter of some doubt. The chief indication of this, which I can perceive, is the increased circulation of the *Reasoner*, and the public discussions which, in various places, have been numerously attended—showing, at least, great interest in the subject. But these are by no means conclusive of the progress of unbelief. Many persons like to hear or read discussions on any topic, not for the sake of arriving at definite conclusions, or satisfying their doubts, but simply to gratify their curiosity. The great evil is, that numbers are estranged in their hearts from true religion, as well as from its existing modes, and whilst this is the case, it signifies but little what they profess.

28 The growth in class feeling*

The textile areas – and particularly Lancashire – were centres of radical activity. Here whole communities of men and women had been transformed by the factory system, and with increasing economic differentiation came nascent class consciousness among masters and men alike. Many observers, not least the Germans Marx and Engels, noted this in the 1840s. The following is an account left by a French visitor.

The factory has invaded the family hearth. To enlarge this circle, hitherto too contracted, it has commenced by breaking it. Life in the future, both for the employer and for the employed, will have two phases—the domestic hearth, and society. Whatever we do we cannot accord to the relation between the husband and the wife—between the children and the father, that exclusive importance which attached to it when men had few other duties. Other associations have arisen which absorb, and justly so, a portion of these sentiments. The workmen united in masses in their workshops, have learnt to study

* From L. Faucher, *Manchester in 1844* (1844) pp. 121–3.

in common their interests, and to form in concert, their opinions. Hence the mutual aid societies, the combinations, and the secret societies. The women have their clubs as well as the men, and claim enjoyment with the same privileges as those with whom they share the fatigues of labour. Manchester, which contains the greatest number of labourers, is the capital of these associations. The workshop depraves, but it throws open to the minds of the operatives a whole world of ideas. Spurred on now by destitution—now by high wages—they are continually struggling to attain a higher position, and feel the necessity of cultivating their minds. No county buys so many books as Lancashire. Chambers's Edinburgh Journal, which circulates to the extent of 85,000 per week, is read principally in the manufacturing districts; and Lancashire alone takes 20,000 of them. There is no portion of society which struggles with greater avidity for a better Future.

The operatives of Lancashire seek to organize themselves, but in vain. Every organization presumes a hierarchy, and in their chimerical projects, they commence always by isolating themselves, and by excluding the natural heads of society from all part in their proceedings. The manufacturers, on the other hand, are little more sensible. One would think they had adopted the brutal motto *"Every thing for the people, but nothing by the people."* So much do they keep the operative at a distance, and negotiate with government, and address public opinion in their own proper name, just as if their hands were so many automata.

29 Rank and file – John Spencer*

When alive, most of the rank and file of popular movements remained anonymous to the wider world, but occasionally death brings them to our notice. Obituary notices submitted to the periodicals by admiring friends in the cause, tell us a little about the characters of the men who meant so much to the quality of a local movement. The following gives us some picture of nineteenth-century ultra-radicalism as lived out by ordinary men and women.

* From *National Reformer*, 21 Jan 1883.

OBITUARY.

JOHN SPENCER is dead, and Secularism, Freethought, Bradlaugh, have lost one of the most faithful workers in the north of England. A rough-spun, rugged man; a true likeness of the hills among which he was born; a plodding, unremunerated worker, except so far as he was repaid for his labor in the knowledge that faithful performance of duty brings its own reward. A familiar figure is gone; one known to all Freethinkers throughout this and surrounding districts; a form which has played a part in many well-remembered scenes in this West Riding of Yorkshire, in many of our public halls in these later years, and on common and moorland in the troubled Chartist times. His outward form was rough—aye, rough and rugged as some of the immense blocks of coarse sandstone which lie upon our moors; and I could never liken the stubble upon head and face to aught but the strong, sturdy heather which straggles to surround and cover up the moorland rocks. And yet beneath this exterior there lay a great human heart—the finer, the grander, the better, because it was simple as a little child's. John Spencer was the first Freethinker who ever attracted me; and it was not his education or culture that called my attention, for he possessed neither, but it was his earnestness. I shall never forget his spelling out in slow fashion, one afternoon, a few sentences from the *National Reformer*, and after he had done, with what simple pride he said he had learned to read, so that he could read what Bradlaugh said. I am young and know men, and may yet know more, of greater fame, but a man to teach me a more direct lesson I shall never know; and so long as I live I shall remember that John Spencer and earnestness are terms of like meaning to me[1].—FRANK ROPER.

NOTE

1. The Halifax Secular Society was re-formed at the home of John Spencer in 1863, and Spencer was elected secretary. *National Reformer*, 3 Oct 1863.

From Above

30 Leadership – James Watson*

The leaders were men of many parts, who in their persons made a unity out of the multiplicity of radical movements. One such man was James Watson who, from his opening speech at the Carlile birthday celebration in Leeds in 1819 until his death in 1874, took part in most ultra-radical movements for social and political reform. As a printer and publisher he had learned his trade under Carlile, but when the Holyoake brothers opened their Fleet Street House in 1853 he transferred much of his publishing to them and went into semi-retirement. In a speech to mark the occasion he recalled his career up to that point.

MR. JAMES WATSON, on rising to respond, was very cordially received. He said:—

MY FRIENDS,—Few persons at their outset in life had less right to expect the warm reception you have given me to-night than the humble individual now before you.

Born of poor parents, in an obscure town (Malton, in Yorkshire) in the year 1799; our family consisted of my mother, my sister, and myself, my father having died when I wanted about a fortnight of a year old; so that I had but one parent to do the duty of two, and, I am proud to say, that duty was performed with all a mother's kindness and devotion. My mother, although poor, was intelligent, as a proof of which I may state that she was a teacher in one of the Sunday-schools of the town. To my mother I owe my taste for reading, and what school edu-

* From *Reasoner* supplement, 5 Feb 1854.

cation I received. I could read well, write indifferently, and had a very imperfect knowledge of arithmetic. At twelve years of age a clergyman, in whose family my mother had lived before her marriage, and who paid for the last three or four quarters of my schooling, induced my mother to bind me to him, as an apprentice, for seven years, to learn field labour, work in the garden, clean horses, milk cows, and wait at table; occupations not very favourable to mental development. At that time there were no cheap books, no cheap newspapers or periodicals, no Mechanics' Institutions to facilitate the acquisition of knowledge. The government was then in the hands of the clergy and aristocracy, the people, ignorant and debased, taking no part in politics, except once in seven years, when the elections were scenes of degradation and corruption. During my stay with the clergyman my mother again became a servant in the family, and well do I remember reading by the kitchen fire, during the long winter nights. My favourite books were two folio volumes, with illustrations—one a history of Europe, the other a history of England. My interest in those books was intense, and many times have I thought, whilst poring over them, 'shall I ever see any of the places here described?' and I *have* seen many of those places since, although my position then seemed so unfavourable. At the end of six years my master's wife died, and he retired into Nottinghamshire, which caused my indentures to be cancelled. After this I lived with my mother and sister; but, not liking to be a burthen on them, myself and a companion, similarly situated, resolved to quit our native town, and seek employment (and some relatives) in Leeds. We succeeded in finding both. I found employment at a drysalter's as warehouseman, and had the charge of a saddle-horse.

It was in the autumn of 1818 that I first became acquainted with politics and theology. Passing along Briggate one evening, I saw at the corner of Union Court a bill, which stated that the Radical Reformers held their meetings in a room in that court. Curiosity prompted me to go and hear what was going on. I found them reading Wooler's *Black Dwarf*, Carlile's *Republican*, and Cobbett's *Register*. I remembered my mother being in the habit of reading Cobbett's *Register*, and saying she 'wondered people spoke so much against it; she saw nothing bad in it, but she saw a great many good things in it.' After hearing it read in the meeting room, I was of my mother's opinion.

In that room I first became acquainted with one who became my friend and constant companion—his name was William Driver. His name and my own were spoken of together amongst our friends in the same manner as, afterwards, my name was mentioned with that of my friend Hetherington. From this time until 1822 I was actively engaged with Mr. Brayshaw, Joseph Hartley, Robert Byerley (my wife's father), Humphrey Boyle, Mr. Gill, and a number of other friends, in collecting subscriptions for Mr. Carlile, spreading the liberal and freethinking literature, and, by meetings and discussions, endeavouring to obtain the right of free discussion. In 1821, the government renewed the prosecutions for blasphemy, and Mr. Carlile (then in Dorchester gaol under a three years' sentence) appealed to the friends in the country to serve in the shop. Humphrey Boyle was the first volunteer from Leeds. He was arrested, tried, and sentenced to eighteen months' imprisonment. On the 18th September, 1822, I arrived in London as the second Leeds volunteer. I served in the shop at 5, Water Lane, Fleet Street, until Christmas, when I spent a week with Mr. Carlile in Dorchester gaol. At that time, Mrs. Carlile, and Mr. Carlile's sister, were his fellow-prisoners. We talked over many plans and business arrangements.

At this time the plan of selling the books by a sort of clockwork, so that the seller was not seen, was in practice. Notwithstanding that precaution, Wm. Tunbridge was arrested, tried, and sentenced to two years' imprisonment, and fined £100. In January, 1823, Mr. Carlile took a shop in the Strand, No. 201. Mrs. Carlile, having completed her two years' imprisonment, resided in the rooms above the shop. Towards the end of February I was arrested for selling a copy of Palmer's 'Principles of Nature,' taken to Bow Street, and, being unable to procure bail in London, was sent to Clerkenwell prison, where I remained six weeks. Two of my Leeds friends, Joseph Hartley and Robert Byerley, then became bail for me. My trial took place on the 23rd April, at Hicks's Hall, Clerkenwell Green, before Mr. Const and a bench of magistrates. I conducted my own defence. Reports had been circulated that the persons who had been taken from Mr. Carlile's shop were but tools in the hands of others, and incapable of defending themselves—which was not true, as Boyle and others of the shopmen *had* defended themselves.

In my defence, I endeavoured to prove from the Bible that Palmer was justified in what he had written, when I was interrupted by the judge, and told that 'I might quote from the Bible, but not comment upon it.' I was convicted, and sentenced to twelve months' imprisonment in Coldbath Fields prison, and to find bail for my good behaviour for two years. I had for fellow-prisoners Wm. Tunbridge and Mrs. S. Wright. Mr. Tunbridge and I had a room to ourselves. During these twelve months I read with deep interest and much profit Gibbon's 'Decline and Fall of the Roman Empire,' Hume's 'History of England,' and many other standard works— amongst others, Mosheim's 'Ecclesiastical History.' The reading of that book would have made me a freethinker if I had not been one before. I endeavoured to make the best use of the opportunity for study and investigation, and the more I read and learnt the more I felt my own deficiency. So the twelve months' confinement was not lost upon me. Mr. Tunbridge did not share my studies. The evenings I usually spent with another fellow prisoner (Mr. Humphrey), an intelligent man, who possessed a good collection of books. For three or four hours after dark we read to each other, after which, until bedtime, we conversed or played a game at cribbage. We found the governor (Mr. Vickery, an old Bow Street officer) a kind-hearted man, more disposed to multiply our comforts than to restrict them. And thus our prison life passed as pleasantly and profitably as was possible under the circumstances. I was liberated on the 24th April, 1824, and shortly after visited Malton, to convince my mother and friends that imprisonment had not made me a worse son or a bad citizen. In May, 1824, the government renewed the prosecutions of Mr. Carlile's assistants, by arresting, trying, and convicting Wm. Campion, John Clarke, T. R. Perry, R. Hassell, and several others, some of whom were sentenced to *three years'* imprisonment.

After visiting Leeds, and the friends there, I returned to London. I applied for employment at a number of places, but found my having been in prison, and shopman to Mr. Carlile, a formidable difficulty, and I incurred in consequence considerable privation. I had, however, a townsman and schoolfellow in London, whose bed and purse were always at my service; that friend, I have the pleasure to say, is now present.

In August of this year, Mr. Boyle, who had managed Mr. Carlile's business sometime, withdrew from it, and I was applied to by Mr. Carlile to supply his place. I conducted the business from that time until Mr. Carlile's liberation from Dorchester gaol, in November, 1825.

In November, 1824, Mr. Carlile's shop (No. 84, Fleet Street) had a narrow escape from fire, the houses on both sides being burnt to the ground.

At the end of 1825, I learnt the art of a compositor, in the office in which Mr. Carlile's *Republican* was printed. Whilst there, I was attacked by cholera, which terminated in typhus and brain fever. I owe my life to the late Julian Hibbert. He took me from my lodgings to his own house at Kentish Town, nursed me, and doctored me for eight weeks, and made a man of me again. After my recovery Mr. Hibbert got a printing press put up in his house, and employed me in composing, *under his directions*, two volumes, one in Greek, the other Greek and English. I was thus employed, from the latter part of 1826, to the end of March, 1828. In 1825 I was first introduced to the advocates of Mr. Owen's New Views of Society, by my friend Mr. Thomas Hooper, and to the end of 1829 I was actively engaged, with others, in forming societies for political and religious liberty, co operative associations, &c., &c. In April, 1828, I undertook the agency of the Co-operative Store, at 36, Red Lion Square, and I remained in that employment until Christmas, 1829.

In the beginning of 1830 I visited Leeds, Halifax, Dewsbury, Bradford, Huddersfield, Todmorden, Wakefield, and other places, to advocate the establishment of co-operative associations. In May, I took the house 33, Windmill Street, Finsbury Square, and *there* commenced the business of bookseller. During the excitement occasioned by the French Revolution in July, I took an active part in the numerous enthusiastic meetings following that event.

In 1831 I became a printer and publisher. My friend, Mr. Julian Hibbert, gave me his press and types. The first use I made of them was to print 'Volney's Lectures on History,' which I composed and printed with my own hands. At this time

I became a member of the National Union of the Working Classes. [For the information of those unacquainted with the struggle for unstamped newspapers, a word or two may here be necessary. At this time, 1831, the price of the newspaper stamp was fourpence for each paper. The object of Mr. Hetherington, Mr. Carpenter, Mr. Cleave, and others, was to get that tax of fourpence abolished. To effect this, the *Poor Man's Guardian*, and other papers of a similar kind, circulating amongst the working classes, introduced *news* into their columns. To suppress the sale of these publications was the aim of the government. After sending 600 persons to prison, they were compelled to reduce the price of the stamp from fourpence to one penny, its present price. To get rid of this penny is the object of the 'Society for the Abolition of the Taxes on Knowledge,' now meeting at 20, Great Coram Street, Brunswick Square, of which Mr. Collet is the active and untiring secretary.][1]

In this year Mr. Hetherington suffered his first six months' imprisonment in Clerkenwell prison for publishing the *Poor Man's Guardian*.

In 1832, the excitement of the people on the subject of the Reform Bill was at its height.

The cholera being very bad all over the country, the government, to please the Agnewites[2], ordered a 'general fast.' The members of the National Union, to mark their contempt for such an order, determined to have a procession through the streets of London, and afterwards to have a general feast. In April I was arrested, with Messrs. Lovett and Benbow, for advising and leading the procession. We were liberated on bail, tried on the 16th of May, each conducting his own defence, and all acquitted. Towards the end of this year Mr. Hetherington was sentenced to his second six months' confinement, in Clerkenwell prison, for the *Poor Man's Guardian*.

In February, 1833, I was summoned to Bow Street for selling the *Poor Man's Guardian*. I justified my conduct before the magistrates in selling unstamped newspapers. They considered me as bad as my friend Hetherington, and sentenced me to six months in the same Clerkenwell prison. I was liberated on the 29th July, and attended the same day a meeting to commemorate the third anniversary of the French Revolution, in which Mr. Julian Hibbert, the Rev. Robert Taylor, Mr.

Hetherington, and others, took part. At the end of this year I was engaged with Mr. Saull, Mr. Prout, Mr. Franks, and Mr. Mordan in fitting up the Hall of Science, in the City Road, as a lecture room for Rowland Detrosier. In January, 1834, occurred the lamented death of Mr. Julian Hibbert. In his will he again gave me a marked token of his regard, by a legacy of 450 guineas. With this sum I enlarged my printing operations. My legacy was soon absorbed in printing 'Mirabaud's System of Nature,' Frances Wright's 'Popular Lectures,' Volney's 'Ruins,' Paine's works, &c. In addition to the legacy, I incurred a debt of 500*l*. in printing and publishing those works. In April I attended the great meeting of the Trades' Unions in Copenhagen Fields, in favour of the Dorchester labourers.

On the 3rd of June I was married. Before the month was over I was again summoned to Bow Street, but preferred a short trip to Jersey, where I stayed three weeks. On the 7th of August the officers again seized me, and I was taken to Clerkenwell for my second six months' confinement. I was liberated on the 21st of January, 1835, and from that time to the present have remained unmolested. 1836, 7, 8, I was engaged with others, in the formation of Working Men's Associations, and assisted to prepare the document called the 'People's Charter.'[3] In 1839 the meeting of the Chartist delegates in national convention. In 1840 took place the trials of John Cleave and Henry Hetherington, for blasphemy[4]. They were convicted and imprisoned. My friend Hetherington honoured me by dedicating his trial to me, and I have been more proud of his testimony and friendship than of anything I ever received. From 1841 to 1846 my bookselling and publishing is so well known to most of my hearers that I need not trespass further on their time.

From 1846 to 1853, my connection with Mr. Holyoake and the *Reasoner* is patent to you all. You are also aware of his new undertaking and our recent changes, and I trust that the responsibilities he has incurred will be shared and sustained by your generous support. I am proud to have assisted in preparing a 'clear stage and no favour' for the Newmans and the Martineaus[5], who are now coming forward to aid the progress of freethought. I hope to see the same freedom extended to our brethren of France and Germany, and throughout the continent; and, more than all, to see the illustrious triumvir,

Mazzini carried back in triumph to the Eternal City.

I have trespassed at great length on your forbearance; but, in what I have said, I have had but one object in view—to show my fellow-workmen that the humblest amongst them may render effectual aid to the cause of progress, if he brings to the task honest determination and unfaltering perseverance. With regard to the question of retirement, I may say that a person who has led the active life I have done cannot relapse into idle indifference. If I leave London it will be to join my friend Linton, and to help him in his republican propaganda; and from an attachment of many years standing, I can truly say that a more devoted and disinterested servant of the people's cause does not exist.

NOTES

1. Holyoake's editorial insertion.
2. The supporters of Sir Andrew Agnew, M.P. for Wigtonshire, who between 1832 and 1837 introduced four unsuccessful Bills to prohibit all labour on the Sabbath.
3. According to Watson's son-in-law, Richard Moore, 'Watson was at the meeting in Cockspur St. when resolutions were agreed to, to prepare the "charter" but was not one of the Committee to draw it up.' R. Moore to G. J. Holyoake, 10 Dec 1874, Holyoake Collection, Manchester, no. 2293. The six names of working men appended to the Charter after the Cockspur Street meeting were those of Hetherington, Cleave, Watson, Moore, Lovett and Henry Vincent – a high proportion of Owenites and infidels.
4. For publishing *Letters to the Clergy of All Denominations*, by C. J. Haslam, a Manchester Owenite.
5. I.e. Francis William Newman (brother of John Henry) and James Martineau. Both men were Unitarians.

31 Lectures – Joseph Barker's list*

The message of freethought was spread mainly by the lecturers who, on a local or national basis, offered their services to the weekly (usually Sunday) audiences. Some lecturers, like Holyoake in the 1850s, charged a fixed fee of two guineas a night. Others, like Bradlaugh and the National Secular Society special lecturers, were entitled to all the takings after the expenses had been deducted. The following is a list of the topics which Joseph Barker was prepared to offer in 1860. Barker changed his

* From *National Reformer*, 29 Dec 1860.

opinions many times, and the year 1860 probably represents the height of his Secularist career. The breadth of the topics is both astonishing and typical.

SUBJECTS OF SOME OF MR. BARKER'S LECTURES.

THE following is a list of some of the subjects on which Mr. Barker lectures:—

1. The Alleged Evidences of the Divine Authority of the Bible, no Evidences at all.

2. Direct Proof that the Bible is *not* of Divine Authority.

3. The Teachings and Example of Jesus,—are they the Perfection of Wisdom and Virtue?

4. A Supernatural Revelation not Necessary.

5. What do you Offer as a Substitute for the Bible? Can you give us anything Better?

6. The Other Side of the Bible Question, or What could you say in Favour of the Bible, if you were to try?

7. How did you Become an Unbeliever?

8. The Sorrows and Perplexities of a Religious Life.

9. The Saint and the Secularist,—which has the best of it?

10. The Principles and Objects of Secularism.

11. The *Model* Secularist, as Young Man, Son, Brother, Companion, Friend, Lover, Husband, Father, Work-man, Employer, Capitalist, Citizen, Old Man.

12. The Bible Plan and the Secularist Plan of Education.

13. The Influence of the Bible.

I. On Morals.

II. On Science, Art, and Literature.

III. On Civil and Religious Liberty.

IV. On Civilisation Generally.

14. Human Progress.

15. Spiritualism as developed in America, with its Bearings on the Great Reforms of the Day.

16. The Truth there is in the Religions of the World.

17. The Deference due to Old Customs and Opinions.

18. The Cause of Infidelity.

19. The Laws of Health.

20. Love and Marriage; or, The Way to Domestic Happiness.

21. Pauperism and the Bible.

22. Temperance.

23. Teetotalism.

24. Legislation on the Drinking System in England and America.

25. Self-culture.

26. Books Worth Reading, and the Right Way to Read them.

27. The Pleasures of Science.

28. Infidel Bigotry and Fanaticism; or the Faults of Reformers.

29. A Word for Every One.

30. The Formation of Character; or a Lesson on Charity.

31. Noah's Flood.

32. Jonah and the Whale.

33. Co-operation.

34. The Absurdities of the Orthodox Theology.

35. Shakespeare.

36. Religious Literature not to be entirely Slighted; or Grains of Gold in Piles of Dust.

37. The Christian Doctrine of Hell a Gross Fiction and a Horrible Blasphemy.

38. The Future of Humanity.

39. The Future of Christianity.

40. An Easy Way open to Great Britain to National Wealth and Happiness.

41. Reviews of Buckle, Darwin, Oxford Essays, Gilfillan, New Relgious Thoughts, Macnaught, Mill, and Baden Powell.

42. On the Right Spirit, and Proper Conduct of Controversy.

43. On the Duties of Parents and Children, Brothers and Sisters.

44. The best Preparation for a Peaceful and Happy Death.

45. The Bible Account of Creation.

46. The Tower of Babel; or the Origin of Language, and the Diversity of Tongues.

47. Amusements and Recreations.

48. The Influence of Scepticism.
49. Paine and his Calumniators.
50. The Life and Character of Voltaire.
51. Pious Frauds.
52. The Six Champions of Orthodoxy; Brewin Grant, John Brindley, J. Rutherford, John Bowes, J. Deadman and Thomas Cooper; and the Honour they do to the Christian Cause.
53. Why do the Respectable and Better Informed of the Clergy Leave the Defence of the Church and Christianity to Men of no Character or Influence?
54. Novels and Novel Reading.
55. Plutarch as a Moral Instructor.
56. Lessons I have Learned on my Way Through Life.
57. What I would *not* do, if I were Young again.
58. Review of my own old Writings in Favour of the Bible and Christianity, with Answers to those things in them that are Answerable.
59. Colonial Reform.
60. The Origin of Religion.

32 Preparations for a visiting lecturer*

Lectures and audiences did not just happen – they had to be organised – and where lecturers were breaking new ground there had to be special preparations demanding much dedicated hard work by one or two individuals. This letter, from one such local convert, illustrates what was involved.

8 Feb [18]56
2 Lacon Terrace
Northfleet   *Friday*

Dear Sir,

I write a line in haste, to 'report progress'. I have been more than usually busy this week or I would have written sooner.

I have had the large placards out for a fortnight. I have also had 50 strips announcing "Mr Holyoake's Lectures on Mon & Wed evenings next, Feb 11 & 13. Commence at 8 o'clock",

* E. S. Cathels to G. J. Holyoake, 8 Feb 1856, Holyoake Collection, Manchester, no. 834.

which will be posted this evening.

In addition to the 600 hand-bills sent from your house, I have had 800 printed in Gravesend, 300 of which I enclosed in directed envelopes and had left in the shops and houses of principle [sic] inhabitants of Gravesend and Northfleet.

I had also upwards of 500 distributed at the Dockyard gates yesterday.

Last week I wrote a respectful letter to each of the ministers in Gravesend informing them of your lectures and enclosing a shilling ticket, copies of which I will show you.

I therefore think you will agree with me in saying that we *ought* to have an audience.

I am afraid we won't be able to have a chairman. I wrote Mr. Crosse the other day soliciting him but I have not received a reply. I also wrote Dr. Ridge, one of the most liberal gentlemen of Gravesend, and rec[eive]d a courteous reply regretting his inability, having multifarious duties on hand, engageing [sic] every moment of his time.

I much regret being unable for want of room to accomodate you Sir in my house, but I have bespoke lodgings in the house of a friend who lives directly opposite the Institution where I am sure you will be very comfortable. I hope you will be able to stay until the conclusion of the lectures, and if you are not otherwise engaged I should be glad to spend the Tuesday with you. You will perhaps kindly walk over and breakfast with us in the morning when we could have a nice stroll in the country returning in time to take tea at my house and spend the evening.

Will you be kind enough to let us know by return what train you will come by on Monday, and whether you will stop at Northfleet and have a cup of tea with us before walking into Gravesend?

The bigots are at work here. You are being terribly denounced, as also your humble servant, or to put it in Christian phraseology, 'poor dupe'.

I am in the meantime
Dear Sir, yours in haste
Ed S Cathels

P.S. I forgot to say that I have had the lectures advertised in two local newspapers.

Ed S C

I will await you at the train. You will find an extra pair of boots convenient, the roads are so bad.

33 A lecturer on tour*

In the 1880s Arthur B. Moss was living in London, working as a London School Board visitor, and spending his weekends as a Secularist lecturer. After protests from the M.P. for North Camberwell in 1888 this latter occupation had to be stopped on pain of dismissal, but a year later Annie Besant succeeded in her campaign to get the Board to reverse its decision. With great dedication Moss used to devote his annual holidays to a lecture tour of the provinces. Through his eyes we get a picture both of the work of a lecturer and of Secularism in the north-east in 1890.

'MY TOUR NORTH'

On Saturday afternoon I made my way to Ox Hill. But Oh, the journey! First a slow railway ride to Birtley; then on a brake to West Pelton, up hill and down dale, now at jog trot pace, anon at full speed along the dusty roads. How vividly the old coaching days of Dickens came back to my imagination as the driver blew his horn to arouse the villagers, and prepare them for our coming. How carelessly too he threw out the parcels that had come down from Newcastle; and how perilously near he ran the coach to the children who played in the road, and who seemed to fancy that they were specially designed to dodge the horse's feet as they scampered through each village. At last we reached West Stanley, and in a few moments, from a trap, the shafts of which rested rather insecurely between two wires that formed a railing, I delivered my first lecture, entitled "Saviors of Mankind". My audience was composed mainly of miners and their wives. On the whole the lecture was listened to very attentively and save one interruption, from an enthusiastic Christian, who challenged my statement that Jesus was alleged to have cured a blind man by daubing some clay upon his eyes, the proceedings passed off well; and I was subsequently told that they produced a marked effect upon many who had heard a Freethought lecture for the first time.

A night at the house of an elderly signalman, who with his

* From *National Reformer*, 17 Aug 1890.

wife had been a Freethinker before I was born, and remembered some of the early advocates of our cause; and then on Sunday morning I was driven in company with several young and enthusiastic members of our party in a small trap over to Newcastle. In the Nelson Street lecture hall I delivered three lectures. In the morning on "Voltaire and Paine"; afternoon "The Bible and Evolution"; and in the evening, "Saviors of Mankind". Considering the attractions elsewhere, Mrs. Besant being at South Shields, and a large number of the Newcastle friends being interested in supporting a Sunday band on the moor, my lectures drew very fair audiences.

On Monday evening the 28th July I spoke in the Bigg Market, at Newcastle, on "Secularism, the religion of everyday life". There was a large crowd, but two drunken Christians contrived to interrupt the proceedings somewhat by their coarse and brutal interjections. Two opponents offered opposition. One of them, who meant well, told the audience that though I had said I did not believe in prayer he knew that I did—indeed he had heard me pray—"for," said he, "I heard him pray that the two noisy gentlemen in the rear would be quiet". "If", I replied, "I had prayed—and I was quite unconscious of it—one thing was certain, there was no efficacy in such prayer, for the interruptions had continued throughout the whole of the lecture." At this there was a laugh, and soon after the proceedings terminated.

On Tuesday I lectured at the Hall of the Sailors' and Firemen's Institute, South Shields, Mr. Peacock presiding. There was a large audience, from which I received a most cordial reception.

Wednesday found me at Sunderland. Freethought unfortunately has been under a cloud for some time in this district, chiefly on account of the difficulty of getting a suitable hall for lectures. I think, however, there is a prospect of good work in the near future, and of recovering some of the lost ground.

My lecture on "Bible Makers" was delivered to a large and appreciative audience on Roker Sands; and one gentleman, a stranger to our movement, dropped a five shilling piece in the hat in order to mark his appreciation of the lecture. Mr. Weightman and other friends worked with great energy in making the necessary arrangements to ensure the success of the meeting.

The audience was composed mainly of visitors to the seaside, with a sprinkling of our own friends to maintain order. A Presbyterian minister, who did not venture to offer opposition when invited, suggested to the policeman on duty, in tones loud enough for me to hear, that the only suitable reply to my arguments would be to throw me into the sea. However, as he did not attempt to put his implied threat into operation, his brave words were allowed to pass unnoticed.

At Blyth, on Thursday, I attracted an audience of over a thousand persons to hear me discourse on "Saviors of Mankind". After the lecture, I had one opponent who nibbled round the subject without ever coming near enough to touch the heart of it; and a Salvationist who found some pleasure in telling the audience how he had been a drunkard and starved his wife and beaten his children, and consequently found his way to gaol, but at last the Lord had caught hold of him, changed his heart, and converted him into a teetotaler and a new man. Then having given a sort of "breakdown" dance on the van from which we were speaking, he exclaimed "What could Charlie Bradlaugh do for me?" at which the audience roared with merriment. My reply was simple, but I think effective. I challenged any Christian present to show me one passage in the Bible in favor of total abstinence. Of course they could not do it; so the proceedings terminated, and the great audience, which had behaved splendidly throughout, quietly dispersed.

From Blyth to Bedlington is a short journey and a very pleasant one, some of the most picturesque scenery in the county of Northumberland lying between these two towns. At Bedlington I got a huge crowd to hear me, estimated at between fifteen hundred and two thousand persons, towards the close of the lecture. Two opponents appeared; one said nothing in particular, and the other told the audience a few pretty stories that would have done very well for the *Christian Herald*, but were in no sense an answer to my arguments. Mr. Saddler presided, and among the audience were Dr. Trotter and Dr. Charlton, and an old Freethinker, who informed me that he had taken the *National Reformer* from the first number in 1860. A large number of *National Reformers* were sold here containing the report of the debate on the Eight Hours Question.

My last lecture was delivered on Saturday, near the Bridge at Chester-le-Street, on "Christian Theories and Christian Practice", to a large audience; but as two or three excited opponents kept up a running fire of interruption, and the band of the Salvation Army played vigorously all the while, I cannot say that I was pleased with my own effort; but when I heard the opposition and the way in which it was received, I was soon satisfied that the lecture was not altogether wasted on the audience.

ARTHUR B. MOSS.

Leisure

34 A Paine birthday celebration*

Radicalism in small communities across the face of industrial Britain was not a mere dogma but a whole way of life. Class consciousness merged with community consciousness, particularly in the textile villages of Lancashire and Yorkshire and the mining villages of Durham.

STOCKPORT.

SIR,

THE Republicans of Stockport assembled in various places to celebrate the natal day of Mr. Paine, whom Englishmen ought to consider the greatest man their island ever produced, and according to your desire those excellent toasts and sentiments published in No. 4, of "The Republican," were given, and received with the warmest enthusiasm, as also many other appropriate toasts and songs on the occasion: Some of which I am particularly requested to forward to you, if you think them worthy a niche in the pages of "The Republican," the proposers will think themselves highly favoured.

1. Mr. Richard Carlile, his Wife and Sister, and may they triumphantly leave their unmerited dungeons, and exult over their dastardly and cowardly persecutors. 3 times 3.

2. May the principles of Thomas Paine, which we are this night met to celebrate, be extended over the Globe, and speedily be acted upon.

3. May every honest Republican soon have the pleasure of

* From *Republican*, 22 Feb 1822.

seeing every Priest and superstitious Bigot become good Citizens.

4. William Cobbett, and may he soon see the propriety of adopting and disseminating the opinion of Thomas Paine.

5. The Captive of Ilchester[1], Sir Charles Wolseley, and the great Northern Union, and may their pens, and the funds of the Union soon be appropriated to the patriotic purpose of destroying Priestcraft and promulgating the doctrines of unsophisticated Republicanism. 3 times 3.

6. Mr. Wooler, Mr. Lewis, Mr. Knight, Mr. Davison, and the old veteran Mr. Burtenshaw, who has just left his dungeon, after two years imprisonment, and in the 70th year of his age, and may they live to enjoy the reward of their labours.

7. May the Republicans of England never cease their exertions until they have obtained justice for the wanton, cruel, barbarous, and horrid Massacre committed on the Plains of St. Peter's, August 16, 1819.

This was received in solemn silence, after which a gentleman gave the following Song which was composed for the last Anniversary of the 16th of August, 1819.

> Pitiful, I behold St. Peter's,
>   Pitiful, oh! pitiful, oh!
> Saw the sad distorted features,
>   Pitiful, oh! pitiful, oh!
> Gazed upon the fiends back'd by knavery,
> Rivetting the chains of Britain's slavery,
> Saw the mad blood thirsty creatures,
>   Pitiful, oh! pitiful, oh!
>
> Cruelly I beheld them trample,
>   Cruelly, oh! cruelly, oh!
> Saw them set the dire example,
>   Cruelly, oh! cruelly, oh!
>
> If the hirelings' pranks be requited,
> By a Tyrant's thanks be united,
> Prepare to shew them vengeance ample,
>   Cruelly, oh! cruelly, oh!
>
> Terribly will the tyrants tremble,
>   Terribly, oh! terribly, oh!

When their victims they resemble,
Terribly, oh! terribly, oh!
Soon shall Freedom's sons be rewarded,
And the Tyrant's thanks be unregarded;
Gladly would the knaves dissemble,
Terribly, oh! terribly, oh!

Liberty, thou shalt be our motto,
Liberty, oh! Liberty, oh!
We'll shout through mountain, vale, and grotto,
Liberty, oh! Liberty, oh!
'Tis slavery alone that can harm us,
Liberty alone that can charm us,
Loud through Palace, Town, and Cot, oh!
Liberty, oh! Liberty, oh!

There were many other songs and toasts on the occasion, but these are the general outline.

Yours, respectfully,
WILLIAM PERRY.

NOTE

1. Henry Hunt, sentenced to two and one-half years for sedition.

35 A Bradlaugh victory celebration*

VILLAGE RADICALISM AND MR. BRADLAUGH.

ON Saturday evening, the 6th instant, the Radicals of the village of Holdsworth, near Halifax, held a "public tea and entertainment", in honor of the termination of Mr. Bradlaugh's litigation *re* the rights of constituencies to select unmolested their own representatives. About one hundred ladies and gentlemen (amongst whom could be seen the faces of many veterans in the cause of reform), partook of an excellently provided tea.

The tables being cleared, a lengthened and enjoyable entertainment was proceeded with. Recitations were given by Messrs. Widdop, Robertshaw, Wakefield, and Mrs. A. B.

* From *National Reformer*, 14 Nov 1886.

Wakefield; and songs by Messrs. E. Dean, Pallier, and Dorsey—the two latter introducing some pump and clog dancing, which was received favorably.

About midway through the proceedings the following resolution was submitted to the assemblage by Mr. Robertshaw: "That this meeting heartily congratulates Mr. Bradlaugh on the termination of the litigation so long pending, and on carrying his law cases to a successful and triumphant issue; and thanks him for his efforts to establish once and for ever the right of each constituency to send its own representative to the Commons House of Parliament." This was seconded and supported by Messrs. Crowther and Ramsden, and passed unanimously with loud cheers. To the air of the National Anthem the meeting, standing, sang:-

> People throughout the land,
> Join in one social band,
>   And save yourselves;
> If you would happy be,
> Free from all slavery,
> Banish all knavery,
>   And save yourselves.
>
> Why will you always toil,
> While others share the spoil?
>   Work for yourselves!
> Let them who live so high,
> Work for themselves, or die,
> Tell them 'tis time to try
>   To keep themselves.
>
> Parsons and Peers may preach,
> And endless falsehoods teach,
>   Think for yourselves:
> Then let your watchword be,
> "Justice and Liberty,"
> And toil unweariedly
>   To save yourselves.

Thus we brought to an end one of the most pleasant evenings spent by the Radicals of the district for some time past. The arrangements—it is only due to say—were admirably carried out by Messrs. Walmsley and John Davis.—*Communicated.*

36 The Hall of Science classes*

One of the most important elements in radical activity was education. 'Knowledge is Power' was the cry, and many examples can be found of the attempt to realise such power through the acquisition of rational knowledge. At first such education was completely outside the framework of any national educational system. The emphasis was on self-help for adults and Sunday schools for the children on a completely voluntary basis. In this respect radical education corresponded in form to that provided by the Mechanics' Institutes and the various religious denominations. This pattern persisted but was supplemented by more formal provisions as the state became more involved in educational activities, and in this connection the work done at the Hall of Science schools (1879–88) was outstanding. Begun under the inspiration of Edward Aveling, the schools were continued by his three star pupils – Annie Besant and the Bradlaugh girls – until the death of Alice Bradlaugh in 1888. This extract indicates the quality of the pupils and the wide variety of courses taught.

SCIENCE CLASSES.
RESULTS OF SOUTH KENSINGTON EXAMINATIONS.

THE returns from South Kensington are very satisfactory and encouraging. Taking them in the order of their return: Mathematics. Eleven students presented themselves, of whom one obtained a Second Class in the Advanced Stage, two a First Class in the Elementary, three a Second Class in the latter stage. Remembering that many entered the Class without knowledge of either Algebra or Geometry and minus the preliminary mathematical training in the early days, this is not discouraging. In Botany, of the ten students, all passed. One takes a First Class Advanced, six First Class Elementary, three Second Class Elementary. In Chemistry of the Junior Class, taught by Miss Hypatia Bradlaugh, eight entered, and two take a First Class, five a Second. Of the Advanced Class, nine entered; two pass in the First Division, three in the Second.

* From *National Reformer*, 31 July 1881.

Finally, in the Elementary Physiology, taught by Mrs. Besant, fourteen students presented themselves, of whom two take a First Class, twelve a Second. In the Advanced examination in the same subject ten examinees yield two successes in the First Division, and six in the Second. Summing up the whole of the examinations, sixty-two students enter; five take a First Class Advanced, ten take a Second Class Advanced, twelve a First Class Elementary, twenty-three a Second Class Elementary. In all, fifty out of sixty-two pass.

SCIENCE SCHOOLS.
(In connexion with the Science and Art Department, South Kensington.)
HALL OF SCIENCE, 142, OLD STREET, CITY ROAD, E.C.

Winter Session—October 1881 to May 1882.

PHYSIOLOGY.

	s.	d.
Elementary Course—Alice Bradlaugh	5	0
Advanced Course—Edward B. Aveling	5	0

CHEMISTRY.

Elementary Course—Hypatia Bradlaugh	5	0
Advanced Course—Annie Besant	5	0

BIOLOGY—Edward B. Aveling	5	0
NATURAL PHILOSOPHY—Edward B. Aveling	5	0
GEOLOGY—Edward B. Aveling	5	0
SOUND, LIGHT AND HEAT—Annie Besant	5	0
MATHEMATICS—Hypatia Bradlaugh	5	0

Members of the N.S.S. or of the Club and Insitute pay half the above fees. Intending students are requested to forward their names, with fees, to E. B. AVELING, Practical Science Laboratory, 13, Newman Street, W.

The lessons are of one hour each. Monday: 7—8, Geology; 8—9, Advanced Physiology; 9—10, Biology. Tuesday: 7—8, Sound, Light and Heat; 8—9, Advanced Chemistry; 9—10, Elementary Physiology. Wednesday: 7—8, Natural Philosophy; 8—9, Mathematics; 9—10, Elementary Chemistry. Session opens on Monday, October 3.

Classes will also be held under the above scheme at the Practical Science Laboratory, 13, Newman Street, W., on Friday evenings, at 7 p.m. and 8 p.m., in—

	s.	d.
ADVANCED BOTANY—E. B. Aveling	10	0
PRACTICAL CHEMISTRY (1½ hrs.)—E. B. Aveling	10	0

EDWARD B. AVELING, D.SC.

37 Huddersfield Secular Sunday School*

The informal education provided by Mechanics' Institutes, Secularist schools and the like meant a great deal to intelligent working men whose natural abilities were not matched by their opportunities. One of the most active Secularist bodies in the provinces was in Huddersfield, where a thriving Sunday school was run between 1862 and 1886. Ben Turner, later the textile workers' leader, was born near Huddersfield, and when his family moved into the town itself he experienced the Secularist school at the height of its success.

My whole outlook was changed by our removal from village to town. I had been a good Sunday school scholar in the orthodox sense of the word in the village, but my father had other notions when we got to Huddersfield, and he took my two brothers and myself to become Sunday school scholars at its noted Secular Sunday School. This was a great adventure, and it did me a world of good. They had two sessions each Sunday, at which we were taught reading, writing, arithmetic, geography, history, elocution, singing, etc. Sometimes there was no school in the afternoons, and noted Secular lecturers came and gave afternoon and evening addresses. It was there I heard Annie Besant, George Jacob Holyoake, Harriet Law, Charles Watts, Dr. Aveling, and many others whose names slip from my memory. I heard Bradlaugh several times; he was a big draw, and they used to engage a big hall for his visit and folks would walk miles to hear him. These secularists didn't always lecture on Secularism. Many of their addresses were on social subjects

* From B. Turner, *About Myself* (1930) pp. 47–9.

like the land question, perpetual pensions, republicanism, home rule, etc., and I learnt a bit about many subjects, but more still, I learnt how to learn about these things. Anti-religion didn't enter much into it, but we were not orthodox religionists, and our workmates, etc., were always running us down as young infidels.

It was at this school, through its elocution and singing classes, that I got my further stimulus in reading. I learnt scores of recitations, took part in many little plays, and we had our own debates, when we thrashed things out rudely and crudely, but, by jove! it was rich life for young fellows like me, from fifteen to nineteen years of age.

At eighteen I became Secretary of this Sunday School, and had even begun to take the chair for the lesser lights that turned up or for the social evenings we arranged. It was the time when young folks did a bit of rhyming, and one bit I inflicted upon them was about Thomas Paine. I am glad nobody has a copy of it, for I know it was poor stuff, but it did me no harm, and certainly it kept me alive to events of the day, for it made us read the newspapers and know about the politics of the time.

PART THREE
The Springs of Protest

Reasons why men became infidels were many and various, but there were at least three phases in the process. Firstly faith in the orthodox religious establishment had to be shaken, traditional beliefs questioned and traditional authority rejected. For many people this stage seems to have been largely an emotional one, inspired by the practical conduct of Christians in general and by the political Conservatism of the Establishment and the moral conservatism of Anglican and Nonconformist Evangelicals in particular.

To this source of protest was added intellectual conviction. The leaders usually insisted that this was an essential ingredient of true infidelity, but whatever may have been true of themselves (and whether it was always true is doubtful), its seems plausible to suggest that many of the rank and file, especially on the fringes, never reached this stage, or reached it only painstakingly after gradually absorbing the teachings of the movement – beginning with Paine's Age of Reason.

The third stage was probably reached by fewest of all – that is, acceptance of an alternative system. The freethinkers not only had to provide an alternative social system to the chapel – in which they were usually highly successful – but most of the leaders sooner or later felt they also had to provide an alternative intellectual system. In a general sense such a system was already to hand in the shape of Enlightenment rationalism and utilitarian ethics – a belief in the power of rational men to organise the perfect secular-based society in which to promote the greatest happiness – but beyond this lay the question of how far an alternative religious system was needed. Paine with his Theophilanthropists, Carlile and Taylor with their Zetetic services and, later, Carlile's own brand of mystical Christianity, were all attempts at religion substitutes; but the most powerful influence in this latter direction came from Owenism, which offered both an alternative economic system and vision of society, and an alternative ethical system and a 'Rational Religion'. In the Secularist movement this latter was perpetuated, particularly whilst under the control of Holyoake who felt that freethinkers' criticisms of existing ideas could only become widely acceptable when the critics themselves could produce a better alternative system.

Destructive Protest

38 Moral revulsion at the Atonement*

The initial protest against Christianity was often a moral one, coupled with a sense of incredulity at the claims made in the Bible. Here, as in so many other things, Paine's Age of Reason led the way. Part 1 was written in Paris in 1794, and towards the end of the work Paine set down his own earliest doubts.

From the time I was capable of conceiving an idea and acting upon it by reflection, I either doubted the truth of the Christian system or thought it to be a strange affair; I scarcely knew which it was, but I well remember, when about seven or eight years of age, hearing a sermon read by a relation of mine, who was a great devotee of the Church, upon the subject of what is called *redemption by the death of the Son of God.*

After the sermon was ended, I went into the garden, and as I was going down the garden steps (for I perfectly recollect the spot) I revolted at the recollection of what I had heard, and thought to myself that it was making God Almighty act like a passionate man who killed His son when He could not revenge Himself in any other way, and, as I was sure a man would be hanged who did such a thing, I could not see for what purpose they preached such sermons.

This was not one of that kind of thoughts that had anything in it of childish levity; it was to me a serious reflection, arising

* From T. Paine, *The Age of Reason*, part 1 (1794) Foner edition, p. 497.

from the idea I had that God was too good to do such an action, and also too almighty to be under any necessity of doing it. I believe in the same manner at this moment; and I moreover believe that any system of religion that has anything in it that shocks the mind of a child cannot be a true system.

39 A street-corner lecture on the Atonement*

The doctrine of the Atonement provided many infidel lecturers with good debating material. The written work of the freethought leaders was often well expressed, appealing to the critical sense, but the message could come over quite differently in the lecture hall or on the street corner. Some of the most striking pictures of freethought meetings come from the pen of the Rev. C. M. Davies, a well-disposed critic of the London Secularists in the 1870s. In the following extract he is describing the performance of W. J. Ramsey at the corner of Gibraltar Walk, Bethnal Green. Ramsey was having to compete for a hearing with a Mr Harrington who was a Christian lecturer endowed with a louder voice than the unfortunate infidel.

Mr. Ramsey, who had a rooted aversion to the letter "h," except where a smooth breathing is usual, began by saying that Christianity differed from other religions in the fact of its having an eternal 'Ell. The Mahometans had their beautiful ladies; the North American Indian looked for his 'Appy 'Unting Grounds; but 'Ell was a speciality of the Christian system. On the other side was the fact that you continually had salvation inundated upon you. Tracts were put into your hand, asking—"What must I do to be saved?" We had to pay for this salvation about 11,000,000*l.* a year to the Church of England, and something like an equal amount to the Dissenters. In fact every tub-thumper went about preaching and ruining servant girls, and for this we paid over twenty millions a year—more than the interest on the whole National Debt. After this elegant exordium, Mr. Ramsey said he proposed to divide his remarks under four heads. 1. Is Salvation necessary? 2. What are we to be saved from? 3. What for? 4. How?

* From C. M. Davies, *Mystic London* (1875) pp. 246–9.

1. According to the Christian theory, God, after an eternity of "doin' nothin'," created the world. He made Adam sin by making sin for him to commit; and then damned him for doing what He knew he would do. He predestined you—the audience—to be damned because of Adam's sin; but after a time God "got sick and tired of damning people," and sent His Son to redeem mankind.

This flower of rhetoric tickled Bethnal Green immensely; but Mr. Harrington was equal to the occasion, and thundered out his orthodoxy so successfully that Mr. Ramsey took a longer drink than usual, and complained that he was not having "a free platform"—it was so he dignified the rickety stool on which he was perched. He then meandered into a long dissection of Genesis i., appearing to feel particularly aggrieved by the fact of the moon being said to "rule the night," though I could not see how this was relevant to the Christian scheme of salvation; and a superb policeman, who had listened for a moment to Mr. Ramsey's astronomical lucubrations, evidently shared my feelings and passed on superciliously. I devoutly wished my duty had permitted me to do the same.

The speaker then went into a long dissertation on the primal sin; the gist of which was that though the woman had never been warned not to eat of the Forbidden Fruit, she had to bear the brunt of the punishment. Then—though one is almost ashamed to chronicle such a triviality—he waxed very wroth because the serpent was spoken of as being cursed above all "cattle." Who ever heard of snakes being called cattle? He was condemned to go on his belly. How did he go before? Did he go on his back or "'op" along on the tip of his tail? These pleasantries drew all Mr. Harrington's audience away except a few little dirty boys on the wall. Mr. Ramsey clearly knew his audience, and "acted to the gallery."

2. But what were we to be saved from? Eternal 'Ell-fire. This 'Ell-fire was favourite sauce for sermons, and served to keep people awake. Where was 'Ell? It was said to be a bottomless pit; if so, he should be all right, because he could get out at the other end! Then, again, 'Ell was said to be a very 'ot place. When the missionaries told the Greenlanders that, everybody wanted to go to 'Ell; so they had to change their tune and say it was very cold. Mr. Ramsey omitted to mention his authority for

this statement.

Into his pleasantries on the monotony of life in 'Eaven, I do not feel inclined to follow this gentleman. The Atonement, he went on to remark, if necessary at all, came 4000 years too late. It should have been —so we were to believe on his ipse dixit— contemporaneous with the Fall. This atonement we were to avail ourselves of by means of faith. Idiots could not have faith, but were allowed to be saved. Consequently, argued Mr. Ramsey, in conclusion, the best thing for all of us would have been to have been born idiots, and, consistently enough, Christianity tried to turn us all into idiots.

40 The horrors of the Bible*

The horrors of the Bible were confirmed by the horrors committed by Christians since then. The rhetoric of the following article by William Chilton was engendered by the heat of the moment at the height of the Scottish prosecutions in 1843.

SECOND ARREST OF PATERSON,
AND
ROBBERY OF HIS SHOP
BY
THE PRESBYTERIAN THIEVES
OF EDINBURGH.

Awake! what, ho! Infidels! thieves! thieves! thieves!
Look to your homes, your liberties, and your rights!
Thieves! thieves! – *Othello* (traverstied.)

———

He (god) is a merchant, the balances of *deceit* are in his hand; he *loveth* to OPPRESS. – Hosea xii. 7.

With such a monster-god, as an object of adoration and imitation, we should never be surprised that christians are the villains we find them. A moral christian would be a greater curiosity than a gentle shark – there could not be, in fact, a particle of morality in a so-called christian, without his being so much the less a christian than he who had none. Neither is this to be wondered at, for

* From *Oracle*, 9 Sep 1843.

THE GOD OF THE CHRISTIANS IS
A LIAR,
And a lover of lying,

For he sent the people "strong delusions, that they should believe a lie" – he put "a lying spirit" into the mouth of the prophets – "I, the lord god, have deceived that prophet" – he bade Samuel tell a lie to deceive Saul – and he instigated Jael to deceive Sisera.

THE GOD OF THE CHRISTIANS IS
AN ADULTERER,
And a lover of adultery, incest, and
whoredom,

For Mary, the wife of Joseph, and mother of Jesus, was with child by god, the *bastard* Christ being the result – David, a man after god's own heart[1], was a murderer and adulterer, and he found favour in his eyes – god directed Hosea to take him "a wife of whoredoms" – Moses, acting under his instigation, directed all the women children that had not known man by lying with him to be kept alive for the soldiers – Abraham, his chosen servant, married his sister – Lot was *specially* saved from destruction by him, and his wife enchanted, *that he may commit incest with his own daughters.*

THE GOD OF THE CHRISTIANS IS
A MURDERER,
And a lover of bloodshed,

For he murdered the first-born of Egypt – he slew Onan for not raising up seed to his brother – he sought to kill Moses, or his first-born – he burnt many of the people in the wilderness – he swallowed up 250 for offering strange fire, and *afterwards* burnt them – he sent lions amongst the people, and slew them – he inspired Jael to deceive Sisera, and afterwards horribly murdered him, for which bloody act she was declared to be "blessed above women."

THE GOD OF THE CHRISTIANS IS
A THIEF!
And a lover of thievery,

For he gave Israel favour in the eyes of the Egyptians, that the Israelites may despoil them of their jewels of silver and jewels of gold – he sanctioned and directed the numberless robberies perpetrated upon surrounding nations by his people – and, during his human incarnation, stole a donkey.

THE GOD OF THE CHRISTIANS IS A DEBAUCHEE!

And a lover of drunkenness,

For he made the princes, wise men, captains, and rulers drunk – he commanded Jeremiah to order the people to drink and be drunken – he got drunk himself, and made others drunk as well, at the feast of Cana – and Noah and Lot, whom he had spared when he had murdered thousands of others, both got drunk and acted indecently, as soon as their danger was over.

THE GOD OF THE CHRISTIANS IS A CRUEL TYRANT!

And a lover of tyranny and cruelty,

For he most barbarously tortured the Egyptians, for what he had compelled them to do – he plagued the people of Israel with fiery serpents, starved them, and subjected them to the horrors of thirst – and the man after his own heart, put men "under saws, and under harrows of iron, and under axes of iron, and made them pass through the brick-kiln."

THE GOD OF THE CHRISTIANS IS A LEWD, IMPURE, GROSS, AND OBSCENE PERSON

And a lover of lewdness, impurity, grossness, and obscenity,

For he wrote the bible, which is a lewd, impure, gross, and obscene book – and he permitted the lewdness, impurity, grossness, and obscenity therein recorded.

The above is a true picture of the christian's god – the object of their reverence and love – taken from his own recorded acts, described by his own pen. Who then can wonder at the crimes of christians? The goddess of the Thugs delights in blood and murder – and the Thugs, therefore, are murderers by profession. The god of the christians is a liar, an adulterer, a whore-monger, a murderer, a thief, a debauchee, a cruel tyrant, a lewd, impure, gross, and obscene person – and christians are liars, adulterers, whoremongers, murderers, thieves, debauchees, cruel tyrants, and lewd, impure, gross, and obscene persons, from love and respect for their god.

NOTE

1. A favourite phrase in infidel literature, from *The Life of David, or A History of the Man after God's own Heart* (1761), attributed to (among others) Peter Annet. It was republished by Carlile in 1820.

41 Anti-clericalism*

Such protests took place against a background of anti-clericalism. Priest-craft was attacked not only on the grounds that it upheld a bigotted religion but also that it maintained a persecuting state. These spiritual and secular roles were most clearly associated in the person of the clerical magistrate. One such man, the Rev. W. R. Hay, had ordered the yeomanry to advance at 'Peterloo', and for this act William Hone caricatured him in the following verses.

THE CLERICAL MAGISTRATE.

"*The Bishop*. Will you be diligent in Prayers—laying aside the study of the world and the flesh?——*The Priest*. I will.
The Bishop. Will you maintain and set forwards, as much as lieth in you, quietness, peace, and love, among all Christian People?——*Priest*. I will.
¶ The Bishop laying his hand upon the head of him that receiveth the order of Priesthood, shall say, RECEIVE THE HOLY GHOST."

The Form of Ordination for a Priest.

——"The pulpit (in the sober use
Of its legitimate peculiar pow'rs)
Must stand acknowledg'd, while the world shall stand,
The most important and effectual guard,
Support, and ornament of virtue's cause.

*   *   *   *

Behold the picture! Is it like?

THIS IS A PRIEST,

made 'according to Law',

* W. Hone, *The Political House that Jack Built* (1819) appendix.

Who, on being ordain'd,
      vow'd, by rote, like a daw,
That, he felt himself call'd,
      by the Holy Spirit,
To teach men the Kingdom of Heaven
      to merit;
That, to think of the World and the flesh
      he'd cease,
And keep men in quietness,
      love and peace;
And, making thus his profession
      and boast,
Receiv'd, from the Bishop,
      the Holy Ghost:
Then—not having the fear of God
      before him—
Is sworn in a Justice,
      and one of the *Quorum*;
'Gainst his spiritual Oath,
      puts his Oath of the Bench,
And, instead of his Bible,
      examines a wench;
Gets Chairman of Sessions—leaves his flock,
      sick, or dying,
To license Ale-houses—and assist
      in the trying
Of prostitutes, poachers, pickpockets
      and thieves;——
Having *charged* the Grand Jury,
      dines with them, and gives
"CHURCH AND KING without day-light;"
      gets *fresh*, and puts in—
To the stocks vulgar people
      who fuddle with gin:
Stage coachmen, and toll-men,
      convicts as he pleases;
And beggars and paupers
      incessantly teazes:
Commits starving vagrants,
      and orders Distress

On the Poor, for their Rates—
        signs warrants to press,
And beats up for names
        to a Loyal Address:
Would indict, for Rebellion,
        those who Petition;
And, all who look peaceable,
        try for Sedition;
If the People were legally Meeting,
        in quiet,
Would pronounce it, decidedly—*sec. Stat.*—
        a Riot,
And order the Soldiers
        'to aid and assist',
That is—kill the helpless,
        Who cannot resist.
He, though vowing 'from all worldly studies
        to cease',
Breaks the Peace of the Church,
        to be Justice of Peace;
Breaks his vows made to Heaven—
        a pander for Power;
A Perjurer—a guide to the People
        no more;
On God turns his back,
        when he turns the State's Agent;
And damns his own Soul,
        to be friends with the————[1]

NOTE

1. [Prince] Regent.

42 A de-conversion*

Many freethinkers were 'converted' to infidelity from Evangelical Christianity, and a number have left their recollections of the reasons why they renounced their former beliefs. One of Carlile's earliest shopmen–victims had been a Methodist lay preacher. He became a deist and set out his

* From *Republican*, 17 May 1822.

explanation in the Republican.

REASONS FOR RENOUNCING CHRISTIANITY.

HAVING been in the habit of going about to preach the Gospel, whilst I was a Methodist, I think it proper that I should give some reasons for renouncing the religion of Jesus the Jew, on whom I once built all my hopes of happiness.

I. Because in reading the Bible I constantly found contrary doctrines, that raised doubts in my mind, and which doubts I could never get satisfactorily cleared up by those who were my "spiritual pastors and masters.'

II. Because I found that all the various sects of which the Christian world is composed brought the proofs of the truth of their different systems from the Bible, and they all declare that their own is only right, and every other wrong.

III. Because I found, (upon watching closely the conduct of Christians, and those who denied Christianity,) more morality and consistency of conduct in those who denied the revelation of God, than in those who professed Christianity. This, in my mind, stript religion of its pretended divine power to effectually reform all those who heartily embrace it.

IV. Because the Christian doctrine asserts, that the heart of man is continually set to do evil; that he is prone to evil as the sparks fly upward. This I deny, because I find in my own nature more propensity to do good than evil, and that satisfaction arising from doing good is to me a constant incentive to virtuous actions.

V. Because I found in Christianity a most baneful influence in setting the interests of the people at variance, thereby giving occasion for a set of lazy Kings and Priests to lord it over them to their great distress.

VI. Because having been told by Christians that "The Age of Reason" was a stupid, vulgar, and blasphemous production, and having read it, and found it quite the reverse, and also found it to contain the most convincing proofs that the book which Christians call the word of God would dishonour any man to have it ascribed to him. I think this a sufficient reason alone to renounce the Christian mythology.

VII. Because, though Atheists, Deists, and Sceptics are all

willing to be convinced by fair argument and reason—the supporters of the Christian system not being able to do it, resort to the unconvincing arguments of fine, imprisonment, and brute violence.

VIII. Because I am convinced, had God chose to reveal his will, he would have done it in a manner that would have satisfied every man that it was the production of a Divine being: whereas the book that is imposed upon us as the word of God is so full of absurdities, contradictions, inconsistencies, not to mention the obscenity of it, that if any other book which has been handed down to us from antiquity had had but one-third of the palpable contrarieties in it as the Bible has, it would have long ago been condemned and held as nothing worth. And I believe God has not made any revelation but what we see in the works of Nature.

W. V. HOLMES.

Giltspur Street Compter,
    April 19, 1822.

Constructive Criticism

43 Biblical criticism*

The nineteenth century saw great advances in biblical criticism, both internal and external, and long articles in freethought journals and pamphlets were devoted to a reasoned attack on the Bible. Paine's Age of Reason was primarily a work of internal biblical criticism. Much that he wrote was not new. In the following extract, the point about Moses's grave had been made by Thomas Hobbes in his Leviathan (chapter 33) in 1651, but the reference to tithes gives a good example of the way in which Paine could always infuse his arguments with popular appeal.

In Deuteronomy, the style and manner of writing marks more evidently than in the former books that Moses is not the writer. The manner here used is dramatical: the writer opens the subject by a short introductory discourse, and then introduces Moses as in the act of speaking, and when he has made Moses finish his harangue, he (the writer) resumes his own part, and speaks till he brings Moses forward again, and at last closes the scene with an account of the death, funeral and character of Moses.

This interchange of speakers occurs four times in this book; from the first verse of the first chapter to the end of the fifth verse it is the writer who speaks; he then introduces Moses as in the act of making his harangue, and this continues to the end of the 40th verse of the fourth chapter; here the writer drops Moses and speaks historically of what was done in consequence of

* From T. Paine, *The Age of Reason*, part 2 (1797) Foner edition, pp. 522–4.

what Moses, when living, is supposed to have said, and which the writer had dramatically rehearsed.

The writer opens the subject again in the first verse of the fifth chapter, though it is only by saying that Moses called the people of Israel together; he then introduces Moses as before, and continues him, as in the act of speaking, to the end of the 26th chapter. He does the same thing at the beginning of the 27th chapter; and continues Moses, as in the act of speaking, to the end of the 28th chapter. At the 29th chapter the writer speaks again through the whole of the first verse and the first line of the second verse, where he introduces Moses for the last time and continues him, as in the act of speaking, to the end of the 33rd chapter.

The writer, having now finished the rehearsal on the part of Moses, comes forward and speaks through the whole of the last chapter; he begins by telling the reader that Moses went to the top of Pisgah; that he saw from thence the land which (the writer says) had been promised to Abraham, Isaac and Jacob; that he, Moses, died there in the land of Moab, but that no man knows of his sepulchre unto this day; that is, unto the time in which the writer lived who wrote the book of Deuteronomy. The writer then tells us, that Moses was 110 years of age when he died—that his eye was not dim, nor his natural force abated; and he concludes by saying that there arose not a prophet *since* in Israel like unto Moses, whom, says this anonymous writer, the Lord knew face to face.

Having thus shown, as far as grammatical evidence applies, that Moses was not the writer of those books, I will, after making a few observations on the inconsistencies of the writer of the book of Deuteronomy, proceed to show from the historical and chronological evidence contained in those books, that Moses was not, because *he could not be,* the writer of them, and consequently that there is no authority for believing that the inhuman and horrid butcheries of men, women and children, told of in those books, were done, as those books say they were, at the command of God. It is a duty incumbent on every true Deist, that he vindicate the moral justice of God against the calumnies of the Bible.

The writer of the book of Deuteronomy, whoever he was (for it is an anonymous work), is obscure, and also in contradiction with himself, in the account he has given of Moses.

After telling that Moses went to the top of Pisgah (and it does not appear from any account that he ever came down again), he tells us that Moses died *there* in the land of Moab, and that *he* buried him in a valley in the land of Moab; but as there is no antecedent to the pronoun *he,* there is no knowing who *he* was that did bury him. If the writer meant that *He* (God) buried him, how should *he* (the writer) know it? or why should we (the readers) believe him? since we know not who the writer was that tells us so, for certainly Moses could not himself tell where he was buried.

The writer also tells us, that no man knows where the sepulchre of Moses is *unto this day,* meaning the time in which this writer lived; how then should he know that Moses was buried in a valley in the land of Moab? for as the writer lived long after the time of Moses, as is evident from his using the expression of *unto this day,* meaning a great length of time after the death of Moses, he certainly was not at his funeral; and on the other hand, it is impossible that Moses himself could say that *no man knows where the sepulchre is unto this day.* To make Moses the speaker would be an improvement on the play of a child that hides himself and cries *nobody can find me;* nobody can find Moses!

This writer has nowhere told us how he came by the speeches which he has put into the mouth of Moses to speak, and therefore we have a right to conclude that he either composed them himself or wrote them from oral tradition. One or the other of these is the more probable, since he has given in the fifth chapter a table of commandments in which that called the fourth commandment is different from the fourth commandment in the twentieth chapter of Exodus.

In that of Exodus the reason given for keeping the seventh day is, "because (says the commandment) God made the heavens and the earth in six days, and rested on the seventh": but in that of Deuteronomy, the reason given is that it was the day on which the children of Israel came out of Egypt and *therefore,* says this commandment, *the Lord thy God commanded thee to keep the sabbath day.* This makes no mention of the Creation, nor *that* of the coming out of Egypt.

There are also many things given as laws of Moses in this

book that are not to be found in any of the other books; among which is that inhuman and brutal law, chapter xxi., verses 18, 19, 20 and 21, which authorizes parents, the father and the mother, to bring their own children to have them stoned to death for what it is pleased to call stubbornness.

But priests have always been fond of preaching up Deuteronomy, for Deuteronomy preaches up tithes; and it is from this book, chap. xxv., ver. 4, that they have taken the phrase, and applied it to tithing, that *"thou shalt not muzzle the ox when he treadeth out the corn";* and that this might not escape observation, they have noted it in the table of contents at the head of the chapter, though it is only a single verse of less than two lines. Oh, priests! priests! ye are willing to be compared to an ox, for the sake of tithes.

Though it is impossible for us to know *identically* who the writer of Deuteronomy was, it is not difficult to discover him *professionally,* that he was some Jewish priest, who lived, as I shall show in the course of this work, at least three hundred and fifty years after the time of Moses.

44 Scientific criticism (1)*

The Mosaic chronology was also open to external criticism, and the developments made in geology, palaeontology and medicine raised profound questions about the origins and nature of man which freethinkers were not slow to exploit. The alternative theory of the Creation to that found in Genesis *(which rested on the special creation of all life by divine intervention) was the Theory of Regular Gradation. This theory, based on the work of the French philosopher Lamarck, was developed in England by Robert Chambers of Edinburgh, first in* Chambers's Journal *and then in his anonymously written* Vestiges of the Natural History of Creation *(1844). The ideas popularised in* Chambers's Journal *were taken up in the early freethought periodicals by William Chilton, the Bristol compositor who had helped Southwell start the* Oracle *in 1841. The first extract gives a summary of the argument against special creation as developed by Southwell and Chilton in the* Oracle. *The second extract gives a 'behind the scenes' glimpse of Chilton at work, just over a year after the appearance of the* Vestiges.

* From *Oracle,* 7 Oct 1843.

THEORY OF REGULAR GRADATION.
XLVI.

Those of my readers who have long since thrown off the fetters of superstitious prejudice, and who upon the dawn of geology saw the consequences which would result from the establishment of the truth of its revelations, must not suppose that all the world, nor even all the thinking and intellectual world, are of the same opinion as themselves—for if they do imbibe so flattering a notion, they will be most grievously deceived. Far from christians generally of the present day, giving up the mosaic cosmogony, some of the ablest writers of the day contend for its truth over geology. In the *Morning Herald* of September last, is a long extract from the "Church of England Quarterly Review," on Scripture Geology. Upon the subject of creation is the following:. . . .

"Now there is one volume *which we rank higher than the book of nature,* or the volumes of science, *and to the standard of which we would bring the book of nature, assured that where they differ we have not read the book of nature aright.* We are sure that the bible speaks of only *one* creation, and at the beginning—that it speaks of only *one* revolution or catastrophe, and at the deluge—and we, therefore, scrutinise narrowly that interpretation of the book of nature which professes to discover *many* creations, and *many* catastrophes—and we assert that on scrutiny, we find it to be manifestly erroneous—inconsistent with itself and with science—and, therefore, even leaving the bible out of the question, this interpretation cannot stand."

It is unnecessary that I should endeavour to controvert these absurd dogmas, for I have already given my readers a sufficient number of geological *facts,* from the highest authorities, in disproof of the mosaic cosmogony . . .

Although I said, but a few minutes since, that I would not trouble you with a refutation of the Church of England Review, yet the monstrous folly of such arguments, and the unblushing effrontery of the men who can submit them to the light of day, and to the scrutiny of reason is so great, that I will, for the satisfaction of the tyro, offer one single fact as damnatory of the doctrine contended for. They say, "We are sure that *the bible* speaks of only *one* creation, *and at the beginning*—that it speaks of only *one* revolution or catastrophe, *and at the deluge,*" and they thence insist that all the phenomena belonging to the science of geology, was the result of the noachian deluge. The bible declares that the noachian deluge was a consequence of man's iniquity, and that all men who were upon the face of the earth, with the exception of Noah and his family, were drowned. The different strata of the earth is crowded with the petrified remains of all other animals, excepting men and monkeys—how comes it then that no remains of these are found, if *one* convulsion was sufficient to entomb all the other varieties of animated nature? Surely, if man's wickedness induced the deity to entirely annihilate *him*, leaving not a wreck behind—the monkeys had not similarly sinned, and their remains might have been preserved, as a monument of their previous existence—but no, they also are not to be found.

45 Scientific criticism (2)*

Feb. 1, 1846
Mr Cooke's, Thomas Street, Kingsdown
Bristol

My dear George,

Received my MS. and your note. Wrote the enclosed notes today, and sent them for your perusal, thinking they may contain, perhaps, an idea or two that may be useful to you, if you persevere in your intentions respecting "Vestiges." If you have any friends in G[lasgow] or E[dinburgh] who have given any attention to anatomy or physiology they could furnish you with plenty of illustrations of the close connexion of species, which is one of the important points of the theory of development. A work was published in Edinburgh some years ago, in a folio form, on the animal kingdom – I think the Edin[burgh] Scientific Journal – wh[ich] contains some excellent chapters on the permanence of species, which I sh[oul]d recommend to your perusal. What I send are simply *notes* for subsequent elaboration.

The extracts from *Kosmos* you can keep if of any use, as I have

* W. Chilton to G. J. Holyoake, 1 Feb 1846, Holyoake Collection, Manchester, no. 155.

preserved them in another form – they bear upon the Vestiges theory.

With respect to the authorship of that work I have this day learnt, upon what I may affirm to be the first authority, namely that of one of the first scientific men of the day, both as an experimenter & publisher, that "he has satisfied himself that Mr. Robert Chambers, of Edinburgh, is the author". It leaked out, I believe, through one of the printers. As you are in the neighbourhood, be cautious how you use this information. I am inclined to think that the gent[leman] referred to from his writings, is an advocate of the general principle of the "V." I quoted largely from him in my digest of the Vestiges. . . .

Yours very truly
W. C.

46   The principles of naturalism*

Although Paine himself had not been a materialist, the freethought tradition usually maintained a materialistic position, drawing on such classics as Mirabaud's System of Nature *and Volney's* Law of Nature. *Materialism lay at the heart of the atheism which Carlile espoused in the early 1820s, and which Southwell and Holyoake adhered to in mid-century. Their argument was a negative one: matter is eternal and so no Creator is needed; as there is no evidence of a Creator, none need be supposed; it is for those who believe in a Creator to show why. The writer here is Holyoake.*

The Atheist is one who believes nothing of any designer, mind, intelligence, cause, power, spirit, principle, or person, distinct from the material universe.

The principles of the Atheist are fair and simple, and may be thus stated —

The Atheist believes in the eternity of matter. This is the first of the great principles on which he rests. He believes that something must have existed from all eternity, for in the words of Paley—"Most assuredly, there never was a time in which nothing existed, because that condition must have continued. The universal *blank* must have remained; nothing could rise up

* From *Movement,* 16 Dec 1843.

but of it; nothing could ever have existed since; nothing could exist now." But as matter exists now—matter—or in other words, the material universe, is that something which has existed from all eternity. The opinion that matter is eternal is founded on the self-evident truism, *Ex nihilo nihil fit*,—"From nothing, nothing can be made,"—or nothing come. But that which came from nothing could have had no beginning, therefore matter had no beginning; and what had no beginning is uncaused, therefore the universe is uncaused and, consequently, self-existent.

The Atheist believes in the infinity of matter. Matter is universal. Imagination cannot bound it. The child instinctively enquires what is there at the end of the world? Infancy pictures something there; and when the telescope has pierced beyond the remotest star, the astronomer still finds new worlds to contemplate. The sailor who said he had travelled until he could not thrust a sixpence between his nose and the moon, only expressed the general truth, that matter is present everywhere.

These are the ancient principles of Atheism, and hence the Atheist concludes that, since the universe is eternal, it could not have had a Creator; and since it is self existent, a sustaining deity is not wanted; and, as matter is infinite, the existence of anything independent of matter is impossible.

47 An argument for atheism*

A more sophisticated philosophical argument was also developed, principally by Charles Bradlaugh, which attempted to turn the logic of the seventeenth-century Dutch philosopher, Spinoza, in favour of pantheism into a justification of outright atheism.

The line of thought pursued in the following pages, was originated by a perusal of the works of Benedict Spinoza, and while acknowledging the source from which my argument is drawn, I beg most distinctly to assert my right, to think unfettered by any conclusions to which the powerful brain of Spinoza attained. He was but a man, and I strive to be one also. I accept him as one who has "gone before" in the toilsome path, but

* From C. Bradlaugh, *Is there a God?* (1860) pp. 5–6

while borrowing the light of his investigations, I do not pledge
myself to follow in all his steps. My definitions are as follows:-

By eternity of duration I simply mean unlimited duration,
duration without limit, duration which I cannot limit, to which
I cannot conceive either beginning or end. I will, for con-
venience, number the following definitions and axioms—1. By
existence, or substance, I mean that which is in itself and is conceived *per se*, that is, the conception of which does not require
the conception of anything else as antecedent to it. 2. By attribute, I understand that by which I am enabled to take cogni-
zance of the various modes of existence. 3. By mode, I
understand each cognized condition or accident of existence
which is included in existence, which is not absolute existence,
per se, but which exists relatively. 4. By eternity, I mean indefiniteness of duration, that is, unlimited duration. 5. By infinity, I
mean indefiniteness of extension, that is, unlimited extension.
The axioms, so far as I shall give them, are in the precise language of Spinoza. "1. Everything which is, is in itself, or in some
other thing. 2. That which cannot be conceived through
another *per aliud* must be conceived *per se*. 3. From a given determinate cause the effect necessarily follows, and *vice versa*. If no
determinate cause be given, no effect can follow. 4. The knowledge of an effect depends on the knowledge of the cause, and includes it. 5. Things that have nothing in common with each
other cannot be understood by means of each other—that is,
the conception of one does not involve the conception of the
other."

Propositions:—Existence is prior to its modes. This follows
from definitions 1 and 3, because modes of existence are conceived relatively and in dependence on existence which is absolutely precedent in such conception.

Existences having different attributes have nothing in common with each other. This is founded on definition 1.

Existences having nothing in common with each other,
cannot be the cause of, or affect one another.

If they have nothing in common, they cannot be conceived by
means of each other (per axiom 5), and they cannot be conceived as relating to each other, but must be conceived *per se*
(per def. 1), and as (per axiom 4), the knowledge of an effect
depends on the knowledge of the cause and includes it, it is im-

possible to conceive any existence as an effect so long as you cannot conceive it in relation to any other existence.

Having used the word "cause" several times, I should add that by "cause" in the absolute, I mean "existence." In its popular or relative sense, I use "cause" as an effect of some precedent causative influence, itself the cause of some consequent effect.

Archimedes is alleged to have said that, given a place whereon to rest his lever, he would move the world. Such a resting place is needed in our present argument. Some fact on which our lever of reason may rest while we remove the world of error which now eclipses the sun of truth. What fact is there so certain, that I may base all my reasonings upon it? My existence is this primary fact; this, to me, indubitable certainty. I am. This logic can neither prove nor disprove. The very nature of proof is to make a proposition more clear to the mind than it was before, and no amount of evidence can increase my conviction of the certainty of my own existence. I do not affirm that I am existence, but I affirm that there is existence. This existence is either eternal, that is, unlimited in duration, that is, indefinite in duration; or else it had a beginning, that is, it has been created. If created, then such creation must be by some existence the same as itself, or by some existence differing from itself. But it cannot have been created by any existence the same as itself, because to imagine such, would be to conceive no more than a continuation of the same existence—there would be no discontinuity. But, says S. T. Coleridge "where there is no discontinuity there can be no origination." And it cannot have been created by any existence differing from itself, because things which have nothing in common with one another, cannot be the cause of, or affect, one another. Therefore this existence has not been created, that is, its duration is indefinite—that is, you cannot conceive a beginning—that is, it is eternal. This eternal existence is either infinite in extent, that is, is unlimited in extent, or it is finite, that is, limited. If limited, it must be limited by an existence the same as itself, or by an existence differing from itself. But the same arguments which applied to a limitation of duration, also apply to a limitation of extension. Therefore this existence is unlimited in extent; that is, is infinite and eternal—that is, there is only one existence. It is at this point that Atheism separates from Pantheism. Pantheism demonstrates one existence, but affirms for it infinite attributes. Atheism denies that attributes can be infinite. Attributes are but the distinguishing characteristics of modes, and how can that be infinite which is only the quality of finity? Men do not talk of infinite hardness or of infinite softness; yet they talk of infinite intelligence. Intelligence is not an existence, and the word is without value unless it strictly comprehend, and is included in, that which is intelligent. The hardness of the diamond, the brilliancy of the burnished steel, have no existence apart from the diamond or the steel. I, in fact, affirm that there is only one existence, and that all we take cognisance of is mode, or attribute of mode, of that existence.

The New System

48 The Law of Nature*

The basis of any positive system of freethought was Nature, as set out in such classics as the American Elihu Palmer's Principles of Nature *(1801 or 1802) or the Frenchman C. F. Volney's* The Law of Nature *(1794). The political as well as ethical implications of this theory are apparent in the following extract from Thomas Davison's edition of Volney's work.*

CHAP. XI.

OF THE SOCIAL VIRTUES, AND OF JUSTICE.

Q. *What is society?*

A. Every aggregate re-union of men living together under the regulations of a contract, tacit or expressed, for their common preservation.

Q. *Are the social virtues many in number?*

A. Yes; we may count as many as there are actions useful to society; but they may be all reduced to one principle.

Q. *What is this fundamental principle?*

A. Justice; which itself alone comprehends all the social virtues.

Q. *Why do you say that justice is the fundamental, and almost only virtue of social life?*

A. Because it alone embraces the practice of all those actions

---

* From C. F. Volney, *The Law of Nature* (1819) pp. 25–7.

which are useful to society; and that every virtue, under the name of charity, humanity, probity, love of country, sincerity, generosity, simplicity of manners, and modesty, are but varied forms, and diversified applications of this axiom, "Do unto another only that which thou would he should do unto thee;" which is the definition of justice.

Q. *How does the law of nature ordain justice?*
A. By means of three physical attributes which are inherent in the organization of man.

Q. *What are these attributes?*
A. Equality, liberty, property.

Q. *In what sense is equality a physical attribute of man?*
A. Because all men, having equally eyes, hands, a mouth, ears, and being alike under the necessity of making use of them for their life's sake, are by this very fact equally entitled to life, and to the use of the elements which contribute to its support. They are all equal before God.

Q. *Do you pretend that all men hear, see, and feel equally well; that they have equal wants, and equal and like passions?*
A. No; for it is a matter of certainty and daily experience, that one man is short and another long-sighted; that one eats much and another little; that has one moderate and another violent passions; in a word, that one grown person is weak both in body and mind, while another is strong in both.

Q. *They are in fact, then, really unequal?*
A. Yes; in the unfolding of their faculties and powers, but not in the nature and essence of these powers; it is a stuff of the same kind, but whose dimensions are not equal, nor its weight and value the same, with those of some other pieces: our language has no word calculated to express at the same time, sameness of nature and diversity of form and employment. It is a relative equality, and for this reason I said, equal before God, and in the order of nature.

Q. *Why is liberty called a physical attribute of man?*
A. Because all men possessing senses fitted and sufficient for their preservation, no one having need of the eye of another man in order to see, of his ear to hear, of his mouth to eat, or of his foot to walk; they are all made by this means, naturally independent and free. No one is of necessity subjected to another's rule, nor has right of dominion over him.

Q. *But if a man is born strong, has he not a natural right to master and rule over him who is born weak?*

A. No; for it is neither with respect to himself a matter of necessity, nor a convention between the two; and in this instance we make improper use of the word right, which in its true sense signifies nothing more than justice, or reciprocal faculties and power.

Q. *How is property a physical attribute of man?*

A. Since every man is formed equal and similar to his fellows, and consequently free and independent, every one is the absolute master, the entire proprietor of his body, and the products of his labour.

Q. *How is justice derived from these three attributes?*

A. From this circumstance; that men being equal, free, and owing nothing to each other, have no right to demand any thing of their fellows, but in proportion as they return for it something equivalent; in proportion as the balance of what is given to what is paid remains in equilibrium; and it is this equality, this equilibrium, which is called justice and equity—that is to say, equality and justice are synonymous words; are the same natural law, of which all the social virtues are but applications and derivatives.

49 The New Moral World*

Owenism sought to introduce a new religion – the Rational Religion – in which man would find true happiness by realising the great environmentalist truths which Owen proclaimed. The ideas he expressed were commonplaces of Enlightenment thought, but he was able to give them a new urgency and appeal to working men whose social and economic circumstances were undergoing rapid and uncertain change. The turning point in Owen's career came in 1817 when he combined his own plans for relieving the poor with an appeal to the wider public. The apocalyptic nature of his revelation is apparent in the following extract.

I may now be asked,—What are the characteristic differ-

* From R. Owen, 'Letter, dated Sept. 6th, 1817, containing a further Development of the Plan for the Relief of the Poor, and the Emancipation of Mankind', *Life of Robert Owen*, vol. 1A (1858) pp. 135–7.

ences between Old and New Society?

They are decisive and manifold.

Old society has supposed, contrary to every fact that has been observed from the earliest period of known time to this hour, that MAN FORMS HIS OWN CHARACTER!! *and all the transactions of mankind have been governed by this absurd notion!!*

New society will be instructed, by close and accurate attention to all existing and provable facts, THAT THE CHILD DOES NOT FASHION ITSELF IN THE WOMB; OR DIRECT THE LANGUAGE, MANNERS, HABITS, SENTIMENTS, AND ASSOCIATIONS, WHICH SHALL BE AFTERWARDS IMPRESSED UPON ITS NATURAL PHYSICAL AND INTELLECTUAL POWERS; *and that the whole character of man is a compound of these combined circumstances.* Old society, therefore, from the hour the child was born, began a system of conduct diametrically contrary to fact, *and Nature was counteracted by all the efforts of Ignorance.* Nature, however continually opposed Ignorance, and all the force and violence of the latter could not keep the former in subjection. Ignorance then called in Superstition and Hypocrisy to its aid; and together they invented all the faiths or creeds in the world;—a horrid crew, armed with every torture both for body and mind. A dreadful conflict ensued; Nature was overcome, and compelled for a long season to receive laws from her conquerors, and to be the slave of Ignorance and Superstition. Nature was then treated with indiscribable severity; and would have been put to death if she had not been immortal, and possessed of powers capable of gradual reaction, equal, and superior, to any force that could be permanently exerted against her. As time advanced, the appalling terrors of Ignorance and Superstition, Faith and Hypocrisy, imperceptibly diminished. Experience united herself to Nature, and produced Real Knowledge and Demonstrable Truth. These grew up together; and, in close bond of union with their parents, they became strong, felt conscious of their strength, and were soon eager for attack. But Nature and Experience knowing the wiles and power of their opponents, restrained their ardour, but inured them to continual opposition and severe contest, until Knowledge and Truth became assured that their united efforts would be irresistible. War was then openly declared against Ignorance, Superstition, Faith, Hypocrisy, and all their dire associates. The latter instantly sounded the alarm, collected their forces, and began to prepare for battle. To their utter dismay, however, Charity, who till now had been compelled by force, contrary to her nature and inclinations, to be their ally, and to appear in their front ranks, escaped their toils, and declared she would henceforward unite herself solely with Nature, Experience, Real Knowledge, and Demonstrable truth; but, to prevent all future devastation and misery, she would use her mediation and obtain the best possible terms for the weakened and now disheartened enemies of Nature and her invincible allies. This offer, seeing all resistance vain and hopeless, was readily accepted, and Truth and Charity dictated the terms, which, in consequence, were kind and benevolent, evincing that they were not influenced by anger, revenge, or any evil motive whatever. Ignorance, Superstition, Faith, and Hypocrisy, were permitted to retain all their possessions;—to remain free and unmolested in the conquered country. But they were to leave it solely to the government of Nature, aided by Experience and Real Knowledge, as counsellors. And Charity, assisted by Demonstrable Truth and Sincerity, was to preside as the active agent over the whole dominions of the New State of Society.

50 The principles of Secularism*

Out of Owenism, and under the influence of the liberal theism of men like W. R. Greg and F. W. Newman and the utilitarianism of Bentham and J. S. Mill, G. J. Holyoake evolved the positive ideas of Secularism which were to constitute the basis of popular freethought for the rest of the century. Its major points were set out by Holyoake as follows.

Secularism is a development of freethinking, including its *positive* as well as its *negative* side. Secularists consider freethinking as a *double* protest—a protest against specific speculative error, and in favour of specific moral truth. The term Secularism has not been chosen as a concealment, or a disguise, or as an apology for free inquiry, but as expressing a certain positive and ethical element, which the terms 'Infidel,' 'Sceptic,' 'Atheist,' do not express. *When* the term 'Infidel' is used to

* From *Reasoner*, 8 Jan 1854.

express fair dissent from Christianity, or 'Sceptic,' to express honest doubt of its principles, or 'Atheist,' to signify pure intellectual inability to account for the Origin of the Universe, or to accept the Christian theory of its government, none of the Secularists object to the application of such terms respectively to themselves. But as these terms usually connote guilt and dissent, they prefer the term *Secularism*, as expressive of opinions which they hold to be affirmative, virtuous, and reasonable.

A Secularist is one who gives primary attention to those speculations, the issues of which can be tested by the experience of this life.

Secularism, looking over human society, discerns numerous persons who stand outside Christianity, who, for conscientious reasons, reject one or other of its fundamental principles. At this point of sight, a serious question arises—are good citizenship, personal virtue, a calm conscience, and fair desert in death, possible to such persons? Secularism undertakes to solve that problem, and answers—*Yes*.

Its moral basis is, that Justification by conduct is a higher and more reliable truth than 'Justification by Faith in Christ.'

Its province of Study is the Order, rather than the Origin, of Nature, the study of the Laws or Operations of Nature being the most fruitful in human guidance.

Its Practical Result is the discovery that Science is the Providence of Man, and the development of this truth as a protection against false dependencies.

Its Theory of Morals.—That there exist guarantees of Morality in Human Nature, in Utility, and Intelligence.

Its Sphere of Controversy.—The criticism of Sacred Books and existing Religions only in those respects in which they seem to contradict ascertained Moral Truths, and are impediments to a Rational progress.

PART FOUR

The Politics of Liberation

Freethinkers believed in the natural rights of man, and in the absolute sovereignty of reason. All human political institutions which were an affront to natural rights or which could not stand up to rational criticism, were deemed in need of a thoroughgoing reform.

This was the theoretical basis for the political ultra-radicalism of the infidels, but in practice they were not always so advanced in social terms. Paineite radicalism was individualistic — a reflection of the atomistic, mechanical and rationalistic universe of the eighteenth century — and, despite the more sophisticated analyses of the Socialist thinkers, individualism remained the key feature of infidel political thought; hence the preoccupation with freeing men's minds from the shackles of priestianity. Once a man could think straight, reform would be inevitable.

But if a system of individualistic natural rights did not always lead to the sort of proto-Marxist thinking about the class basis of power in society, which kept threatening to break out in the radical periodicals (especially those connected with J. B. O'Brien), it did nevertheless offer a great deal to the oppressed, or at least to those who were willing by thrift and sobriety to raise themselves from the irrational state of wilful poverty. Natural rights were, by definition, undeniable and therefore to be won by all, including foreigners and women. When freethinkers were not among the vanguard of the proletariat at home, they were among the most faithful supporters of republicanism abroad, and were consistently among the leaders of the struggle to improve the lot of women.

Domestic Radicalism

51 Paineite republicanism*

The infidel radicals were republicans, but they did not accept the contemporary connotations of the word, which implied an anarchic and violent change in the political system. By republicanism the radicals from Paine to Bradlaugh meant a thoroughgoing reform within a context of representative, democratic constitutionalism.

What is called a *republic*, is not any *particular form* of government. It is wholly characteristical of the purport, matter, or object for which government ought to be instituted, and on which it is to be employed, RES-PUBLICA, the public affairs, or the public good; or, literally translated, the *public thing*. It is a word of a good original, referring to what ought to be the character and business of government; and in this sense it is naturally opposed to the word *monarchy*, which has a base original signification. It means arbitrary power in an individual person; in the exercise of which, *himself*, and not the *res-publica*, is the object.

Every government that does not act on the principle of a *Republic*, or in other words, that does not make the *res-publica* its whole and sole object, is not a good government. Republican government is no other than government established and conducted for the interest of the public, as well individually as collectively. It is not necessarily connected with any particular form, but it most naturally associates with the representative

* From T. Paine, *Rights of Man*, part 2 (1792) Collins edition, pp. 200–1, 206.

form, as being best calculated to secure the end for which a nation is at the expense of supporting it.

Various forms of government have affected to style themselves a republic. Poland calls itself a republic, which is an hereditary aristocracy, with what is called an elective monarchy. Holland calls itself a republic, which is chiefly aristocratical, with an hereditary stadtholdership. But the government of America, which is wholly on the system of representation, is the only real republic in character and in practice, that now exists. Its government has no other object than the public business of the nation, and therefore it is properly a republic; and the Americans have taken care that THIS, and no other, shall always be the object of their government, by their rejecting everything hereditary, and establishing government on the system of representation only. . . .

In the representative system, the reason for everything must publicly appear. Every man is a proprietor in government, and considers it a necessary part of his business to understand. It concerns his interest, because it affects his property. He examines the cost, and compares it with the advantages; and above all, he does not adopt the slavish custom of following what in other governments are called LEADERS.

It can only be by blinding the understanding of man, and making him believe that government is some wonderful mysterious thing, that excessive revenues are obtained. Monarchy is well calculated to ensure this end. It is the popery of government; a thing kept up to amuse the ignorant, and quiet them into taxes.

The government of a free country, properly speaking, is not in the persons, but in the laws. The enacting of those requires no great expense; and when they are administered, the whole of civil government is performed—the rest is all court contrivance.

52 Carlile's republicanism*

This theme was taken up by Carlile, but the tone of his writings was more violent and the emphasis on 'priestcraft' more pronounced than in the Rights of Man. *To Carlile the war on religion was a vital part of*

* From *Republican*, 23 Aug 1822.

radical reform; this he saw to be the true Paineite legacy, and anyone who did not agree — such as Henry Hunt — could not be regarded as a true reformer. The following letter is both a veiled attack on Hunt and a rallying call to Carlile's own brand of republicanism to which he had attached the name of Paine.

TO THE REPUBLICAN BASKET MAKERS AND OTHERS, OF SHEFFIELD.

CITIZENS,   Dorchester Gaol, August 18, 1822.

I RETURN you thanks for your subscription towards my support, and more particularly for the sentiments you have expressed in accompaniment with them. With you I have not failed to notice the apathy which pervades Sheffield at this moment, distinguished as that town has been, ever since the commencement of the French Revolution, for its warm support of all reforms that can ameliorate the condition of the human race. When I read the reports of the speeches made at the Sheffield Meetings during the existence of the Corresponding Society; when I recollect that Sheffield was one of the towns that openly addressed Thomas Paine, and thanked him for his "Rights of Man," and when I know that Redhead Yorke distinguished your town by addressing his "Essay on Civil Liberty" to its inhabitants; I-feel assured that Sheffield must abound with real Republicans, though many of that day must be advanced in years at this, and though a man never loses a true Republican spirit, yet a course of disappointments may render him silent or more secret in propagating his sentiments.

Your townsmen want some new stimulus for union and co-operation, and I will call upon them to come forward upon the principles of the only Radical Reform; that which shall root out all unnecessary taxation, that which shall put down Priestcraft as well as Parliamentary abuses, that which shall venerate nothing for custom or antiquity's sake, that which shall make the whole system of Government representative, from the highest to the lowest officer of the state, or its law; and that which shall establish that species of equality as to leave no man more power than another, but what is delegated to him by some body of Electors, and such as they can recal whenever they think proper. I call for the co-operation of the inhabitants of Sheffield upon these only true principles of Republicanism. I ask their assistance in my attempt to root out idolatry both political and theological, as the only true Radical Reform.

[Richard Carlile]

53 An attack on apolitical Owenism*

Robert Owen did not share these views, though many of the radicals other-wise influenced by him did. Henry Hetherington had been associated with the Owenites since 1821, and he was to continue active among them until his death in 1849, but he was infuriated at the way official Owenism refused to become involved in the agitation for parliamentary reform in 1831–2.

I reiterate what I then said, that Mr. Owen's principles are "practicable and beneficial," if the working people have fair play—not else. Independent Co-operation cannot be success-fully established in this country—*even as an experiment*—till the working classes obtain their political rights, or an alteration takes place in the existing laws. I could, were it judicious to do so, state several important facts in corroboration of this asser-tion. Mr. Owen is generally esteemed, and without doubt is, a kind-hearted man —benevolently disposed to do his utmost to better the condition of mankind; but he exhibits a strange per-versity of mind in expecting to realize his political millenium before working men are placed on an equal footing with the other classes of community with regard to political rights; and I consider him, on this point, in almost as hopeless a condition, as the individual who believed he was made of glass; it was use-less to knock his head against the wall to convince him to the contrary—the notion was immoveable. So it is with Mr. Owen—he entertains an absurd idea, that with the aid of a plundering aristocracy he shall be able to establish Co-operative principles, notwithstanding the unjust and inquitous laws which at present exist in this country. In his case, experi-ence is unavailing; for after more than twenty years' exertion he

* From *Poor Man's Guardian*, 14 Jan 1832.

is not a jot nearer the attainment of his object. His mental vision must have some peculiar defect, or he would perceive that he was "dipping buckets into empty wells, and growing old in drawing nothing up."

54 A defence of apolitical Owenism*

The Owenites had a point, though, and their socialist analysis of economic power was far more sophisticated than Carlile's 'priestcraft' interpretation. The socialists correctly perceived that, even though political reform might be desirable, the realities of power made it highly unlikely, whereas by direct economic action working men could successfully by-pass the state and live in their own communities. This case was put by John Finch, the Liverpool ironmaster, Owenite and Temperance reformer, in a series of letters on the Ralahine community effort in Ireland, which appeared in the Northern Star *and then in the* New Moral World *during the summer of 1838, just as the Socialists were preparing to start their own community on English soil at Queenwood in Hampshire.*

No country on earth, not even America, in these respects, is so free as our own. It is not practical, political, or religious liberty, then, that we so much want; and, if we did want them, with the present constitution of Parliament, and the present state of political parties, we have no chance at present of obtaining them. We have a Whig ministry, supported by a very large and powerful party both in and out of the House of Commons; apparently (I think not really) opposed by a large majority of the bishops and peers in the Lords, and a party of Tories nearly as numerous as themselves in the Commons; *and both these parties have declared themselves determinedly against any further political reform.* It is true, there is a third party in the House of Commons, the Radicals; but they are few in number; and though supported by the great body of the working classes, and by many of the most liberal and thinking of every other class, their friends being princially non-electors, there is no chance of their numbers being much increased; and the utmost they can accomplish, and which, I trust, they will accomplish, will be to hold the balance of power between Whigs and Tories, and prevent a

* From *New Moral World*, 1 Sep 1838.

retrograde movement. The working classes may hold large meetings, petition, talk big, and bluster, but in political reform they can at present do no more.

My friends! what the working class is now wanting is employment and a fair reward for their labour, good food, clothing, lodging, and education. Annual Parliaments, Universal Suffrage, and the Vote by Ballot, cannot procure any of these for them, or they would have done it for America. The want of these is not the great cause of the evils they suffer: *it is because 7s. 6d. in the pound of all they earn is spent by those who merely distribute the articles they make, 2s. 6d. in the pound by the government, 1s. by their teachers, and 4s. 6d. by idlers, leaving only 4s. 6d. in the pound for themselves; and because competition has reduced every man's means of purchasing, these are the true reasons why they are unemployed, and in want and poverty.* Remove the cause and the effects will cease; *and nothing short of that complete change in society, which it has been my object to develope [sic] in these letters, can effect this desirable change.*

55   Dreams of a new radicalism*

Such differences of opinion were of little importance to most radicals. They were seen as mere differences over strategy or of emphasis. The dream was of one united radical movement which would embrace the aims of all causes. This need for unity became increasingly apparent as individual popular movements failed. By the mid-1840s both Chartism and socialism were past their peaks, and this gave George Julian Harney, among others, much cause for thought. Harney had been imprisoned as a vendor of the unstamped, he was an ardent radical and an infidel, and thoroughly committed to the English Jacobin tradition. As sub-editor of the Northern Star *he showed every sympathy for the infidel socialists, especially for G. J. Holyoake, whose Chartist opposite number he had been in Sheffield in 1841. Holyoake had just written a text book entitled* Practical Grammar, *which he hoped (successfully) that Harney would review in the* Northern Star. *The following letter, in Harney's handwriting, is unfortunately incomplete.*

* G. J. Harney to G. J. Holyoake, 23 Apr 1844, Holyoake Collection, Manchester, no. 115.

Leeds, April 22[18]44.

Dear H[olyoake]

Much obliged for your good wishes for Mrs. H[arney]'s better health who still continues very unwell.

If you send your Grammar I will try to give it a notice in some shape, though how I'm to do so I can hardly tell as I know no more of grammar than does a cow of handling a musket. Grammar is *my* "great difficulty." Could I overcome that I think I could see my way clear for a living for the future, without that knowledge my present occupation is but precarious. I could never muster sufficient resolution yet to read a page of any grammar book though I have several by me. If you send yours I *must* read it in the way of business, perhaps it may lead me to read further.

If you send me the Trials[1] when complete I will contrive to give them a second notice.

Much pleased with your article in No 18 Move[men]t "What ought Congress to do?"[2] The fact is that Owenism is by. It strikes me that we shall yet see a new party in this country combining the good of Socialism and Chartism. The latter *ism* cannot stay where it is, it must advance. Here is my idea of Chartism in the *Present* and the *Future*

Political

Present	Future
The 6 Points	Republicanism – including the 6 points

Social

Present	Future
Protection to Labour Fair Days wage for Fair days work	Communism – Destruction of Landlordism and Profitism

(Anti) Theocratical

Present	Future
Anti-State Churchism	War with all Priesthoods and Priestcrafts.

You may smile at these notions, but I have for some time past entertained them; and as the showman says 'We shall see what we shall see.'

I send you the enclosed article from the *Star* of April 13th not because I think it any very grand affair but because of the Republican and Anti-Priestly sentiments which I have endeavoured to thereby give currency too [sic] . . .

NOTES

1. 'The Trial of Thomas Paterson for Blasphemy', with a preface by Holyoake, was reviewed in the *Northern Star*, 6 Apr 1844. The volume was completed with the addition of the trials of Finlay and Roalfe (Doc. 67) under the composite title, *The Scotch Trials*. Harney printed extracts in *Northern Star*, 15 June 1844.

2. The coming Socialist Congress was that at which pro- and anti-Owen factions finally split. Holyoake had argued in his article that, though atheism was subordinate to the principal feature of Owenism (i.e. its science of society), it was nevertheless a necessary part of the whole. *Movement*, 13 Apr. 1844.

56 A plea for compromise*

The question of strategy continued to be discussed, and Owenite fears about the ineffectiveness of Chartism proved to be all too well founded. The need for collaboration between middle- and working-class radicals was increasingly voiced, and the Owenites with their 'all classes of all nations' approach were well equipped to press for this. Holyoake was a prominent moderate, but even more extreme freethinkers like Robert Cooper came to adopt the strategy of political and class compromise. In the following letter he explained to Joseph Cowen Jr of Newcastle why he and his Manchester friends differed from Cowen's Northern Reform Union.

8, Moss Side View,
Manchester, July 28th 1862

My dear Sir,

I have just seen in the *Chronicle* of the 12th inst. a report of the meeting of your council[1]. In your own speech no more than justice is done to the Manhood Suffrage views, more especially as respects the noble efforts of your own association, but you scarcely appreciate the labours of those who introduced the original

* R. Cooper to J. Cowen, 28 July 1862, Cowen Collection, Newcastle, no. C. 1738.

as well as the amended resolution at the late Conference². However, I will not be captious. I only ask that justice should be awarded to those who have precisely the same object in contemplation – the enfranchisement of every male adult, not a criminal. We merely differ as to the *speediest* mode of attaining that object. My antecedents are known to many gentlemen who spoke at your council meetings, and I trust I am entitled to say that I should be one of the last men in our ranks to compromise or betray the interests of the working classes. I will at once avow that should the programme adopted at the Conference – a programme drawn up, and *unanimously* approved by a Committee of which you were a member as well as myself³ – fail to secure justice to the people, I shall be the first to abandon it for any other that would more readily consummate our common purpose. I will never rest till Manhood Suffrage is the law of the land. Nevertheless, as a practical man, who has had some experience both amongst the working and middle class, I hold it to be perfectly legitimate to inquire, – how can we best accomplish that measure? There are only two modes – by the working class, as hitherto, isolating themselves from all other classes, or by their seeking the co-operation of the liberals of the middle class. I believe the latter is the more feasible, since every great measure, political or social, has only been carried by the joint action of the two classes. Experience has demonstrated that the middle class – whether justly or unjustly is not now the question – exercise, in the *present* political scale, a determining power in settling national concerns. If they and the aristocracy unite, they beat the people, – if they and the people combine they defeat the aristocracy – and the *latter* are the natural enemies of popular power. Is it not worth while, therefore, to make some sacrifice to secure the help of that class which would give the preponderance in the political scale in favour of popular interests? It may not be that the middle class would go for manhood suffrage – I know they would not *as a class*, but the more advanced portion, if we earnestly sought their support, would go just so far, that a liberal majority would be secured in almost every borough in the Kingdom. And would not such a House of Commons be likely, at the first favourable opportunity, to grant a *further* extension of the suffrage, until, by degrees, a House of Commons would be returned that would pass a Manhood Suffrage Bill? On the other hand, if we take a position at first so advanced as to repel the Middle Class, we at once strengthen the hands of the common enemy – the aristocracy, who will concede nothing to the people unless sustained by the commercial community. By raising the standard of Manhood suffrage *now*, we *might* rouse the people, get up monster meetings – in short, revive the agitation of 1839, '42 and '48. But what then? Why, the landed aristocracy, having at present the military power under their control, and knowing the middle class were not with us, our "extreme" proceedings having converted the sympathy of the latter into distrust, if not opposition – the government would be instigated to put down our meetings, and, if need be, incarcerate our leaders, leaving the people once more a prey to disappointment and suffering. The ultimate issue would be the complete cessation of popular agitation till a new generation arise. Why not, Sir, at least, *try* the opposite plan? Let us work for an instalment, as a means of securing a larger instalment, until the whole is gained? There is no inconsistency in this, no abandonment of principle. The plan is clear, reasonable and practical. When it is seen that the first instalment of the suffrage has only tended to elevate the people, to render them more peaceable citizens, and therefore more industrious and skilful workpeople, strengthening the hands of their employers, and facilitating the extension of free trade in new fields of commerce, rest assured that the fears and prejudices of those above the people, would be immensely diminished. The obstacles to further instalments would rapidly become less and less, till the final triumph of complete emancipation would crown our efforts.

Here then, my dear Sir, rest the points of difference between your association and ours. You prefer the first plan – we the last. Now is it not possible to settle this difference before another Conference? I repeat we both mean the same thing. We have only to agree as to the mode of obtaining that end. I would respectfully suggest that a deputation of the Northern Union, should meet a deputation of our association at Leeds – being the most central – where, in conjunction with the Leeds association, we could consult together and determine upon the most satisfactory mode of rendering the conference of October next of truly national importance. Let us come to some arrangement by which we can thwart, not each other, but the open foe. I am wearied with mere party strife amongst men of the same opinions. I will never again impair health and waste mental strength in squabbles. We had better, indeed, not move at all except *unitedly* – Hence union is the *sine qua non* to either immediate or permanent success, in a cause dear to us all.

This letter you may make use of as you deem advisable, and awaiting your reply, I remain, dear Sir,

> Yours faithfully,
> Robert Cooper,
> President of the Manchester Working
> Mens Parliamentary Association.

J. Cowen Esq.,
President of the Northern Reform Union.

NOTES

1. For Cowen, see the *Dictionary of Labour Biography*, vol. 1. Cowen, whose father had risen in the ranks to become a manufacturer of clay bricks and retorts, owned both the *Newcastle Daily Chronicle* and *Weekly Chronicle*. His Northern Reform Union (1858–62), for which Holyoake was the London agent, became the northern branch of the Reform League in 1866.
2. The Reform Conference had been held in London, 20, 21 May 1862. The original motion had proposed a £10 household franchise; the amended motion, proposed by Washington Wilks and supported by Cowen, Bradlaugh, George Thompson and Benjamin Lucraft, proposed manhood suffrage. Finally a compromise was agreed which proposed a householder and lodger franchise to all those who paid the Poor Rate or were liable to it. Bradlaugh commented in the *National Reformer*, 'This was not quite what we could have wished, but rather than stand in the way of united action we concurred; reserving it to ourselves to declare that manhood suffrage is *the right*, while the proposed basis of the Conference only recognises *the politic.*' *National Reformer*, 31 May 1862.
3. The original motion had been drafted by a committee which included Cowen, Cooper, Wilks and Richard Moore. It had been Cooper's task to put the motion to the full meeting. Ibid.

57 In praise of Mr Gladstone*

The political product of this class compromise was Gladstonian Liberalism, to which many ultra-radicals became firmly committed. The appeal of Gladstone was an emotional one, based only partly on what Gladstone

* From *National Reformer*, 30 July 1865.

had done as Chancellor of the Exchequer. What really wedded the radicals to him, despite many practical disillusionments, was the ideal of moral integrity which he represented. A leading article by John Watts in the National Reformer *in 1865 makes the appeal of Gladstone clear. The occasion was the defeat of Gladstone by Gathorne Hardy at Oxford University in the general election, and the consequent election of Gladstone to represent South Lancashire. The quotations from Gladstone's speeches are not only typical of the prolixity of his grammar but also illustrative of the way in which they actually mean the opposite of what radicals took them to mean, despite Watts's admiration of their 'distinctness'.*

NATIONAL PROGRESS.

THOSE who profess to be National Reformers cannot but take interest in National Progress. And happily there have not been wanting, during the last few weeks, many indications that such progress is being rapidly attained. The recent elections afford numerous instances of the triumph of intelligence, of tolerance, of honesty, and of truly liberal principles. The last great victory gained was Mr. Gladstone's defeat at Oxford. Never were the Tories more shortsighted than when they "unmuzzled" Mr. Gladstone; and however much they may for the moment exult over his defeat, the time is not far distant when they will exclaim, as the *Telegraph* puts it, "Oh, Oxford, Oxford, you have carried Gathorne Hardy, but you have given Liberalism an irresistible leader." Yes, they have set free from ecclesiastical shackles one whose claim to be the representative of South Lancashire, and, beyond that, the leader of the Liberals in Great Britain, may be thus stated. His early sacrifices and distinguished services in the promotion of free trade; his equalisation of direct taxation, by making the wealthy men of Ireland pay the income-tax, by widening the contributions to it in England, and by subjecting real property to the succession duties; his completion of the removal of the taxes on knowledge by the removal of the paper duty; his prosecution of the measure of the Post-office savings' bank for the working classes; his measures for life annuities and for life insurances for the same classes; his promotion of the freedom of internal communication by a commission of inquiry into the means of railway reform in the transport of persons and goods, including in the scope of the inquiry

a cheap parcel-post delivery, and a cheap postal electric telegraph system—measures of vast importance to manufacturing
and commercial communities; his early adoption and promotion of measures for the administrative reform of the civil service
of the country; and above all, his early adoption and the practical promotion of the principle of an open and fair field for the
junior appointments to the public service, by open competitive
examination, thus cutting up corrupt political patronage by the
roots.

The good results of the rejection by Oxford of such a man is
already to be seen. In his Lancashire speeches immediately
upon his "disgrace," Mr. Gladstone said, "I don't hesitate to
say, and I said it while I represented the University of Oxford,
that I believe no greater error can be committed by those who
call themselves friends of the Church, but who are in reality
least of all its friends, than to endeavour to maintain its preponderance, not by the free adhesion, not by the cordial love and
admiration, of the people to whom it ministers, but by miserable legal contrivances, that are available for no purpose whatever but of placing an offensive badge on certain members of the
community, and taking security, as far as human folly can take
it, that those members of the community shall be, from age to
age, bitter enemies of that Church which, I am thankful to say,
is still the Church of the nation." Of Reform Mr. Gladstone
speaks with equal distinctness: "I have ever been, and I still am,
opposed to every sudden and violent change; but this I say, that
the true and just balance of powers would not be destroyed, but
improved, by a fair, and liberal, and sensible—not a sweeping
nor overwhelming—admission of our brethren of the labouring
community to the privileges of the subject." These views were
not, as a matter of course, in accordance with those great par-
sonic nobodies who rejected the recent ornament to their university. But their loss is our gain. Mr. Gladstone was evidently
fettered by his University ties, and his devotion to the task he
undertook may be gathered from his own words. Speaking to
his new friends, he said:—"But, gentlemen, do not let me come
among you under false colours or with false pretences. I have
loved the University of Oxford, with a deep and passionate love,
and as long as I breathe that attachment will continue. If my affection is of the smallest advantage, to that great, that ancient,

that noble institution, that advantage, such as it is, albeit most insignificant, Oxford will possess as long as I live." Doubtless an "attachment will continue;" but we shall lose our faith in the power of circumstances, if Mr. Gladstone, the elected of the people, does not become more and more the servant and benefactor of the people. It is, in fact, to such men as the Chancellor of the Exchequer that we look for aid in the future. The mere oscillation of numbers between Whigs and Tories is a matter of no moment to the people. Lord Palmerston will no doubt get a good majority from the elections, but of what service will either he or his majority ever be to the nation? Under existing circumstances we fear very little. But the time will come when Lord Palmerston and the "old school" will have passed away, and then the value of such men as Mr. Gladstone will be appreciated, and the advantages of their principles fully recognised. Such a time is at once our hope and our consolation.

58 Bradlaugh's election manifesto, 1868*

Despite this adhesion to Liberalism, Bradlaugh's political views remained extreme. As a member of the Reform League from 1865 to 1867 he was an advocate of confrontation with the government, and after the Reform Bill had been passed he expressed his dissatisfaction with household suffrage by embarking on an outspoken campaign for republicanism and land reform. His views are clearly expressed in his first election manifesto, issued at Northampton in the general election of 1868.

TO THE PRESENT AND FUTURE

ELECTORS OF THE BOROUGH

OF

NORTHAMPTON.

In seeking your suffrages for the New Parliament I am en-

* Copy in Bradlaugh Collection, no. 192.

couraged by the very warm feeling exhibited in my favour by so many of the inhabitants of your borough, and by the consciousness that my own efforts may have helped in some slight degree, to hasten the assembly of a Parliament elected by a more widely extended franchise than was deemed possible two years ago.

If you should honour me by electing me as one of your representatives, I shall give an independent support in the New Parliament to that party of which Mr. Gladstone will probably be chosen leader; that is to say, I shall support it in so far as its policy and action prove consistent with the endeavour to attain the following objects, which I hold to be essential to the progress of the nation:—

1. A system of compulsory National Education, by which the State shall secure to each child the opportunity of acquiring, at least, the rudiments of a sound English education preparatory to the commencement of the mere struggle for bread.

2. A change in our Land Laws, commencing with the abolition of the Laws of primogeniture and entail; diminishing the enormous legal expenses attending the transfer of land, and giving greater security to the actual cultivator of the soil for improvements made upon it.

3. A thorough change in our extravagant system of national expenditure; so that our public departments may cease to be refuges for destitute members of so-called noble families.

4. Such a change in the present system of taxation, that for the future the greater pressure of imperial taxes may bear upon those who hold previously accumulated wealth and large tracts of devised land, and not so much upon those who increase the wealth of the nation by their daily labour.

5. An improvement of the enactments relating to capital and labour; so that employer and employed may stand equal before the law; the establishment of Conciliation Courts for the settlement of Trade disputes, and the abolition of the jurisdiction in these matters of the unpaid magistracy.

6. A complete separation of the Church from the State; including in this the removal of the Bishops from the position they at present occupy as Legislators in the House of Lords.

7. A provision by which minorities may be fairly represented in the legislative chambers.

8. The abolition of all disabilities and disqualifications consequent upon the holding or rejection of any particular speculative opinion.

9. A change in the practice of creating new Peerages; limiting the new creations to Life Peerages, and these only to be given as rewards for great national services: Peers habitually absent from Parliament to be deprived of all legislative privileges, and the right of voting by proxy in any case to be abolished.

10. The abolition as a Governing Class of the old Whig party, which has long since ceased to play any useful part in our public policy. Toryism represents obstructiveness to Radical progress, but it represents open hostility. Whiggism is hypocritical; while professing to be liberal, it never initiates a good measure or hinders a bad one. I am in favour of the establishment of a National Party which shall destroy the system of Government by aristocratic families, and give the members of the community born, poorest fair play in their endeavour to become statesmen and leaders if they have genius and honesty enough to entitle them to a foremost place.

In order that my competitors shall not have the right to object that I unfairly put them to the expense of a contest, I am willing to attend a public meeting of the inhabitants of your Borough, at which Mr. Gilpin and Lord Henley shall be present[1], and to be governed by the decision voted at such meeting as to whether or not I persist in my candidature.[2]

In asking your support I pledge myself, in the event of a contest, to fight through to the last moment of the Poll a fair and honest fight. It would give me special pleasure to be returned as the colleague of Mr. Gilpin, whom I believe to be a thoroughly honest and earnest representative; and if you elect me I shall do my best in the House of Commons for the general enfranchisement and elevation of the people of the United Kingdom.

CHARLES BRADLAUGH.

Sunderland Villa, Northumberland Park,
    Tottenham, N.

NOTES

1. Gilpin was the Liberal candidate, first put forward in 1857 by the Northampton Secularist leader, Joseph Gurney. Just before his death in 1874,

Gilpin accepted Bradlaugh as his natural successor but, through the intervention of a Whig banker, William Fowler, a Tory took the seat and Bradlaugh did not secure election until 1880. Henley was the Whig candidate, probably defeated in the 1874 general election by a Tory because some of the usual Gilpin/Henley electors voted Gilpin/Bradlaugh.

2. Bradlaugh was hailed by the public meeting but secured only fifth place in the poll with 1086 votes, 292 short of the nearest Tory. Gilpin and Henley topped the poll with 2632 and 2105 votes respectively. The Radical vote had been split by F. R. Lees, the religious Temperance advocate, who polled 485.

59 Republicanism for England*

In the early 1870s Bradlaugh became the leader of the popular republican movement, with close support from his fellow Secularists. The ideal remained the same as that envisaged by Paine in 1791. In a paper read to the London Dialectical Society in 1871, Austin Holyoake put the case for an English republic. The background to the strong republican feelings of the early 1870s was the seclusion of the Queen since the death of Prince Albert in 1861, and the disreputable capers of the Prince of Wales.

At the present moment, England is perhaps better prepared for a Republican form of Government than any other nation in Europe. We owe this state of things to several causes, chief among them being the Queen herself. She, perhaps more than any other Monarch who ever occupied the throne, has shown us how easy it is to do without a Sovereign. For ten years past she has been of less service in the State than any single member of the Cabinet. Mr. Disraeli, by his extravagant laudations, has done more to show the shortcomings of the head of the State, than her own persistent avoidance of duty has done. Why, if the Queen were gifted with an iron constitution and enormous energy, and were blessed with two very good heads, instead of possessing one of very moderate capacity, she could not perform the work mapped out by the late Prime Minister.

The Monarchy is not a necessity, as has been shown, and it has long ceased to be an ornament. But then we are told that it is undoubtedly a blessing to the country in restraining ambitious men from seeking to rise to supreme power. That may

* From A. Holyoake, *Would a Republican Form of Government be suitable to England* (1873) pp. 4, 6–7.

be true so long as we have a Monarch so extravagantly endowed, that it makes it worth the trouble of any man to seek to rise to regal honours. This brings me to the consideration of what should be done to improve the present costly mode of government.

First of all, as the Monarchy has long ceased to be either useful or ornamental, I would, at the demise of the present occupant of the throne, disestablish and disendow it. I would serve it like the Irish Church; I would pay it a tolerably good sum to go away quietly. Though having a very strong opinion as to its right to claim any compensation at all, I would choose the lesser of two evils, and pay rather than fight; and from what we know of the family, I think they would take the money rather than run the risk of losing all if it came to a contest. The question is rapidly resolving itself into one of finance, if it has not reached that stage already; and he will be a wise statesman who counsels the claimants to the throne to give up without anger what is no longer deemed necessary to the State, lest the people, who have remembrances of wrongs, should forget in the hour of excitement the wise policy of mutual concession and compromise.

.   .   .

We want cheaper government in this country. Mr. Gladstone and all our best statesmen say the same thing. Those at the head of affairs see how shamefully the hard earnings of the people are frittered away in the hands of incompetent officials, and also in the working of our cumbrous and antiquated machinery. Mr. Gladstone in his electioneering speeches proclaimed the evil, but expressed his inability to alter it single-handed. And no one man can alter it—it must be done by the nation itself. It is the nation's work, and when properly done will benefit the whole nation. It is therefore the urgent duty of every one to speak out, even at the risk of being charged with presumption, and with being an anarchist.

I protest against the present costly and ruinous system—a system which is demoralising and pauperising millions of our countrymen. But I am prepared to do more than protest—I will work and subscribe to bring about an improvement; and, what involves a great amount of courage, I will venture to suggest what I think would be a remedy for at least some of the evils under which we suffer.

"Some writers," says Paine, "have so confounded Society with Government, as to leave little or no distinction between them: whereas they are not only different, but have different origins. Society is produced by our wants, and Government by our wickedness; the former promotes our happiness *positively*, by uniting our affections; the latter *negatively*, by restraining our vices. The one encourages intercourse, the other creates distinctions. The first is a patron, the last a punisher. Society, in every state, is a blessing; but Government, even in its best state, is but a necessary evil; in its worst state, an intolerable one; for when we suffer, or are exposed to the same miseries *by a Government*, which we might expect in a country *without Government*, our calamity is heightened by reflecting, that we furnish the means by which we suffer. Government, like dress, is the badge of lost innocence; the palaces of kings are built on the ruins of the bowers of paradise. For, were the impulses of conscience clear, uniform, and irresistibly obeyed, man would need no other lawgiver; but that not being the case, he finds it necessary to surrender up a part of his property to furnish means for the protection of the rest; and this he is induced to do by the same prudence which, in every other case, advises him out of two evils to choose the least. *Wherefore*, security being the true design and end of Government, it unanswerably follows, that whatever *form* thereof appears most likely to ensure it to us with the least expense and greatest benefit, is preferable to all others. I draw my idea of the form of Government from a principle in nature, which no art can overturn—viz., that the more simple anything is, the less liable it is to be disordered, and the easier repaired when disordered."

We have the giant evil of land monopoly to abolish, and there seems no chance whatever of that being done so long as the present system of aristocratic ascendancy is maintained. The people will press for a redress of grievances. All they want is political equality, that they may have a voice in the making of laws which shall give them an opportunity of enjoying the fruits of their daily toil. They do not fairly enjoy those fruits to-day. It is a struggle between those who have not enough, and those who have too much. Till these things are altered there can be no peace in the land. Among all peoples, where enormous fortunes are accumulated by particular individuals, a spirit of aristocracy is engendered on the one side, and abasement on the other. It is therefore desirable in a Republic that easy circumstances should be enjoyed generally by the citizens, without so great a disparity of condition as to lead to the destruction of every kind of civil equality.

60 The new socialism*

The Secularists, and particularly Bradlaugh, were republicans and individualists. They deplored measures which would restrict the freedom of the individual, and they deplored violence. So they were at odds with those republicans who envisaged the use of force in Britain, and they were antipathetic towards the new generation of socialists who were largely inspired by Karl Marx and other German refugees. The Liberal and socialist positions were highlighted in 1884 when Bradlaugh and H. M. Hyndman of the Social Democratic Federation met to debate 'Will Socialism benefit the English people?'. The following report is by Annie Besant who was later herself to be converted to Fabian Socialism.

THE DEBATE ON SOCIALISM.

St. James' Hall was filled on Thursday evening last, to listen to a debate on Socialism between Charles Bradlaugh and Mr. H. M. Hyndman. The latter appeared as the champion of the Democratic Federation, a curious body, part Tory, part Democratic, built largely on the lines suggested by the late Lord Beaconsfield, and likely to find its future leader in Lord Randolph Churchill. Various wealthy men, some of marked Tory proclivities and some holding the queer semi-democratic opinions of the late Napoleon III., formed this association. Prominent in it we have now Mr. Hyndman, who appeared as a Jingo candidate for Marylebone at the election of 1880, a gentleman whose sympathy with the workers is a plant of very recent and very rapid growth, and whose sudden conversion is, not unnaturally, looked on with considerable suspicion by the workers themselves. This suspicion will be a good deal deepened by an unfortunate phrase let slip by Mr. Hyndman during the

* From *National Reformer*, 27 Apr 1884.

Socialist debate. Worried and annoyed at the demand for details put forward by Mr. Bradlaugh, and forgetting for a moment his *rôle* as sympathiser with the poor, he exclaimed contemptuously that he did not expect to be required to "explain all the details of bottle-washers, cooks, and cabmen in the remote future." The retort came sharp and trenchant from the true Democrat, whose Democracy, instead of being skin-deep, has grown through thirty years of honest work in the cause of the people: "Why do you jeer at the bottle-washer? Is not the bottle-washer as good as the prince? I belong to the bottle-washers, and I want to know how our bottles are to be washed?"

During the debate, I was seated with my friends in the body of the Hall at the side, and so had a good view of the whole proceedings. Among other things, I observed that although the Democratic Federation had refused to allow Mr. Bradlaugh to have a single seat kept on the platform for his special friends, they kept a number of seats for their own; his daughters and myself were not allowed to have seats near him, but chairs were kept for Mr. Hyndman's friends.

There were a considerable number of Socialists present, mainly Germans, and at the beginning of Mr. Bradlaugh's first speech they tried to disconcert him by yelling, some of the stewards (who were supposed to be there to keep order) leading the *claque*. The arrangement, however, broke down, from the simple reason that the Socialists were hopelessly outnumbered by the Radicals, and on recognising this fact—borne in upon their understandings by the roars of applause that followed Mr. Bradlaugh's sharp retorts—they subsided, and the remainder of the meeting was fairly orderly. One individual, acting as a leader, made himself prominent by his gross insolence to everyone whom he regarded as a friend of Mr. Bradlaugh's, and by his endeavors to bully the people about him. I am not altogether sorry to see the rough intolerance manifested by the Socialists, for it serves as a fair warning of the intolerable tyranny they would establish if they were in the majority. The Germans, who form the greater part of the party in England, may be readily pardoned their bullying ways, for they have revolted against a despotism, and, like all suddenly-freed slaves, desire to use over others the tyranny from which they have themselves suffered.

But a party will never succeed in England which has not learned the alphabet of liberty. It is all very well for the Germans to revolt against the repression of Bismarck; it is not so well for them to try to pose as petty Bismarcks in England, and to try to play a sixteenth-rate "blood and iron" farce among the sons and daughters of a nation whose political liberty is the envy of their own enslaved and police-ridden land.

Mr. Hyndman, as will be seen by the report of the debate, did not condescend to explain to us what Socialism is, beyond that it was "organised co-operation for existence," and "a distinct historical theory which accounts for the progress of man in society by his command over the forces of nature, by the economical development, the power he has of producing wealth." But everyone is agreed that man has progressed in society by his command, etc. That is not Socialism. It is a historical truth recognised by Tory and Radical, by Socialist and Democrat. The phrase "organised co-operation for existence" needs a very special definition to make it agree with Socialism; co-operation, both productive and distributive, has been and is being carried on by persons who are anti-Socialists. Mr. Bradlaugh has been one of its strong supporters all his public life through, and the "stores" of Lancashire, with their libraries and reading-rooms, are one of the most splendid proofs of what can be done by "the wage-slaves" without the help of the State.

Mr. Hyndman devoted the remainder of his first speech to a disquisition on the poverty and evils of our present society; granted; we all acknowledge these; the point at issue is, how they shall be cured? On this Mr. Hyndman threw no light; he poured out vague phrases, that "production and exchange must be social," that all must be organised for the good of all. How organised he did not condescend to explain.

Mr. Bradlaugh defined what he meant by Socialism, in default of any definition by his opponent, and his definition was not challenged by Mr. Hyndman. Basing his attack on the published statements of the Federation, he analysed their high-sounding phrases, and as against froth put figures. He showed how every part of life would be disorganised by Socialism, and asked what the re-organisation would be. In his answer Mr. Hyndman objected to details, as though people were likely to destroy society as it is at the bidding of those who are unable to say what social arrangements they propose to substitute for the present. And this is scientific(!) Socialism. A scientific theory is exact, based on facts, explaining facts, classifying facts. Socialism despises the pettiness of facts and then arrogates the name of scientific.

Mr. Hyndman showed a curious ignorance of English history in classing together Robert Owen, O'Brien, Oastler, Stephens, and Feargus O'Connor, as working "hard for the cause which we call Socialism to-day." When Mr. Bradlaugh pointed out the extreme divergence of their views, Mr. Hyndman in reply shifted his ground, and only claimed to inherit from them as "we inherit the learning of Aristotle and Plato although they were absolutely opposed." In that sense—which was not the sense in which Mr. Hyndman originally spoke—we all inherit the wisdom of these men, as of all others.

The impression left on my mind by the debate was that Mr. Hyndman was very clever, very fluent, very shifty, and very shallow in his knowledge of the history of English working-class movements. He very much toned down and modified the threats and menaces with which he delights the most ignorant and reckless of his ordinary hearers, much to the disgust of some of those present. "Bah! he doesn't give it them half strong," said a wrathful Socialist, when Mr. Hyndman sought to explain away some of the violent language he had printed, and this feeling seemed pretty general among a considerable portion of his supporters. On this point, the debate will have done good, as showing that the violent Socialist of the lecture-hall becomes meek and mild when confronted with an antagonist, and that the menaces arc used for effect, not from conviction.

There was only one matter on which Mr. Hyndman made a momentary point, and that only by resorting to misrepresentation of what his opponent said. Mr. Bradlaugh stated that an individual motive entered into all actions, whether the motive were love of gain, desire of approval, or other. Mr. Hyndman twisted this into meaning that actions were always prompted by desire for "direct personal gain," and said, quite truly, that in every great advance, a higher motive had come in, the good of the human race. Mr. Bradlaugh, in his answer, pointed out the misconception, but I see, in Mr. Foulger's article in *Justice*, that he repeats the unfair deduction. Yet when Mr. Foulger says: "Socialists are now informed that over against their Social ideal, their opponents, whether the friends of monopoly or the friends of the people, have nothing to place but self"—he might surely have hesitated if only in glancing at the life of the man he libels. If "personal gain" were the object aimed at by one like Mr. Bradlaugh, he most certainly would not be an Atheist and a Republican in England. And Mr. Foulger ought surely to be a little more careful when he remembers that he has himself only proclaimed himself a Socialist since Socialism became a passing fashion in consequence of the help of the wealthy men, of whom Mr. Hyndman spoke; before that he was one of the superfine Radicals who had always a hard word to throw at those who were doing the work that he was too timid to touch. It scarcely befits one so careful of personal gain while Democracy was less attractive, to taunt with selfishness those who worked for her ere Mr. Morris and others made silver slippers for her foreign cousin. Socialism is just now fashionable, as æstheticism was a little time ago, and it is especially favoured by those whose political principles have no firm basis, who are easily moved by the associates of the movement, and who like to pose as "extreme," without bearing the penalties imposed on practical dissent from orthodox views. To all these "Scientific Socialism" is alluring, and its utter unpracticalness is its especial charm, since they will never be called to suffer by putting their theory into practice, and so coming into conflict with the prejudices of society. It just suits those who like to play in artistic, dainty, dilettante fashion with problems of life and death, which they have not the earnestness, the courage, nor the self-sacrifice to solve.

None of these will have been touched by the debate. But many whose good hearts have led them to assume a name which they identified with the cause of the poor, without trying to realise what the name really means, will have been led to turn away from a fanciful and useless dream, and to cast in their lot with the workers for the redemption of mankind from poverty, misery, and degradation.

ANNIE BESANT.

61 Secularism and socialism in Leicester*

Secularism nevertheless led to socialism, as local branches could not ignore the new radical interest. However, some local leaders found the ideas of the socialists difficult to swallow. Sydney Gimson of Leicester, son of the old Owenite and Secularist Josiah Gimson, was one such, as emerges from his recollections of the Leicester Secular Society in the 1880s.

Notwithstanding our Individualism we decided, on pursuance of our policy of a free platform, to give our audiences an opportunity to hear the best that could be said for the new Socialism which was then coming rapidly to the front. So we arranged for a lecture by H. M. Hyndman on "Constructive Socialism" on Wednesday, Jan. 16. 1884, and one by William Morris on "Art and Socialism" on Jan. 23. These were to be followed by a lecture in opposition by the Rev. J. Page Hopps on "Sensible Socialism", on Monday January 28th.

. . .

In the autumn of 1888 we arranged to have the series of lectures by seven members of the Fabian Society which were afterwards, in December 1889, published under the title "Fabian Essays in Socialism". These lectures were delivered in Willis's Rooms, London, at one of the Universities and on Sunday evenings in the autumn of 1888 and the first months of 1889 in our Hall. We felt it an honour that we were able to have such an important series given to our audiences. The seven speakers were Sidney Webb, G. Bernard Shaw, Sydney Olivier, William Clarke, Graham Wallas, Mrs. Annie Besant, and Hubert Bland.

. . .

Mrs. Eleanor Marx Aveling lectured for us twice, first on December 20th 1886, and secondly 12 years later, in November, 1897. I have no definite remembrance of her lectures, except that to her Freethought was at least as important as Socialism, but I well remember her as a very lovable woman. She stayed with us and, the second time in particular, we felt

* From S. A. Gimson, *Random Recollections*, series 1, pp. 21, 25, 32–3, Leicester Secular Society records, Leicester Museum.

that we were getting very friendly and both my wife and I looked forward to a growth of the friendship, but, alas! soon afterwards came Mrs. Aveling's tragic death[1]. Thinking of the importance of Freethought to Socialism I call to mind that one of the first things that William Morris said to Ernest[2] and me was, "I expect that the reason so many of you Secularists don't like Socialism is because a lot of parsons come to us; well, I don't know why they come, we don't want them!" No doubt he was thinking of the so-called "Christian Socialists", a label which attracted some of the politically "advanced" parsons of that time.[3]

Socialists in England seem to less and less appreciate the importance of Freethought to their movement. They adopt the conventional religious attitude, no doubt quite sincerely in most cases, and do not recognise how loose thinking in that direction re-acts on their judgement in all Social problems. I suppose it gets them more votes for the time being, and they are in a hurry.

NOTES

1. She shot herself in 1898 when she discovered that Aveling, her common law husband, had remarried secretly.
2. Sydney's brother, who was so impressed by Morris on art that he went to work with him.
3. Stewart Headlam, a leading Christian Socialist, was in fact on very good terms with Bradlaugh and acted as the 'statutory clergyman' for the Hall of Science schools. He also worked closely with Mrs Besant on the London School Board.

European Republicanism

62 Hopes and fears in 1849*

The republicans of Britain wished to see the triumph of peoples all over Europe. The Holy Alliance powers, mainly Russia and Austria, were thought to be at the heart of all political oppression, and as late as 1877 Cowen, Harney and Linton could not bring themselves to support Gladstone's apparently pro-Russian policies. The greatest chance for liberation appeared to come in 1848, when revolutions shook most of the thrones of Europe. The English radicals watched the scene keenly and, when necessary, provided support for republican refugees. The English Chartists had failed in their attempted 'rising' in 1848 and were now once more concerned to restore their own fragile unity. In France the revolution had succeeded, but the new republic turned sour as the government opened fire on the socialist barricades in Paris in June 1848, and as the December presidential elections brought a Bonaparte back to power. Of the speeches which follow, Hetherington's in particular points out the close connection between reactionary politics and the Church.

HONOUR TO ROME, TO HUNGARY, AND THE RHINE!

A densely crowded public meeting was held at the Literary and Scientific Institution, John-street, Tottenham Court-road, on Tuesday evening, June 19th, to sympathise with the brave

* From *Northern Star*, 23 June 1849.

and heroic peoples now struggling against allied despots, in defence of their democratic and social liberties.

Mr. H. HETHERINGTON was called to the chair, amidst loud applause, and after reading the placard convening the meeting, said:— We find the people moving in favour of progress from one end of Europe to the other. When the people are in misery we find the government telling them that they have duties secular and religious to perform, whilst a hireling priesthood tells them that they must submit to 'their spiritual pastors and masters, and all that are put in authority under them;' – (laughter, and 'Hear, hear;') – and they also profess the greatest veneration for the book from which they profess to draw their religion, which book tells us 'that men of all nations are made of one flesh and blood;' yet, at the same time, they mow down their brethren with grape shot and cannister. The rulers of France deserve the execration of all mankind; whilst the patriots of Hungary, for their noble and heroic conduct, have won, and richly merit honour from all nations. (Immense cheering.) Look at Austria, headed by a brutal monster of an Emperor, who, while he brutally flogs women and tortures men to death, calls himself the father of his people. (Laughter, and groans.) Why there is a league of kings and scoundrels – the Guizots and Metternichs – to put down democracy in all nations – (hear, hear) – and what is it that democracy asks, that governments should be so desirous of keeping it down? Why the political, moral, and social happiness of the whole people. (Loud cheers.) Under such circumstances it should be our duty to unite all sections of the Democratic party. Let us have a league of peoples against the league of kings and despots, and make kings proclaim equality of rights to all men; but this will never be done until a thorough republican feeling pervades all countries. (Tremendous cheering.) Kings were frequently very mean people; look at the Kings of Hanover, ruling a portion of Germany, and at the same time dipping his hand into our pockets to the tune of £23,000 per annum. He could not think what the Queen Dowager wanted with £100,000 per annum. When he compared his income with her's [sic] he could not think what she did with it – (loud laughter) – and then it appeared she had some £6,000 a year of pocket money, which she could throw in the gutter if she liked. These things must be altered. This meeting was a step in the right direction, and he said go on, and success must follow. (Loud cheers.) . . .

Mr. G. J. HOLYOAKE moved the following resolution:—

'That as all nations are formed of one flesh, and are consequently brethren, despotism and usurpation are contrary to, and subversive of, the great laws of humanity; and as the end of all government should be the happiness and well-being of the governed, those who by an assumption of unnatural power trample on and destroy their fellow men, deserve to be held up to scorn and execration; while those who are enslaved, and are nobly struggling to free themselves from bondage, and those, too, who having won liberty, are defending their freedom at the cost of their lives, merit the admiration, the applause, the sympathy, and support of the people of this and every other country.'

JULIAN HARNEY, who on coming forward was received with loud applause, said: This resolution asserts two great principles: that all men are brethren; and that it is the duty of the nations to afford each other mutual aid as members of the same human family. I should like to see the man who would stand here and attempt to demonstrate the unsoundness of these principles. It is true that in the history of the human race there has hitherto been but little of Fraternity. Hitherto kings, and priest, and aristocrats, and capitalists – and I am sorry to add to the disreputable list, sham-republican rulers – have set the nations rearing at the throats of each other, when, instead of which, it was the interest and duty of the people of all countries to have marched together, shoulder to shoulder, in pursuit of the one great end of life, – happiness. (Hear, hear.) . . . I implore all the able and true leaders and instructors of the people to forget their jealousies, their injuries – real or imagined – to abandon the rivalries of petty ambition, forget the quarrellings of the past, and cordially unite to advance the great cause we are wedded to. (Great applause.) Then should our brethren on the continent be compelled to succumb for a time – then by our union, judgment, and energy, we may extend the movement from England to the continent, and sustain it until oppression shall everywhere be overthrown, and the reign of Justice be universally, triumphantly, and permanently established. (Enthusiastic and prolonged cheering.)

63 Arms for Garibaldi*

Harney's vision of England as the conserver of European liberty was not to be fulfilled in the radical way he had envisaged in 1849, but in the case of Italy his dream was at least partially fulfilled. With the help of Joseph Cowen, republican Chartists like Harney, Holyoake and Linton had continued throughout the 1850s to organised financial and even military support for the European republican movement. The climax came in 1860 when a group of middle-class radicals organised a British Legion to fight with Garibaldi in southern Italy. To avoid the Foreign Enlistement Act, the Legion posed as an excursion of tourists, and about 700 men were sent out in two ships, the Melazzo and the Emperor. The Legion itself arrived almost too late to be of much use, and was beset with administrative difficulties largely caused by untrustworthy characters such as 'Major' Hicks. The following minutes are of the Garibaldi Committee's third meeting and are concerned with initial preparations.

Garibaldi Special Fund
Committee Meeting
Volunteer Service Club St James's
September 3rd 1860 6 p.m.

Present E. H. J. Craufurd M.P. in the Chair
W. H. Ashurst[1]
G. B. C. Leverson (Treasurer)[2]
W. J. Linton
H. B. Edenborough
G. J. Holyoake
J. S. Barker

Mr. De Carteret not being present and previous minutes not being before the Chair – they were stated in substance by Mr. Craufurd.

Mr. Holyoake reported that he had received from Mr. Ashurst and paid to Mr. Leverson the sum of £70.

Mr. Leverson reported that he had paid to Major Beach Hicks the sum of £500 in accordance with the instructions of the

---

* From the Minute Book of the Garibaldi Committee, Holyoake Collection, Bishopsgate Institute.

Committee.

Major B. G. U. Hicks being present stated in answer to questions from the Chair that he had paid £225 to the London Armoury Company that day on account of a special contract for Rifles and that Eighty Rifles in consequence lay at his order: that he held in hand £275 intended for a further contract for Rifles with Bates of Birmingham.

Mr. Ashurst moved and Mr. Holyoake seconded this resolution:—that Major Hicks be requested to be so good as to give to the Chairman on or before the next meeting of this Committee the voucher for the payment he had made of £225 and the order for the Rifles bought therewith.

On the motion of Mr. Barker and Mr. Leverson Mr. Linton was requested to sign the Circular prepared by Captain Minchin relative to a Fete at Cremorne.[3]

A placard and advertisement to the following effect was on the motion of Messrs. Barker and Holyoake ordered to be issued.

GARIBALDI EXCURSION. –

NOTICE is hereby given, that the applications to join this excursion having been much more numerous than the funds yet available for the purposes of the committee enable them to provide for. NO FURTHER APPLICATIONS can be received after this date unless the intending excursionist be prepared to pay the expense of his outfit and passage. Indeed so numerous are the applications to join the excursion that many most eligible gentlemen must necessarily be left behind.

Sept 4, 1860

Committee Room 8, Salisbury-street, Strand, London W.C.

On the motion of Mr. Linton and Mr. Leverson Mr. Ashurst was requested to procure the services of a paid secretary.[4]

NOTES

1. Ashurst was the son of Robert Owen's lawyer (d. 1855).
2. Leverson was the brother of Bradlaugh's employer.
3. Cremorne was a famous London pleasure garden.
4. Holyoake was appointed at the next meeting at a salary of five guineas a week, 'tho the sum he w[ou]ld consent to receive from the Committee would not half remunerate him for the engagements he must forgo'.

Women's Rights

64 A plea for divorce*

All the ultra-radicals were advocates of the rights of women as well as of men. But by the rights of women they more often meant sexual than political rights, and the sexual emancipation of women involved easier divorce and freedom from unwanted childbearing.

Owen's Lectures on Marriage *were originally delivered in 1835 and published in the* N.M.W.*, but they were not given a wide circulation until republished unofficially by Joshua Hobson in 1838, when they furnished useful material for those Christians wishing to prove that socialism was immoral.*

The human law which binds one man to the same woman, and the woman to the man through life, whether or not they can retain an affection for each other, has produced more hatred, and destroyed more love between these parties than would otherwise have taken place, probably many thousand-fold. It has produced a general practice of the most gross as well as refined falsehood, and the deepest deception between these parties, and to the public. It has given rise to the most extensive jealousy and revenge, and severed those, for ever, from each other, who were compelled, by their natures, to entertain the strongest and most sincere mutual affection, competent by their union to create as much happiness as their forced separation produced misery. This permanent artificial union of a single pair for life has forced a system of promiscuous inter-

* From R. Owen, *Lectures on the Marriages of the Priesthood of the Old Immoral World*, 4th ed. (1840) pp. 66–7.

course, in those countries in which this law prevails, most degrading and injurious to the physical, intellectual, and moral
character and conduct of both sexes; and thereby produced an
extent of injustice, cruelty, and misery, especially to the female,
beyond the power of any written statement or mere wordy
document to enable the present race of man to comprehend.

In fact, this forced continued union of a single pair of human
beings through life, with or without affection, as it may happen
to be, is calculated, in all its consequences, to the old, young,
and middle-aged, to create an extensive ramification of the
most immoral external circumstances. And through the natural effect of these vicious institutions of the priesthood, acting
and re-acting continually upon human nature, they are also
calculated, as well as if they were devised for the purpose, to
constitute a weak, artificial, heartless, miserable condition of
human society. This Christian custom cannot, therefore, be
intended to be the practice of the human race when they shall
acquire sufficient experience to become rational creatures.

65 The Knowlton Pamphlet *

*From the very start of his public career in the Secularist movement, Brad-
laugh was an advocate of birth control, so when Charles Watts pleaded
guilty to being the publisher of an immoral work, the Knowlton Pamphlet,
in 1877, Bradlaugh and Besant reissued the book with the following explanation.*

PUBLISHERS' PREFACE TO DR. KNOWLTON'S
"FRUITS OF PHILOSOPHY."

THE pamphlet which we now present to the public is one which
has been lately prosecuted under Lord Campbell's Act, and
which we republish in order to test the right of publication. It
was originally written by Charles Knowlton, M.D., an American physician, whose degree entitles him to be heard with
respect on a medical question. It is openly sold and widely circulated in America at the present time. It was first published in
England, about forty years ago, by James Watson, the gallant

* From *National Reformer*, 25 Mar 1877.

Radical who came to London and took up Richard Carlile's work when Carlile was in jail. He sold it unchallenged for many years, approved it, and recommended it. It was printed and published by Messrs. Holyoake and Co., and found its place, with other works of a similar character, in their "Freethought Directory" of 1853, and was thus identified with Freethought literature at the then leading Freethought *depôt*. Mr. Austin Holyoake, working in conjunction with Mr. Bradlaugh at the *National Reformer* office, Johnson's Court, printed and published it in his turn, and this well-known Freethought advocate, in his "Large or Small Families," selected this pamphlet, together with R. D. Owen's "Moral Physiology" and the "Elements of Social Science," for special recommendation. Mr. Charles Watts, succeeding to Mr. Austin Holyoake's business, continued the sale, and when Mr. Watson died in 1875, he bought the plates of the work (with others) from Mrs. Watson, and continued to advertise and to sell it until December 23, 1876. For the last forty years the book has thus been identified with Freethought, advertised by leading Freethinkers, published under the sanction of their names, and sold in the headquarters of Freethought literature. If during this long period the party has thus—without one word of protest—circulated an indecent work, the less we talk about Freethought morality the better; the work has been largely sold, and if leading Freethinkers have sold it—profiting by the sale—in mere carelessness, few words could be strong enough to brand the indifference which thus scattered obscenity broadcast over the land. The pamphlet has been withdrawn from circulation in consequence of the prosecution instituted against Mr. Charles Watts, but the question of its legality or illegality has not been tried; a plea of "Guilty" was put in by the publisher, and the book, therefore, was not examined, nor was any judgment passed upon it; no jury registered a verdict, and the judge stated that he had not read the work.

We republish this pamphlet, honestly believing that on all questions affecting the happiness of the people, whether they be theological, political, or social, fullest right of free discussion ought to be maintained at all hazards. We do not personally endorse all that Dr. Knowlton says: his "Philosophical Proem" seems to us full of philosophical mistakes, and—as we are neither of us doctors—we are not prepared to endorse his medical views; but since progress can only be made through discussion, and no discussion is possible where differing opinions are suppressed, we claim the right to publish all opinions, so that the public, enabled to see all sides of a question, may have the materials for forming a sound judgment.

The alterations made are very slight; the book was badly printed, and errors of spelling and a few clumsy grammatical expressions have been corrected: the sub-title has been changed, and in one case four lines have been omitted, because they are repeated word for word further on. We have, however, made some additions to the pamphlet, which are in all cases kept distinct from the original text. Physiology has made great strides during the past forty years, and not considering it right to circulate erroneous physiology, we submitted the pamphlet to a doctor in whose accurate knowledge we have the fullest confidence, and who is widely known in all parts of the world as the author of the "Elements of Social Science;" the notes signed "G. R." are written by this gentleman.[1] References to other works are given in foot-notes for the assistance of the reader, if he desires to study the subject further.

Old Radicals will remember that Richard Carlile published a work entitled "Every Woman's Book," which deals with the same subject, and advocates the same object, as Dr. Knowlton's pamphlet. R. D. Owen objected to the "style and tone" of Carlile's "Every Woman's Book" as not being "in good taste," and he wrote his "Moral Physiology," to do in America what Carlile's work was intended to do in England. This work of Carlile's was stigmatised as "indecent" and "immoral," because it advocated, as does Dr. Knowlton's, the use of preventive checks to population. In striving to carry on Carlile's work, we cannot expect to escape Carlile's reproach, but whether applauded or condemned we mean to carry it on, socially as well as politically and theologically.

We believe, with the Rev. Mr. Malthus, that population has a tendency to increase faster than the means of existence, and that *some* checks must therefore exercise control over population; the checks now exercised are semi-starvation and preventible disease; the enormous mortality among the infants of the poor is one of the checks which now keeps down the population.

The checks that ought to control population are scientific, and it is these which we advocate. We think it more moral to prevent the conception of children, than, after they are born, to murder them by want of food, air, and clothing. We advocate scientific checks to population, because, so long as poor men have large families, pauperism is a necessity, and from pauperism grow crime and disease. The wage which would support the parents and two or three children in comfort and decency is utterly insufficient to maintain a family of twelve or fourteen, and we consider it a crime to bring into the world human beings doomed to misery or to premature death. It is not only the hard-working classes which are concerned in this question. The poor curate, the struggling man of business, the young professional man, are often made wretched for life by their inordinately large families, and their years are passed in one long battle to live; meanwhile the woman's health is sacrificed and her life embittered from the same cause. To all of these, we point the way of relief and of happiness; for the sake of these we publish what others fear to issue, and we do it, confident that if we fail the first time, we shall succeed at last, and that the English public will not permit the authorities to stifle a discussion of the most important social question which can influence a nation's welfare.

CHARLES BRADLAUGH.
ANNIE BESANT.

NOTE

1. George Drysdale (1825–1904).

PART FIVE
Law and Public Opinion

The aim of the freethinkers was the attainment of full civil rights – the right to speak and publish their views without civil penalty or other prejudice. There were, of course, other issues to be fought for, such as the abolition of tithes and Church rates, and secular education, but in these matters other groups suffered too and they often took the lead. On three points, though, the infidels were the most active and most vulnerable agitators for a thorough change.

The first objective was to secure freedom of publication. Restrictions could take two forms: financial – the so-called 'Taxes on Knowledge' – which regulated the price of literature and hence its potential market among the poorer classes; and the laws of libel which determined the content of what was published. The financial restrictions were challenged by Hetherington in the 1830s, Holyoake in the 1850s, and Bradlaugh in 1868–9. The laws of libel were contested by Carlile in the 1820s, Southwell and his friends in the 1840s, Charles Bradlaugh in 1877, and G. W. Foote in 1882–3, as well as by dozens of lesser freethinkers throughout the nineteenth century and into the twentieth. These libel laws were in three parts which were to some extent interchangeable, as the prosecution tended to select its own strongest ground – blasphemous, seditious and obscene.

The second objective was equality before the law. The law of Britain was the law of a Christian country, and so those who held no religious beliefs could not take a meaningful oath as jurors, in the courts as witnesses, or in Parliament. The infidel campaign against the oath mounted as various other groups – Unitarians, Roman Catholics, Quakers and Jews – were admitted to their civil rights, but not until Bradlaugh's Act of 1888 did freethinkers achieve parity with other United Kingdom citizens.

The third objective was not in the area of public law, but in what J. S. Mill conceived to be the more fundamental area of public opinion which determined whether such laws which were on the Statute Book were actually enforced. Prejudice against unbelievers was extremely strong. The fear lingered from the days of the French Revolution that blasphemy was seditious, and to this the nineteenth century added a new Evangelical militancy to save souls at all costs. Tract societies, town missionaries, Sabbattarians and moral prudes all saw the infidels as their natural enemy. The task of the freethinkers was to woo public opinion away from such extremism, and in this they were helped by the growing respectability of their intellectual criticisms of Christianity, and by the persistent obscurantism of some of their major critics.

Persecution and Prosecution

66 A history of persecution*

The ultra-radicals had a great sense of their own history, in which the two most important turning points had been the English Revolution of the 1640s and the French Revolution of the 1790s. Many of the laws against which they campaigned had been formulated in reaction to these two events: Sir Matthew Hale's Common Law decision on blasphemy, 1676; the Blasphemy Act of 9 & 10 William III cap. 32; the Stamp Acts of 38 George III cap. 78, 39 George III cap. 79, 55 George III cap. 80, cap. 185, 56 George III cap. 56; and the Blasphemous and Seditious Libels Act of 60 George III cap. 9.

PROSECUTIONS FOR BLASPHEMY,
Or a speaking evil of the Bible and the Christian Religion.

NOTHING of this kind was known under the sway of the Roman Catholic Religion, nor until long after the period called the Reformation, when the Bible became commonly printed, sold and read.

The first case known to the writer is, that of the reign of Charles the Second, during the Chief Justiceship of Sir Matthew Hale. Here a new case arose: some man proclaimed the Bible and the Christian Religion to be a cheat, and the Chief Justice, in the absence of an applicable law, made one by his own authority, to punish him. That piece of Judge made law has not at any time since been sanctioned by the Legislature. It was founded upon the assertion, *that Christianity was part and*

* From *Republican*, 18 Mar 1825.

parcel of the law of the land, or what is called *common law:* an idea, that cannot be supported, until Christianity can be defined to be something tangible by law.

The Christian Religion had assumed so many and such strange, fantastical and ridiculous shapes, among the dissenters from the Established Church, during the reign of the Stuarts, and more particularly during the civil war between Charles and the Parliament, and during the subsequent Commonwealth, that, towards the end of the seventeenth century, knowledge beginning to spread, atheism, deism, and a denial of the doctrine of the Trinity had become very common. During the reign of William and Mary, a statute was made, to make a denial of the doctrine of the Trinity, or a Blasphemy of the Bible, penal; but the moderation of the penalties imposed by that statute, places in no very amiable light, the authors of modern prosecutions and the Judges who have passed the shameful sentences suffered and are suffering.

After the passing of that statute, to its partial repeal in 1813, the chief prosecutions for blasphemy, in point of number, were carried on against the Unitarians. Mr. Locke was expelled from the University of Oxford; and tradition says, that it was fear of his great talents being applied to Deism or Unitarian Christianity, that brought forth the first and only statute in existence against blasphemy in its modern acceptation. Mr. Whiston was also expelled from the University of Cambridge on the ground of Unitarian Blasphemy.

In the early part of the last century [1729], Mr. Woolston was prosecuted in the Court of King's Bench, for his work on the miracles of the New Testament, in which, he attempted to explain them allegorically. He told the Judge and Jury, in his defence, that, in point of knowledge, they were not competent to try him, and since it was a question of knowledge, he ought not to be tried by them, or, if tried, acquitted. He was, however, pronounced Guilty, and sentenced to one year or eighteen months imprisonment in the King's Bench Prison, whence he publicly sold his work.

Later in that century [1761], Peter Annet was prosecuted at the Old Bailey Sessions, and fined, imprisoned and pilloried, for a work that ranks no higher in the scale of knowledge, than the writings which now come from the Unitarians, and almost

pass as Orthodox. Both Woolston and Annet had been educated and ordained as clergymen of the Established Church.

None of the Deistical writings of the last century which
created as much or more noise and prejudice, than the atheistical writings of the present day, can be now considered other
than similar to what are now called Unitarian Christian writings. Thomas Paine excepted. Thomas Paine was the first
Englishman that struck an honest and well aimed blow at the
idolatry of the Christian Church. And, from the publication of
his Age of Reason, modern prosecutions may take their date.

The writer is not positive; but he rather thinks, that a Mr.
Simmons, and a Mr. Crosby, were prosecuted for the publication of the First Part of the Age of Reason, in 1794. But the
first effort of the Vice Society was, to prosecute Thomas Williams, in 1797, for the publication of the First and Second Parts.
Williams was sentenced by the Court of King's Bench to one
year's imprisonment in the Cold Bath Fields Prison.

The Age of Reason was not publicly sold from this time to the
month of December 1818, a full lapse of twenty years. Daniel
Isaac Eaton published Mr. Paine's Examination of the Prophe-
cies, in 1812, under the title of the Third Part of the Age of
Reason; for which he was prosecuted and sentenced to imprisonment for eighteen months, and to the Pillory. It is supposed,
that the Pillory, in this instance, was found to be so great an
outrage on the public mind, or the London public, that it led to
its abolition in the ensuing session of Parliament, for all cases
but unnatural crime. Eaton was an old man, above threescore,
which made the outrage the greater.

67 Blasphemy in Edinburgh*

*After the Carlile period the next series of cases came in the 1840s, with
Southwell's and Holyoake's trials and then the Scottish prosecutions. The
self-defeating nature of such prosecutions, as well as the manner in which
they were carried out, is illustrated by the report of the trial of Matilda
Roalfe in Edinburgh, 1844, following the prosecution and imprisonment
of Robinson, Finlay and Paterson. Like most freethinkers, Roalfe
defended herself because a defence counsel could not be trusted to maintain*

* From *The Scotch Trials* (1844) pp. 75–80.

the principle of the defence; unlike most, however, Roalfe did not make a defence speech lasting several hours, and so it can be reproduced in full. The commentary is by Holyoake.

THE TRIAL OF MISS MATILDA ROALFE.

THIS case is illustrative of the truth, that when persecution is employed against the conscientious and determined, it becomes the finest auxiliary of proselytism. No sooner were Mr. Finlay and his son-in-law imprisoned, by the procurator-fiscal than Mr. Paterson (who is a native of Scotland) returned to his own country, and stepped into the places of the imprisoned, not only to sell what they sold, but to sell books which they had no intention of selling. When the procurator gutted *his* premises, the walls were covered with placards, in characters that they who run might read of Christianity's doings, and young and old were enabled to learn what without the fiscal's friendly aid, would have required years of silent labour to have brought under their notice. Not only did the law's unwise functionaries "stretch the pewer [sic] vested in them" as the *Edinburgh Courant* boasted, but according to the *Pictorial Times* it became necessary for the police force to "stretch their jackets" in the ungracious and undignified office of washing placards from the walls. The efforts of these officials were either defeated or rendered most arduous by persons taking the precaution of *gluing* the obnoxious papers in every conspicuous place. As fast as one set of bill-stickers were apprehended, another volunteered their services, and nightly bands perambulated the City of Edinburgh and its suburbs. Every letter box was favoured with a special inclosure for the better information of its owner.

On the apprehension of Mr. M'Neile of Campsie[1], at the instance of the Rev. Mr. Lee, Messrs. Paterson, Jeffery and Budge, issued from Glasgow and invaded the districts of the Rev. bigot, sold papers, posted placards and delivered addresses to the inhabitants. Atheism, unadulterated and undisguised, was diffused into every corner of the land, and the bold voice of the conscientious unbeliever was heard in remote districts where scepticism had probably never before penetrated. The press was forced to discuss the subject and Mr. Southwell was invited from England to expound the startling

tenets of Atheism, which his talents, enthusiasm and imprisonment, had first brought into general notice.

This ardour and agitation only acquired fresh resolution
from the barbarous sentence passed on Mr. Paterson, and the
disappointed rage which was reeked on Mr. Finlay.[2] It was now
known that Mr. Paterson was shut up in solitary confinement,
and treated with that severity which if not intended, will probably, as it has in too many instances, produce insanity. It was
under these circumstances that Miss Roalfe, with more than
woman's usual courage left London to oppose, as far as lay in
her power, that religious tyranny to which it is no less a duty
than a glory to offer resistance.

Immediately on her arrival in Scotland, she entered upon the
superintendence of the "Atheistical depot, 105, Nicolson
Street, and soon after circulated a Manifesto addressed to the
public of Edinburgh, setting forth her determination to sell
such books as contained sentiments she deemed useful to be
known, "whether they did or did not bring into contempt the
Holy Scriptures and the Christian religion." The Manifesto
concluded by announcing for sale a list of all the prosecuted
works; taking special care to notify that "country orders were
punctually attended to." Just as Mr. Paterson when he announced a collection of the obscene passages of the Holy Bible,
informed the public that he made "a liberal allowance to
Sunday Schools."

In a few day after the sentence on Mr. Finlay, the procurator-
fiscal with a number of officers, like an inquisitor with his fam-
iliars, entered Miss Roalfe's shop, rudely turned over every article in her private dwelling, carried away a considerable
portion of her stock and conveyed her to the sheriff's office for
examination.

Of Miss Roalfe's treatment immediately on her apprehension she thus writes:—

"When committed to prison I was put into a wretched stone
cell, and after waiting in vain for my dismissal I was told by the
turnkey that the lights were about to be extinguished and that I
had better go to bed, as there was very little chance that I
should leave that night. But on preparing for rest guess my sur-
prise and disgust, on discovering my bed covered with *vermin!* I
instantly made an alarm and insisted on being removed into

another cell, which was accordingly done. I stated that I should make a complaint, but as the turnkey was particularly civil I said no more about it. Since my return home however I have had considerable difficulty in freeing myself from the impurities of that place."

"On my liberation on bail, I found my home, as you may well suppose, in a wretched state of disorder on my return from prison. It took the greater part of yesterday to restore it to anything like a degree of comfort. Next I had the shop filled with persons who called to see me, some prompted by regard, and others by curiosity, and last though not least, the house was surrounded by a riotous mob, whose hissings and hootings at times almost stunned me. Never did I witness such a scene as took place the night of my liberation; the moment it was ascertained that I was at home, a crowd began to assemble, and in about half an hour some hundreds of persons had collected, and before ten o'clock their conduct baffled all description. If you can imagine an *Indian war-whoop* then you may form some idea of the yells of these disciples of the meek and lowly Jesus— Several of the committee of the Anti-P. U. were at my house, some of whom attempted to put up the shutters; but part were seized by the mob, and others were struck; one young man in particular was struck by a medical student on the head with his stick, which cut it open. At last with the assistance of a number of the police, we succeeded in dispersing the mob. I fear, however, that I shall experience considerable annoyance for some time to come, as I am blessed with a neighbour who is a Methodist local preacher, and who is the principle actor in the scene."

Miss Roalfe's trial took place in the sheriff's court on Tuesday, January 23rd 1844. At an early hour every part was crammed to suffocation.

Sheriff Tait on the bench.

The indictment having been read, the defendant was asked if she was guilty.

Miss Roalfe.—Not guilty.

Did you vend the books spoken of.

Miss Roalfe.—I did sell them, but am not guilty of doing so with a wicked and felonious intent, I am quite satisfied that the quotations made from the books, may be borne out by reference to the Bible.

Sheriff Tait.—In vending them you are guilty of breaking the law.

Miss Roalfe.—I have read the books bought, and I do not see anything in them that I am not prepared to defend, I do not think that such works are calculated to demoralize the readers of them.

John Buchanan and Abjah Murray were called to prove going to 105, Nicolson Street, on the 11th December last. Campbell the sheriff's officer, proved going to Nicolson Street, saw the defendant there, was in the shop and back room for two hours, took possession of all he considered Blasphemous, Abjah Murray was with him.

William Murray.—I recollect going to a shop in Nicolson-street, last November, on Saturday, November 18th. Abijah Murray and James M'Levie went with me; Abijah Murray went in first, I stood and looked in at the door saw the defendant there and no one else, saw her hand Abijah Murray two books he had purchased. Went back to the shop again, in a few minutes after, the same day, and made another purchase of "A Home Thrust at the Atrocious Trinity." I had some conversation with the defendant when I was in the shop the second time; I said, you have got a fine shop now. She replied—yes it is when put to rights. I told her I thought she would be in a better situation in Register-street, I thought she would sell more.

Cross examined by Miss Roalfe.—How do you get your living?—I am a police officer; I suppose you know that. Did you come to my shop on your own account or were you sent?—I was sent. Who sent you?—I decline answering that question. Miss Roalfe, I insist upon knowing who sent you, it is important to my defence?—I don't know that I may tell you. The witness then addressed sheriff Tait to know if he should tell who sent him. Certainly, was the reply, Mr. Scott sent me, said the witness. Miss Roalfe: Who is Mr. Scott?—The procurator fiscal. Here a strong feeling of disapprobation was manifested. Sheriff Tait said he did not sit there to here approbation or disapprobation, and if it was continued he would have the court cleared immediately. Defendant to the witness, so you were mean enough to come to my shop, knowing I should be imprisoned for it were you?—I had nothing to do with that. Did you know the nature of the book before you bought it?—No. Then you had not read it?—No. Were you given to understand what you were sent for?—No. Where do you say you purchased the book?—Of you in Nicolson-street.

James M'Levie.—I am a criminal officer, William and Abijah Murray went with me to 105, Nicolson-street, and bought *Oracle of Reason*, 91 and 94. Abijah went in a second time and bought "A Home Thrust at the Atrocious Trinity;" saw him buy it, he showed it to me, I went in to buy 91 *Oracle of Reason*, she sold it me, I wanted 93, she had not got it. I showed it to the others.

Cross examined by Miss Roalfe.—Did you get 93 *Oracle of Reason?*—No, you said you would get it for me. Did you ever see me before you saw me in Nicolson-street?—Yes, I saw you once in Register-street. What did you go to Register-street for?—I went there to see some one else. Who was it?—He is not here now. Miss Roalfe, but who was it?—It was Paterson. Did you purchase anything of me in Register-street;—I don't remember. Are you quite sure you did not purchase anything of me there?—I think I did buy something?—What was it. I don't remember, I should have need of a good memory to recollect I think. Yes, I think you would require a better one than you have. Do you know the nature of it?—Oh, it was something similar to what lies here, pointing to some of the numbers of the *Oracle of Reason*. Did you read the books?—Yes I did read some of them. What effect did it have upon your mind?—Here the witness appeared thoroughly bewildered, first looking at the sheriff then at the advocate, and at last said—It had no effect upon me. Miss Roalfe.—Are you quite sure?—Yes, it had not the least effect upon me. Are you the less moral in consequence of having read them?—This question seemed to puzzle the witness more than the other, and after being asked several times for an answer, he said—NO; I do not consider I am the less moral. (*laughter.*)

Abijah Murray examined.—I went to the shop on the 7th December, with John Colquhoun for to purchase some books; John Colquhoun bought "the Bible an Improper Book for Youth, and Dangerous to the Easily-excited brain," and the "Trinity of Trinities;" went again with Campbell the sheriff's clerk, and saw him seize some books and papers on the 11th December.

Cross examined by Miss Roalfe.—Did you read the books you bought?—No. Were you sent to my shop?—Yes. Who sent you?—The procurator-fiscal. Had you any instructions?—No, only to buy. You say you did not read them?—No, only just glanced over them, I stood at the door while you served William Murray and James M'Levie, I don't know where you took the books from; 7th December I was with John Colquhoun. What made you purchase the books you did?—I was told to purchase them.

John Colquhoun examined.—I went with Abjah Murray to the shop in Nicolson Street, saw the defendant there on the 7th December, Murray stood at the door, she came from the back room, I bought the Bible an Improper Book for Youth, &c., and Trinity of Trinities, paid 6d., showed to books to Murray.

Cross examined by Miss Roalfe.—I was sent in by Abijah Murray, I did not read them. Did you know the nature of the books?—I understood they contained something blasphemous. What do you consider blasphemy?—I never read any blasphemy in my life.

Mr. Brown, advocate, was heard on the part of the prosecutor. He contended the case was fully proved, there could be no discussion in a case of this kind, the purchase of the books from the defendant had been fully proved. The criminality of selling them had been settled in the High Court of Justiciary. The indictment comprised six different complaints. The witnesses were criminal officers who had received instructions and that most properly. Their being criminal officers could not in the least invalidate their evidence. That they were sold with a wicked and felonious intent there could be no doubt; he therefore contended the case was fully made out.

There was one thing more he wished to draw attention to, that was the last paragraph of a paper written and published by the defendant herself, entitled "Manifesto of Matilda Roalfe, to the People of Edinburgh which was as follows:—

"To aid in destroying the influence of *such* men, by bringing into contempt the fabulous trash they palm upon the ever-credulous, ever-deceived multitude, as genuine religion, is the great, the *sole* object of my ambition. I neither hope nor fear any thing from authority, and am resolved to supply the public with works of a controversial and philosophical character, whether such works do or do not bring into contempt the "*Holy Scriptures or the Christian Religion.*"

He thought such things should not be tolerated, they were illegal and should be dealt with accordingly.

Miss Roalfe then briefly protested against any book or paper being brought against her that was not named in the indictment; the books were not sold for the purpose of demoralizing the readers of them, nor did she think that they were likely to produce such an effect. When it was shown they did produce the effect ascribed to them, she would cease to sell them. She said the opinions she entertained she held conscientiously, she never read any book but the Bible, it was the Bible that converted her. She was for many years in the capacity of teacher in a Sunday school, and made a practice of telling scholars to ask for an explanation of any passages they did not understand. Was repeatedly asked questions she could not answer, resolved to study Bible more attentively than she had done before; the result was, could not find any evidence to prove Christianity superior to any other religion, accordingly rejected Christian religion and all others as mere fables. Had been much happier since, had derived more pleasure from the study of the sciences than she had ever done from the study of religion. She objected to the work, God *v.* Paterson being brought against her, it was merely the published trial and defence of another individual, and the parts objected to, were merely quotations made by Mr. Paterson in his defence.[3] However, she did not regret what she had done nor did believe that she should; she should have no occasion to do so, and so soon as she was at liberty she should consider it her duty to do the same thing again. It did not appear to her that this was a case demanding many words. The question was not whether Christianity was true or false, but whether Atheists had an equal right with Christians to publish their opinions, she had only to repeat that it was her intention to pursue the same course again, so soon as she should be at liberty.

Sheriff Tait said that two trials that had lately taken place in the High Court of Justiciary, had established the illegality of selling such works, and he could not do otherwise, then follow the example of the High Court; the only difference being that one individual had fifteen months, the other twelve, while he could only give two. If, however, she could prove that she had sold the books innocently, not knowing the contents, why then it would be a very different thing, but as she had admitted she knew the contents of the books, he was satisfied the charge was fully proved, and the sentence was that she be imprisoned for sixty days in the jail of Edinburgh.

Strong disapprobation was expressed on the sheriff passing sentence and he found it necessary to threaten to clear the court if it was repeated.

Miss Roalfe exhibited great firmness, and on being led away to jail the assembled multitude, unable to restrain their feelings, gave her three hearty expressions of applause.

Miss Roalfe's treatment while undergoing her imprisonment was quite in keeping with the brutal indecencies and inhuman barbarities which these Trials have in other places related. Upon her liberation she thus detailed the indignity to which she was subjected. "When I was removed from the bar after sentence was pronounced, I was conveyed in a cab to Calton gaol. On my arrival there, I was placed in the "receiving room" with a number of other prisoners, where I remained until about 7 o'clock, when I was compelled to strip myself of every article of clothing, and was ordered to plunge into a bath in the presence of about half a dozen persons. Against this, however, I strongly protested and neither would nor *did* submit to such an indignity. I was then given the prison dress and locked up in a stone cell without fire, and treated in every respect as a common felon. During the first three weeks of my incarceration I suffered very severely both from cold and hunger. At the expiration of which time I was removed to another cell, which was lighter and rather warmer; I was ordered some additional flannel by the doctor, as I was suffering from severe pains, no alteration whatever was made in my food. I was neither permitted to write nor to receive letters, and although many were sent by persons in various parts of the country, yet was I not permitted to receive them till the morning of my liberation. Amid all the privations I endured there was yet one glorious privilege of which they could not rob me, my thoughts were still unfettered; our persecutors have yet to learn that when they have turned the dungeon key upon us, there is still that, over which they have no controul, thought free as ever defies all their attempts to enslave it, and until they can do this their triumph is incomplete. I still feel the most thorough contempt for that law which will concede to one portion of society those rights which it withholds from another, I therefore resolved to act in defiance of such a system, and having weighed all the consequences before I did so act, I have never for one moment regretted it. Let us unite all our energies, nor relax our endeavours until we have obtained an abrogation of a law, which is an insult alike upon common sense and justice.

The failure of these harsh and foolish steps to prevent the publication of atheistical sentiments is evinced by the fact, that no sooner was Miss Roalfe incarcerated than *The Movement* announced:—

"ARRIVAL EXTRAORDINARY, Mr. Baker of the United order of Blasphemers, London, has arrived in Edinburgh, to take the superintendence of the Atheistical Depot, in Nicolson-street, during the absence of Miss Roalfe."

NOTES

1. For selling *Oracle* no. 91 on his bookstall. The offensive article is Doc. 40.
2. Paterson was sentenced at the High Court to fifteen months' felon's treatment in Perth penitentiary; Robinson, who was ill and pleaded guilty, got twelve months; Finlay was sentenced at the Sheriff's Court to sixty days in Calton gaol.
3. This was the report of Paterson's trial for his earlier escapades in London, Christmas 1842, when he had displayed 'obscene' (i.e. blasphemous) placards in the window of the *Oracle* shop in Holywell Street.

68 A problem for the Newcastle magistrates*

The final prosecutions of Carlile's shopmen in 1824 had been the work of the Home Office, but increasingly the government became unwilling to initiate such proceedings, or, indeed, to encourage local magistrates to do so. In December 1850 John Mill had delivered two lectures in Newcastle upon Tyne on 'The First of Genesis as compared with Tradition – especially with reference to the Hindoo, Greek and Scandanavian accounts of the Creation of the World' and 'The Theology and Philosophy of the Old

* From Home Office papers, 45 O.S. 3537, Public Record Office.

Testament Writings'. The response of the Home Office to the mayor's letter about this was lukewarm: a pencilled endorsement of the letter is full of ridicule; and the Law Officers' advice is given in the knowledge that the magistrates cannot afford to follow it.

Newcastle upon Tyne
9 January 1851.

Sir

I have the honor to transmit to you by desire of the Magistrates of this Borough copies of Reports of two Lectures which have recently been delivered in a Room called the "Lecture Room" in this Town, by a Mr. John Mill.

For sometime past Lectures and Discussions have been given here to the great disgust and annoyance of the Inhabitants generally, wherein Atheism and Infidelity have been plainly advanced and the divine authority of the Bible and of the Christian Religion openly impugned, set at nought and denied.

These Lectures and Discussions have been attended by a considerable number of persons chiefly of the Working and Lower Classes, and they were announced at one period during the Mayoralty of my predecessor in Placards and Hand-bills so offensive, that he and the Magistrates felt it incumbent upon them in the discharge of their duty to prevent one of the meetings taking place; which they did, by sending the Police to the Lecture Room previous to the hour announced for the commencement of the discussion, to forbid the Meeting.

At the discussions Mr. John Mill generally took a part, he being the advocate in favour of Christianity against another party who argued in favor of Atheism. The Lectures at that time were not given by Mr. Mill.

The step taken by the late Mayor and the Magistrates was severely criticised in some infidel publications, which are printed and sold or circulated in this Town, but since then much more caution is apparent in the Hand-bill Notices of the intended Lectures, which are generally couched in such terms as to convey the notion of a philosophical enquiry into the History &c. of the Bible, the Jews, Creation, &c. and to render it doubtful whether the authorities could interfere to prevent the Lectures or not.

Mr. Mill however the former advocate for Christianity, is now the Lecturer who calls in question the divine authority of the Old and New Testament.

Under these circumstances it has been judged proper to have some of these Lectures attended by reporters and Policemen in plain clothes, to watch, and if necessary to speak to, their tendency.

The Reports now sent it is thought merit particular notice, and in order to comply with the requirements of the Law, an information has been laid against Mr. Mill for the Lecture delivered on the   December last. The accuracy of the Report can be vouched for by two Reporters; and two Policemen who were present will be able to confirm it.

I was requested at a Meeting of Magistrates to ask your advice and opinion on these Reports and if a Prosecution for Blasphemy should be undertaken against Mill for the Lecture he delivered on the   December, and which there can be no doubt comes within the meaning of the Statute 9 & 10 Wm IIId Cap. 32, Secs 1, and further I have to ask you whether Her Majesty's Government will undertake the Prosecution as the Magistrates have no fund out of which to pay the requisite expences [sic].

I may state there is reason to believe that a regular system for the delivery of these Lectures &c., is in operation, as on applying to the Proprietor of the Lecture Room under the hope of being able to put a stop to this scandalous evil through him, it was found that a person of the name of Barlow, who Prints and sells infidel and obscene Books had rented the Room, and there is no doubt he engages these Lecturers and disputants, and makes a profit by charging a small fee for admittance. It is requisite that something decisive should be done to put these proceedings down, as they tend greatly to promote infidel and Socialist doctrines amongst the people, and to the disparagement of true Religion, and all constituted authority. The public are keenly alive to them, and are upbraiding the authorities for not putting them down.

I have the honour to remain
Sir
Your Most Obedient Servant
Wm. Armstrong
Mayor

The Rt. Hon[oura]ble
  The Secretary of State
    Home Department
      &c.   &c.   &c.
[This letter was endorsed as follows in the Home Office]
The Mayor a/c Feby. 6. Sends Reports of two lectures by a Mr.
Mill alleged to be Atheistic – asks advice as to a prosecution, for
Blasphemy & inquires whether the Govt. will undertake it as
the Justices have no funds.
[The next sentence is added in pencil]
The Notion of proceeding under the Stat. of W III's is preposte-
rous – as to an Indictment at Common Law the Law Officers
might be consulted.

Letter to Mr. Maude
    14 Jan 1851
Law Officers
  See Law Officers
  Opinions of 1 Feb.
                    Copy of Opinion
We are of opinion that John Mill is liable to prosecution and
that it may be either by indictment or information but we think
it proper to add that we should in this case consider it highly
inexpedient for the Government to institute any such proceeding but that it may be properly left to the magistrates to take
such cause in this matter as they may consider to be most advisable.

                              John Romilly
                              A. E. Cockburn
1 February 1851.

Civil Rights

69 Britain not a free country*

*The Secularists could always rely on encouragement and financial support
from men and women in a higher social position than themselves, and one
of the foremost defenders of the freethinkers in their civil rights campaign
was John Stuart Mill. His essay* On Liberty *was written against a
background of religious bigotry (best brought out in T. H. Buckle's review article in* Fraser's Magazine, *May 1859), and in it Mill makes
specific references to the legal disabilities of those who either would not or
could not take an oath in the courts of law. The footnotes in this extract are
Mill's own.*

It will be said, that we do not now put to death the intro-
ducers of new opinions: we are not like our fathers who slew the
prophets, we even build sepulchres to them. It is true we no
longer put heretics to death; and the amount of penal infliction
which modern feeling would probably tolerate, even against the
most obnoxious opinions, is not sufficient to extirpate them.
But let us not flatter ourselves that we are yet free from the stain
even of legal persecution. Penalties for opinion, or at least for its
expression, still exist by law; and their enforcement is not, even
in these times, so unexampled as to make it at all incredible that
they may some day be revived in full force. In the year 1857, at
the summer assizes of the county of Cornwall, an unfortunate
man,[1] said to be of unexceptionable conduct in all relations of
life, was sentenced to twenty-one months' imprisonment, for
uttering, and writing on a gate, some offensive words concern-

* From J. S. Mill, *On Liberty* (1859) Everyman edition, pp. 90–1, 91–2.

ing Christianity. Within a month of the same time, at the Old Bailey, two persons, on two separate occasions,[2] were rejected as jurymen, and one of them grossly insulted by the judge and by one of the counsel, because they honestly declared that they had no theological belief; and a third, a foreigner,[3] for the same reason, was denied justice against a thief. This refusal of redress took place in virtue of the legal doctrine, that no person can be allowed to give evidence in a court of justice who does not profess belief in a God (any god is sufficient) and in a future state; which is equivalent to declaring such persons to be outlaws, excluded from the protection of the tribunals; who may not only be robbed or assaulted with impunity, if no one but themselves, or persons of similar opinions, be present, but any one else may be robbed or assaulted with impunity, if the proof of the fact depends on their evidence. . . .

These, indeed, are but rags and remnants of persecution, and may be thought to be not so much an indication of the wish to persecute, as an example of that very frequent infirmity of English minds, which makes them take a preposterous pleasure in the assertion of a bad principle, when they are no longer bad enough to desire to carry it really into practice. But unhappily there is no security in the state of the public mind that the suspension of worse forms of legal persecution, which has lasted for about the space of a generation, will continue. In this age the quiet surface of routine is as often ruffled by attempts to resuscitate past evils, as to introduce new benefits. What is boasted of at the present time as the revival of religion, is always, in narrow and uncultivated minds, at least as much the revival of bigotry; and where there is the strong permanent leaven of intolerance in the feelings of a people, which at all times abides in the middle classes of this country, it needs but little to provoke them into actively persecuting those whom they have never ceased to think proper objects of persecution. For it is this—it is the opinions men entertain, and the feelings they cherish, respecting those who disown the beliefs they deem important, which makes this country not a place of mental freedom.

[1] Thomas Pooley, Bodmin Assizes, July 31, 1857. In December following, he received a free pardon from the Crown.
[2] George Jacob Holyoake, August 17, 1857; Edward Truelove, July, 1857.
[3] Baron de Gleichen, Marlborough Street Police Court, August 4, 1857.

70 The Bradlaugh case*

The most celebrated case of all in which an oath was refused came in 1880 when Charles Bradlaugh was elected to Parliament as junior Member for Northampton as the colleague of Henry Labouchere. Exactly what happened during the next five years was often disputed, but the summary of the whole affair given in the Star *newspaper shortly before Bradlaugh's death was quoted by the* National Reformer *as being substantially correct.*

MR. BRADLAUGH'S PARLIAMENTARY STRUGGLE.

VARIOUS queries, and some misstatements in the press, show that the manifold details of Mr. Bradlaugh's five years' Parliamentary Struggle have faded from individual memories. It may therefore be useful to Freethinkers to reprint the following matter, the bulk of which appeared in the *Star* of the 27th ult.:

On May 3, 1880, when Mr. Bradlaugh handed to the Clerk of the House a written paper claiming the right to affirm under the law, the trouble began. A common statement is that he "refused to take the oath", and "obtruded his opinions" on the House. Neither of these things happened then or at any other time. The Speaker, being in doubt, asked Mr. Bradlaugh to withdraw: and Lord F. Cavendish, seconded by Sir Stafford Northcote, moved the appointment of a Committee of Inquiry, which was agreed to, though a week after, on its being formally moved, there were 74 votes against to 171 for it. On May 20th the Committee reported that persons entitled to affirm in courts of justice under the Evidence Amendment Acts were not legally entitled to affirm in the House, this view being come to only on the casting vote of the chairman, Mr. Walpole. Mr. Bradlaugh then publicly intimated that while the oath included words which to him were meaningless, so that it would have been an act of hypocrisy on his part to take it voluntarily if another course were open to him, he should now take the oath, holding himself bound, not by the words of asserveration, but by the explicit affirmation. On the 21st he went to the table, amid uproar, to be sworn. Sir H. D. Wolff objecting, the Speaker again

* From *National Reformer* 15 Feb. 1891.

requested Mr. Bradlaugh to withdraw, going on to admit, however, that he knew of no precedent for refusing the oath to a member offering to take it. Sir Henry moved that refusal be made, on the score, not only of the member's Atheism, but of his "Impeachment of the House of Brunswick"; and Alderman Fowler seconded. Gladstone and Bright spoke powerfully on the other side in the long and fierce debate which ensued, and which, after several adjournments, ended in the appointment of another Committee, this time to report whether Mr. Bradlaugh was entitled to take the oath. On June 16th, this Committee reported that the taking of an oath by Mr. Bradlaugh would not be a genuine swearing in the meaning of the law; but recommended by a majority of four, that after all he be allowed to affirm, and that his right be afterwards tested by action at law.

Over a motion by Mr. Labouchere to this end, there was another long debate, Sir Hardinge Giffard and Alderman Fowler moving a resolution refusing both oath and affirmation. Finally, Jews and Nonconformists and Parnellites helping the Tories, the motion was defeated by 275 to 230.

The situation is edifying, when one looks back on it. It was first decided that Mr. Bradlaugh could not legally affirm in the House, though he had frequently affirmed in the Courts. But the law allowing affirmation in the Courts, being apparently framed to prevent dishonest Christians from evading the oath, puts upon unbelievers the virtual insult of making the judge technically but ambiguously decide that an oath "would not be binding" on their conscience. When, therefore, Mr. Bradlaugh gave his evidence to the effect that he had affirmed in the law Courts, he was held to have admitted that he satisfied judges that an oath "would not be binding on his conscience". Therefore, though he clearly explained that that was only a legal technicality, and that an oath was as binding on his conscience as an affirmation, he must not be allowed to take the oath, though everybody knew that various unbelievers then sitting in the House had done so. The law then clearly ought to be altered, but the majority would not alter it. On this basis of unabashed iniquity, a Christian legislature stood for five years.

All the same, Mr. Bradlaugh again came forward, and was allowed to make his first great speech at the bar; but a rescinding motion was defeated. Requested to leave the House, he respectfully refused, because the order was illegal. Gladstone, then Premier and leader of the House, refused to help the majority out of the fix in which they had placed themselves; and on the motion of Northcote, after much uproar, the offender was "committed to the Clock Tower", from which he had just to be released unconditionally. Mr. Gladstone later moved as a standing order that members be allowed to affirm at their choice; and this was carried by 303 to 249; whereupon Mr. Bradlaugh made affirmation of allegiance, took his seat, and voted. Immediately he was sued for penalties, as having voted illegally, by Clarke, the tool of Mr. Newdegate. Insults all the while rained in from all sides on the member, his family, and his friends, and among others the Rev. Mr. Voysey pronounced the action of Northampton disgraceful, and praised the speeches urging the Atheist's exclusion; while Sir John Hay brutally insulted Mrs. Besant, Mr. Bradlaugh's partner.

At length, in 1881, the action of Clarke v. Bradlaugh was decided against the defendant, who again lost on appeal. Bradlaugh's seat was thus vacated, and he again stood for Northampton, to be again elected after a desperate struggle. Again he came to the table to take the oath, and again, on a division, he was prevented. Removed by the Sergeant again and again to the bar, he again and again returned to the table, till the House adjourned; and again next day he presented himself, till it was arranged that the Government should "give facilities" or do something themselves. The Ministerial Oaths Act making no progress, Mr. Bradlaugh appealed to the country, and again, on August 3rd, 1881, he presented himself at the House, this time to be violently seized at the very door and ejected by fourteen policemen and ushers. Standing on the steps, hatless, with his clothes torn, he might, it is said, by one word, have set his host of enthusiastic followers wrecking the House. The word was not spoken. The immediate result of the outrage, perpetrated by the House on its lawfully elected member, was for him a severe attack of erisypelas in the arms. Once before he had had the same malady, as a result of a bludgeoning by a gang of ruffianly Jingoes who got him down in the course of an open-air meeting held in protest against the Beaconsfield Government's Turcophile policy. On that occasion, it is credibly reported, on getting to his feet, he struck five blows, which sent five men to the hospital; and there are legends of damage to some of the fourteen policemen.

Again, next year, on the assembling of Parliament, the unsubduable member presented himself, and made his third speech at Bar; and again the majority refused to let him swear or sit. A few days later, Mr. Gladstone professing to have no policy, Mr. Bradlaugh took the strategic step of administering the oath to himself and sitting down. Again he was expelled; again he was elected for Northampton, on the largest poll yet reached. Still the House decreed his exclusion; though over a thousand petitions, with a quarter of a million signatures, had been presented in his favor. On May 3rd, 1883, the third anniversary of his appearance in the House, the Government Oaths Act Amendment Bill was lost by three votes; and next day Bradlaugh was once more refused, by a majority of 106, the right to vote. While all this battle was being fought, the Conservatives had further sought, though vainly, to convict him of blasphemy in respect of selling the prosecuted *Freethinker*. On the other hand, he had won in the Lords, on appeal, his action against Newdegate for "maintenance" of Clarke; and Newdegate, it is known, had to sell some of his best timber to meet the accumulated mass of costs.

The rest of the story is soon told. On 9th February 1884, Mr. Bradlaugh again administered the oath to himself and voted: and was again expelled. He then accepted the Chiltern Hundreds, and was yet again triumphantly returned for Northampton. Denied justice throughout the Parliament of 1880–1885, he was allowed by the new Speaker, on the assembling of the first Parliament of 1886, to take the oath and sit, the Speaker firmly refusing to let any protest or question be interposed, and thus virtually pronouncing his predecessor's policy illegal. Later, Mr. Bradlaugh carried his Affirmation Bill and put matters on a safe, legal footing.

Public Opinion

71 The suppression of infidel socialism*

Public opinion was invariably hostile to the infidels, and every attempt was made to tar them with accusations of immorality and sedition as well as blasphemy. The Owenites of Manchester aroused the wrath of the great Evangelical leader, the Rev. Hugh Stowell, and a committee for which he was responsible drew the following letter from a Morning Herald *correspondent. The Owenite* New Moral World *was sufficiently amused to reproduce the letter in large type.*

"SOCIALISM.—Every Christian will rejoice to learn that a committee has been for some time formed and actively at work in Manchester, for the counteraction and suppression of that hideous form of infidelity which assumes the name of Socialism. Besides the circulation of tracts and the delivery of lectures, highly important legal steps have been taken, and with the happiest success,—two convictions having been obtained, and the infidel having been proved to be disqualified to take an oath in a court of justice.[1] A most important and complete chain of evidence on the subject has also been transmitted to her Majesty's Government. It will scarcely be credited, except by those who have taken pains to ascertain the truth, that in the densely-peopled manufacturing districts there are loads of tracts issued every Saturday, filled with *blasphemy, sedition,*

* From *New Moral World*, 22 Aug 1840.

and INDECENCY, for the perusal of the working-classes on the Sabbath-day; that school-books are issued from the same diabolical fountain of evil, filled with IMMORAL POISON for the youthful mind; that *blasphemous* and INDECENT SONGS for children are printed to teach the infant tongue to overflow with the outpourings of impiety; that copy-books are printed for the purpose of conveying the same poisonous instruction to the rising generation of infant poor; and that *laboured attempts are made to corrupt the* MORALS *of the females in the factories and domestic establishments, by the profuse circulation of tracts filled with every* EXCITEMENT TO PROFLIGACY AND CRIME. Lectures are also delivered on Sunday evenings, and are regularly attended by hundreds of the working classes. It is to check the progress of the principles thus inculcated that the Manchester committee has been formed, and it would be well if similar ones were established in every town and village in the kingdom.— *Correspondent, Morning Herald, Wednesday, Aug. 12, 1840.*

NOTE

1. The door stewards at the opening meeting of the new Manchester Hall of Science were prosecuted under 39 George III cap. 79 for taking money at the door of a public hall on a Sunday. Their defence rested on the claim that the hall was registered with the bishop for public worship, but this legally sound defence was disallowed when all the defence witnesses were shown to be incapable of taking a meaningful oath and testifying to the fact. *Manchester Courier,* 13 June 1840.

72 A Christian mob*

Mob violence was always a danger, and the freethinking radicals had much experience of it. Though there was probably some moderating of extremism after the decline of Owenism, the revival of Secularism, particularly under Bradlaugh's vigorous leadership, still provoked a number of local Christians to attempt to defeat infidelity by force.

WILD BEASTS AT HOYLAND.

HOYLAND is about fifty years behind the rest of England; to go

* From *National Reformer,* 17 Sep 1876.

there is to find oneself transplanted to the bad old days when Christianity was strong; to meet Hoyland Christians is to see Christianity in its natural state, and a very ugly and savage state it is. In answer to the invitation of the Barnsley Secular Society—a Society which is gallantly trying to enlighten the dense darkness produced in the district by Christianity—I willingly agreed to go to Hoyland to deliver a theological lecture; I had already delivered there two political lectures, and had been well received, but as a Primitive Methodist parson there, Hebblethwaite by name, had been abusing Atheists in most virulent fashion, showing by the manner of his attacks that he was utterly ignorant of the subject with which he attempted to deal, it was decided that my subject should, this time, be a theological one. As Mr. Hebblethwaite had been slandering Atheism, I decided to defend it, and I elected to speak on the question, "Is there a God?" So far, so good, but a week previous to my visit there arrived in Barnsley two ignorant and bigoted Protestants, who travel about the country libelling and slandering Secularist lecturers; these two set busily to work after their usual fashion; they have two or three lectures between them, and sometimes one delivers them, and sometimes the other. It is a sort of joint-stock slandering business, limited (in brains). Their method of working is as follows: They read up a mass of medical details, and then lecture on them, deducing the most indecent conclusions, and then proclaim their own foul thoughts as the teaching of Secular lecturers. They put into the mouth of Mr. Bradlaugh the most immoral and disgusting doctrines, and the gaping and ignorant Christians swallow it all, and believe that "Charles Bradlaugh, the Atheist," is responsible for the abominable teaching invented by these pious followers of Jesus. The lectures are further garnished with invented stories, which blacken the characters of the Secular lecturers, and which are all believed by those of the hearers who are sufficiently uncultivated to take pleasure in foul language and murdered English. This amusement had been going on in Barnsley for a week previous to my arrival in that town with great vigour, and between placards asking "Will Mrs. Besant defend" certain teachings, and the most libellous platform attacks, the two Christian missionaries had stirred up the lowest and most brutal section of the population, exhorting them to "sweep Secularists out of the town." They then held an open-air meeting at Hoyland, just previous to my lecture, and all was ripe for a row. Arrived at the hall, I found it crowded to excess, the labours of the missionaries resulting in giving me a splendid audience, though the rough element was painfully conspicuous. One of the Christian saints was present; 'the worst of the two thought himself safer out of the way.' This one, however, began at once making a noise, when I announced the conditions of debate, stating that the platform was open to all, save to two disreputable individuals, whom I need not then name. The cap fitted so exactly, that disreputable individual No. 1 began shouting, but desisted when told that if he were not silent he would be pitched out; some Barnsley friends were round the platform, and the disreputable individual subsided. The lecture went through all right, at times interrupted by Christian yells, when any stroke was specially sharp, and by one very lively fight near the door, occasioned by an enthusiastic Theist, who wanted to take God under his protection, but whom God failed to save from ejection. But when the lecture was over, the tumult began; I had, by name, challenged the Rev. A. Hebblethwaite, who was present, but the disreputable individual thought himself the best man, and wanted to speak. I declined, and gave my reasons: he insisted, and his organised roughs jumped on the benches, hooting and yelling with spiritual—or, at least, spirituous—fervour. I explained politely that it was never wise to fight with a sweep, however anxious the sweep might be to fight, because the soot came off and soiled one's hands, and I really could not soil mine by touching the disreputable individual. Mr. Hebblethwaite said he was suffering from nervous excitement, and that his friend, the disreputable, ought to be allowed to speak; Mrs. Besant was shuffling, and was afraid of the D.I. Mrs. Besant laughed at the fun of her being afraid of the very illiterate D.I., and quite declined to be taunted into allowing the Secular platform to be polluted by debate with such a person: it was really a joke to see the Christians as, standing on forms, they yelled, roared, made faces, shook their fists, and generally conducted themselves like maniacs; if one had only had a glass, to show them how silly they looked, with their faces twisted, and their mouths wide open! We had had half an hour of it, and I began to get tired, so I formally challenged Mr. Hebblethwaite to debate, when not suffering from "nervous excitement," and he said he would when some obscure pamphlet of his, unknown to me, had been "satisfactorily answered," to *whose* satisfaction he did not state: no one else wanted to debate, except the D. I., so the Chairman, at my request, declared the meeting closed. Then there was the crowd to get through, still making the air musical with their melody (what good practice for heaven); the Barnsley friends had the cab at the door, and had conveyed three other ladies to it, but they looked doubtfully at the yelling Christians, and thought I had better wait till they had dispersed. Mr. Hebblethwaite tried to increase the riot by shouting out that they should get back their money, and the hubbub was something remarkable. I had no mind to wait the pleasure of a Christian mob, and announced my intention to go through, and through I went. A friend walked in front down the lane of yellers and hooters, and I think it was that good Secularist, Mr. Crookson, who tried to keep off the pressure at the back. Some chivalrous gentlemen shook their fists at me, but I laughed in their faces, and they restrained their feelings; at the door, Barnsley friends, amongst whom was Mr. Bullard, President of the Barnsley Society—who did capitally as Chairman—tried to keep a way to the cab, and here, in the darkness, some specially pious Christians tried kicking, but only one just touched me, enough to remind one of what they would do if they could get loose. A rush was then made at the cab, accompanied by shouts of "Overturn it, overturn it;" but the very sensible driver foiled them by driving quickly away, and the last we heard of Hoyland was the yells of the pious. Such a scene is very instructive, as showing Christian feeling; it is wicked now, as it ever has been, and is only kept under by the strong force of sceptical public opinion; Christians have all the will, but not the power, to persecute and to put to death, and their essentially savage creed breaks out wherever heresy has not spread its civilising influence. Clearly, Hoyland must be looked after; few villages now are in so unenlightened a state; compulsory education will do much to abolish its present brutality, and until that has time to do its work Secular lecturers must persevere there, and tame the wild beasts.

ANNIE BESANT.

73 Signs of progress*

There were signs of improvement, however, and both Holyoake and Brad-laugh survived early obloquy to become respected figures in the political world. More important than this personal acceptance, though, was the general change in the social and intellectual climate. Surveying the scene towards the very end of his life, Charles Bradlaugh noted the progress which had been made as well as the work which was still to be done.

THE PRESENT OUTLOOK FOR FREETHOUGHT IN ENGLAND.
BY CHARLES BRADLAUGH.

. . . So far the progress is very great, and, if measured against the persecution directed at earlier periods to crush out all forms of Freethought, Freethinkers should, perhaps, be content, and should certainly be most grateful to the heretics of the past, who suffered sorely to win for us this freedom. Yet it must be confessed that a Freethought reputation is even to-day in Britain a heavy drag on the climber, unless he is content to treat his opinions as too costly a luxury for every-day expression. France having only one Church to fight, and that Church on the side of divine-right monarchy, scepticism has there been honored in the highest places. In England the various Nonconformist bodies have ever been associated with the struggles for political and civil freedom; but, as if to accentuate their position, the Nonconformists have not been too tolerant of dissent which went to the extent of disbelief in their own tenets. And this is not unnatural. The Church of England is only tolerant when it is indifferent. It is usually indifferent, unless it fears the hand of the spoiler on its enormous revenues. In Ireland the State Church was the Church of the oppressing minority, and it has fallen. In Wales it is the Church of a minority which unfortunately for itself is still entitled to collect tithes, and it will fall. In Scotland Dis-establishment is within measurable distance. In England the Church is very closely bound up with two great estates of the realm, and I strongly doubt if peers and king

* From *National Reformer*, 30 Nov 1890.

will readily consent to allow the Church of England to merely become one of the religious sects of the Empire. I say king and peers, for certainly no Bill for the disestablishment of the Church of England is likely to pass the House of Commons in the present reign. In the meantime, research is each day freer in every department of human thought, and there is great hope that that best minority of men and women is every day growing larger throughout every phase of society, which will treat all honestly held convictions with equal respect, and will rather encourage expression of doubt and inquiry than denounce or condemn it. All progress is marked by flux and reflux, and the occasional heresy-hunts in Scotland show that bigotry is far from dead; but as a very modern sign-post, there is, in North Britain, Lord Gifford's published will, establishing not only a course of critical lectures on such points as the existence of deity, the immortality of the soul, the nature and possibility of revelation; but in the interests of truth providing that his trustees should allow the Atheist his turn amongst the lecturers appointed to search for truth. The trustees have not yet ventured on an Atheist, but the words of the will should remind these gentlemen that the only real limits to human thought are in the ability of the thinker, and the dead Scotch Judge speaks from his grave clearly, and tells them that hypocrisy is worst irreverence, and honest denial may be most reverent tribute to the truth. In the evening decade of this 19th century there is the bright and mature glory of the enormous progress made in the ninety numbered years; and even in the duller clouds of prejudice and obstacle there is the greater promise for the free watcher and active worker of the to-morrow's dawn.

Sources and Further Reading

MANUSCRIPTS

Home Office Blasphemy Papers, series 45, Public Record Office.
Owen Collection, Co-operative Union, Manchester.
Owenite Minute Books, International Institute of Social History, Amsterdam.
Holyoake Collection, Bishopsgate Institute, London.
Holyoake Collection, Co-operative Union, Manchester.
Bradlaugh Collection, National Secular Society, London.
Cowen Collection, Newcastle upon Tyne Central Reference Library.
Records of the Leicester Secular Society, Leicester Museum.
[The Holyoake and Bradlaugh Collections are available on microfilm.]

PERIODICALS

Carlile: *Republican* (1819–26), *Lion* (1828–9), *Prompter* (1830–1), *Gauntlet* (1833–4).
Hetherington: *Poor Man's Guardian* (1831–5).
Owen: *Crisis* (1832–4), *New Moral World* (1834–45).
Independent Owenite: *Oracle of Reason* (1841–3), *Movement* (1843–5), *Herald of Progress* (1845–6).
Secularist: *Reasoner* (1846–61), *London Investigator* (1854–9), *National Reformer* (1860–93).
[Most of the above are available in reprint or microform, except the *Oracle*, the *Reasoner* and the *Investigator* (in British Museum and elsewhere), and the *Herald of Progress* (only in

Manchester).]

GENERAL READING

Slightly more background to the century and topic of this book is given in my *Radical Politics, 1790–1900* (1971), which also contains a limited selection of documents and full bibliography. I have tried not to reproduce here documents which can be found there, but a fuller version of two documents previously used does appear in the present work. For a more detailed survey of the period to 1866, see my *Victorian Infidels* (1974), which has an extensive list of primary and secondary works. A second volume, which will complete the analysis to the end of the century, is now being prepared.

THE IMPACT OF PAINE

The best modern edition of Paine is P. Foner (ed.), *The Complete Writings of Thomas Paine*, 2 vols (New York, 1945). A convenient edition of the *Rights of Man* has been edited and introduced by Henry Collins (1969). W. H. Reid, *The Rise and Dissolution of the Infidel Societies* has been reprinted, together with W. J. Linton, *Life of James Watson*, in V. Neuburg (ed.), *Literacy and Society* (1971).

The most recent life of Paine is A. Williamson, *Thomas Paine* (1973). For the popular societies, see G. S. Veitch, *The Genesis of Parliamentary Reform* (1913, reprinted 1965), G. A. Williams, *Artisans and Sansculottes* (1968), and J. Walvin, *The English Jacobins* (forthcoming). The ethos of Jacobin (and Zetetic) radicalism is vividly recreated in E. P. Thompson, *The Making of the English Working Class*, 2nd ed. (1968).

RICHARD CARLILE AND THE ZETETICS

There is as yet no full biography of Richard Carlile, though J. H. Wiener is working on one. The Carlile agitation is covered in W. H. Wickwar, *Struggle for the Freedom of the Press, 1819–32* (1928, reprinted 1972). Brief lives of Carlile were written by G. A. Aldred (1923) and G. D. H. Cole (1943), and of Robert Taylor by G. A. Aldred (1942) and H. Cutner (n.d.). For the rest, see Carlile's own periodicals and T. C. Campbell, *The Battle of the Press as told in the story of the Life of Richard Carlile* (1899), which is his daughter's commentary to Carlile's own letters. G. A. Williams prints a Zetetic liturgy in *Rowland Detrosier* (1965).

OWENISM

The Life of Robert Owen written by himself is the best way to sample Owen's own writings, and is available either with an introduction by J. Butt (1971), or in a reprint of the original complete with Owen's own selection of his early writings, 2 vols (1857–8, reprinted 1967). His two most important works, *A New View of Society* and *Report to the County of Lanark* are in a convenient edition introduced by V. A. C. Gatrell (1969).

The best biography of Owen is still F. Podmore, *Robert Owen* (1906, reprinted 1968), supplemented by G. D. H. Cole, *The Life of Robert Owen*, 3rd ed. (1965).

Holyoake's autobiographies, *Sixty Years of an Agitator's Life*, 2 vols (1897) and *Bygones Worth Remembering*, 2 vols (1905) are interesting but unreliable. There are also a *Life and Letters* by J. McCabe, 2 vols (1908) and a biography by Lee E. Grugel, *George Jacob Holyoake* (1975). Charles Southwell left a fascinating *Confessions of a Freethinker* (1850) and Robert Cooper *An Autobiographical Sketch* (1868) – both are extremely rare and they are shortly to be reprinted by the Rationalist Press Association.

On Owenism, the starting point for a reappraisal is J. F. C. Harrison, *Robert Owen and the Owenites in Britain and America* (1969) and the two volumes of bicentennial essays, *Robert Owen, prince of cotton spinners,* ed. J. Butt (1971) and *Robert Owen, prophet of the poor,* ed. S. Pollard and J. Salt (1971).

SECULARISM

The most easily available primary sources are Charles Bradlaugh, *Selection of Political Pamphlets* (1970), and Annie Besant, *Selection of Social and Political Pamphlets* (1970), both edited by John Saville. No such volume yet exists for Holyoake, but his autobiographies, cited above, are often available second-hand. H. B. Bonner and J. M. Robertson, *Charles Bradlaugh, his life and work*, 2 vols (1898) contains much primary material but was written too close to the events and can now be supplemented by D. Tribe, *President Charles Bradlaugh, M.P.* (1971). There is a full study of *The Bradlaugh Case* by W. L. Arnstein (1965). Annie Besant also wrote *An Autobiography* (1893) and is the subject of

A. H. Nethercote, *The First Five Lives of Annie Besant* (1961) and *The Last Four Lives of Annie Besant* (1963).

There are two articles dealing with the Secularist movement: J. Eros, 'The rise of organised freethought in mid-Victorian England', *Sociological Review* (1954) and F. B. Smith, 'The Atheist Mission', in *Ideas and Institutions of Victorian Britain*, ed. R. Robson (1967). Smith has also written a biography of the foremost non-infidel Paineite, *W. J. Linton* (1973).

Index

Adams, George and Harriet, 53, 54, 56
Adams, J. P., 65, 85, 86
Annet, Peter, 3, 13, 33, 131, 194
Annual Register, 6–8, 10–11
anti-clericalism, xvi, 14–15, 17, 20, 40, 115–16, 131–3, 139, 161–2
Anti-Persecution Union, 43, 47, 54–7, 198
Ashton under Lyne, 35
Ashurst, W. H., 64, 184–5
Aveling, Edward, 119–21, 180

Baptists, x, 60, 86
Barker, Joseph, 66, 70, 106–9
Besant, Annie, 68, 88, 112, 119–20, 121, 174–8, 179, 180, 187–90, 212, 215–18
Bible and biblical criticism, 13, 42, 83–4, 85, 93–4, 102, 107–9, 112, 125–6, 128–30, 134–5, 136–41, 198–202, 204–6
Birmingham, 4, 39, 40
birth control, 67–8, 70, 86, 87–8, 186, 187–90
Black Dwarf, 16, 100
Blackburn, 36, 71
blasphemy, 16–19, 34, 42, 101, 105, 108, 128–30, 162, 193–207
Blatchford, Robert, 70
Bolton, 19, 33, 35, 57, 71
Bon Sens, 3, 13
Bradford, 35, 71, 81, 103
Bradlaugh, Alice, 119–20
Bradlaugh, Charles, xv, 32, 65–70, 82, 84–9, 91, 98, 106, 117–18, 143–6, 155, 165, 168–71, 174–8, 187–90, 191, 210–13, 215, 216, 219–20; Bradlaugh Case, 67, 68–9, 88, 117–18, 210–13
Bradlaugh, Hypatia, 32, 119–20
Brindley, John, 40, 64, 109
Bristol, 42, 139, 141

British Secular Union, 68
Burke, Edmund, 4, 6, 7
Burnley, 71

Campbell, Alexander, 38
Carlile, Mrs Jane, 23, 24, 32, 101, 115
Carlile, Mary Ann, 23, 25, 26, 28, 29, 31, 32, 115
Carlile, Richard, xi, xv, 3, 16–24, 25–8, 31–7, 38, 39, 40, 42–3, 52–3, 65, 83, 89, 94, 99, 101–3, 115, 123, 131, 133, 156–8, 159, 188–9, 191, 195, 204
Carpenter, William, 47, 48–9, 56, 104
Chambers, Robert, *Vestiges of the Natural History of Creation,* 139, 141–2
Chartism, x, xvi, 40, 43, 63, 65, 66, 71, 91, 98, 105, 106, 159–62, 181, 184
Cheltenham, 42, 52
Chilton, William, 42, 48, 128–30, 139–42
Christian socialism, 65, 180
civil rights, 68, 88, 107, 191, 208–13, 214–15
Cleave, John, 104, 105, 106
Cobbett, William, 32, 34, 116; *Parliamentary History,* 9–10; *Weekly Political Register,* 16, 100–1
Constitutional Association ('Bridge Street Gang'), 28, 31
Cooper, Robert, 43, 57–60, 63–4, 65, 72, 81–4, 162–5
Cooper, Thomas, 78, 109
co-operative movement, 39, 103, 108, 158
Cowen, Joseph, xv, 162, 165, 181, 184

Darwinism, *see* evolution
Davenport, Allen, 36–7
Davison (or Davidson), Thomas, 23, 24, 116, 147

deism, xii, 3, 18, 33, 194–5
Detrosier, Rowland, 18, 105
Drysdale, George, 190; *Elements of Social Science,* 70, 188, 189

Eaton, Daniel Isaac, 5–6, 34, 195
Edinburgh, 31–2, 42–3, 49–50, 52, 58, 128, 141, 195–204
education, 67, 78, 80, 98, 99–100, 107, 111, 119–22, 150–1, 169, 180, 191
eight hours question, 113
Ellis, John, 59, 60
Enlightenment, x, xv, 44, 123, 149
Evangelicals, x, xvi, 89, 93–5, 123, 133, 192, 214
evolution, 108, 112, 139–42

Fabians, 70, 174, 179
Finch, John, 159–60
Finlay, Thomas, 43, 195, 197, 204
Foote, G. W., 68, 69, 191
Forder, Robert, 89
Fox, W. J., 86
France, 4, 5, 9, 22, 94; *see also* revolution
Fraser, D. K., 67
Freethinker, 69

Galpin, William, 50, 52
Garibaldi Legion, 184–5
Gimson, Josiah, 76, 78, 179
Gimson, Sydney, 179–80
Gladstone, W. E., 67, 165–8, 169, 172, 181, 212, 213
Glasgow, 17, 38, 49–51, 58, 60, 61, 64, 65, 71–2, 141, 196
Gloucester, 42, 53
Godwin, William, 14
Graham, Sir James, 53, 54
Grant, Rev. Brewin, 64, 109
Gravesend and Northfleet, 109–10
Gurney, Joseph, 170

Habeas Corpus, 5, 6
Halifax, 81, 98, 103, 117
Hardy, Thomas, 5, 8, 10–11
Harney, George Julian, xi, xvi, 43, 160–2, 181, 183, 184
Headlam, Rev. Stewart D., 180
Herald of Progress, 62
Hetherington, Henry, 39, 47, 56, 83, 101, 104, 105, 106, 158–9, 181, 182, 191, 221
Hibbert, Julian, 103, 104, 105
Hobbes, Thomas, *Leviathan,* 136

Hobson, Joshua, xvi, 186
Holmes, W. V., 31, 133–5
Holyoak, William H., 76, 77, 78
Holyoake, Austin, 64, 68, 85, 86, 99, 171–4, 188
Holyoake, George Jacob, 42, 43, 47–8, 49, 51, 52–3, 54, 56, 57, 58, 60, 61, 62, 63–5, 66, 68, 72, 75, 76–8, 82, 84, 85, 86, 99, 105, 106, 109, 121, 124, 142–3, 151–2, 160–1, 162, 183, 184–5, 188, 191, 195, 196–204, 209, 219
Hone, William, 16, 131–3
House of Commons, Committee of Secrecy (1794), 5, 6, 8, 9–10
Howell, George, 67
Hoyland, 215–18
Huddersfield, 19, 36, 40, 60, 103, 121–2
Hume, David, 102
Hunt, Henry, 19, 116, 117, 157
Hunt, Thornton L., 72, 84
Hyndman, H. M., 174–8, 179

infidels, infidelity, x–xii, xvi, 11–15, 17–18, 19, 41–3, 64–5, 91, 94, 106, 107, 123, 151–2
International Working Men's Association, 67, 70
Ireland, 5, 67, 219
Italy, 105–6, 184–5

Jeffery, Henry, 49–51, 196
Johnson, W. H., 65
Jones, B. B., 25–31
Jones, John Gale, 19, 26
Jones, Lloyd, 19
Justice, 177–8

Keighley, 72
Knowlton, Dr Charles, 68, 87, 187; *see also* birth control

Labour Exchanges, 39
Lamarck, J.-B., 139
Lancashire, 18, 64, 79, 96–7, 115, 166–7
land reform, 67, 161, 169
Law, Harriet, 85, 86, 121
Leeds, 18–19, 35, 40, 99, 100–1, 103, 160
Lees, F. R., 171
Leicester, 75–8, 179
Leigh, 72
Liberalism, 67, 165, 168
Linton, William James, 106, 181, 184–5
Lion, 18, 38

Liverpool, 35–6, 159
London, 11–15, 19, 20, 39, 59, 66–7, 84–5, 87; Bethnall Green (Gibraltar Walk), 87, 126–8; Blackfriars Rotunda, 19, 35, 36; City Road Hall of Science, 63, 66, 84–5, 86, 87, 89, 91, 105, 119–21; Cleveland Street Hall, 85, 86; Corresponding Society, 3, 5, 8, 10, 12, 13, 19; Dialectical Society, 171; Hackney, 87; Hoxton, 65; *Investigator*, 65, 81–4; John Street Institution, 40, 70, 86, 181; Lambeth, 42, 47; school board, 111, 180; Victoria Park, 65, 87; West Ham, xvi; Whitechapel, 57
Love, William, 60, 61
Lovett, William, 39, 106
Lucraft, Benjamin, 165

Manchester, xii, 3, 9, 18–19, 35, 39, 40, 44, 58, 65, 71, 93–7, 106, 165, 214–15
Martin, Emma, 43, 59, 60
Martineau, Rev. James, 105, 106
Marx, Eleanor, 179–80
Marx, Karl, xi, 67, 70, 96, 174
materialism and atheism, 17–18, 142–6
Maughan, John, 65
Mazzini, J., 105–6
Methodism, 66, 86, 133, 198, 216
Miles Platting, 72
Mill, John Stuart, 64, 108, 151, 191–2, 208–9
Mirabaud, *System of Nature*, xii, 13, 17, 32, 105, 142
Moore, Richard, 106, 165
Morris, William, x, 178, 179, 180
Mosheim's Institutes of Ecclesiastical History, 32, 102
Moss, Arthur B., 111–14
Movement, 43, 142–3, 204

National Reformer, 66, 67, 69, 84–6, 97–8, 106–9, 111–14, 117–21, 165–8, 174–8, 210–13, 215–20
National Secular Society, 60, 66–9, 86–9, 91, 106
National Union of the Working Classes, 19, 39, 48, 104
neo-Malthusianism, *see* birth control
New Moral World, 41, 44–6, 51, 62, 159–60, 186, 214–15
Newcastle upon Tyne, xv, 73, 111–12, 162, 204–7
Newdegate, C. N., 68–9, 212, 213

Newman, F. W., 105, 106, 151
newspaper stamp agitation, 39, 48–9, 83, 104–5, 160, 191
Nockles, James, 51, 59, 60
North East (Northumberland and Durham), 111–14, 115
Northampton, 67, 68, 69, 168, 213
Northern Reform Union, 162, 165
Northern Star, xvi, 159, 160, 162, 181–3
Nottingham, 31, 35, 73

Oastler, Richard, 177
O'Brien, J. Bronterre, x, 153, 177
O'Connor, Feargus, 177
Oracle of Reason, 42, 43, 47, 48, 51, 53, 54–7, 128–30, 139–41, 200, 204
Over Darwen, 73
Owen, Robert, 38–41, 47, 52, 60, 62, 70, 94, 149–51, 158–9, 177, 185, 186–7
Owen, Robert Dale, 68, 188–9
Owenism, x, xii, 19, 38–44, 47, 49–51, 57–8, 62, 64, 65, 71, 76, 79, 94, 103, 106, 123–4, 149–51, 158–60, 161, 162, 179, 214–15; Association of All Classes, 40, 44–6; National Community Friendly Society, 40; New Harmony, 39; Queenwood, 40, 43, 49, 51, 52, 58, 68, 159; Ralahine, 159; Rational Society, 40, 63; Universal Community Society, 40, 41, 42, 52

Paine, Thomas, xi, xv–xvi, xvii, 3–6, 10, 18, 19, 21, 32, 36–7, 38, 41, 63, 65, 67, 70, 83, 105, 109, 112, 115, 116, 122, 123, 142, 153, 155, 157, 171, 173, 195; *Age of Reason*, x, xv, 5, 6, 11, 12, 16, 17, 33–4, 123, 125–6, 134, 136–9, 195; *Common Sense*, 16, 37; *Crisis* papers, 37; *Letter addressed to the Addressers*, 4, 5; *Rights of Man*, xv, 4–5, 6, 7, 9, 10, 16, 155–6
Paisley, 60, 73–4
Palmer, Elihu, 17, 101, 102, 147
Palmerston, Henry (Viscount), 63, 168
Paterson, Thomas, 42–3, 162, 195, 196–7, 200, 204
Peel, Sir Robert, 53, 54
'Peterloo massacre', 17, 19, 20, 116–17, 131
Phillpotts, Henry, Bishop of Exeter, 41
Pitt, William, 3, 8
Pooley, Thomas, 209
Poor Man's Guardian, x, 39, 104, 158–9
Potteries, 39

Preston, 74
Priestley, Joseph, x, 4
Prompter, 39

Ramsey, W. J., 126–8
Reasoner, 25–30, 43, 60, 62, 63, 64, 71–5, 76, 82, 96, 99–106, 151–2
Reform League, 66, 67, 165, 168
reform of parliament, 3–4, 19, 104, 158, 162–5, 168–70
Republican, xii, 16–18, 20–4, 31–4, 36–7, 42, 100, 115–17, 133–5, 156–8, 193–5
republicanism, 9, 15, 43, 67, 106, 153, 155–8, 161, 171–4, 181–3
revolutions: American independence, 4, 22, 36–7, 83; English (1640s), 7, 15, 22, 83, 193, 194; English (1688), 6, 9; European (1848), 181–3; French (1789), x, 4, 5, 94, 157, 192, 193; French (1830), 103, 104
Roalfe, Matilda, 43, 162, 195–204
Robinson, Henry, 43, 195, 204
Ryall, Maltus Q., 42, 47–8, 54–7, 58, 60

Salvation Army, 113, 114
Scotland, 8, 61, 64, 128, 195–204, 219, 220; *see also* Edinburgh and Glasgow
Secularism, 63–70, 71–5, 79–80, 83–4, 86–9, 98, 107, 121, 124, 151–2, 174, 179, 215
Sharples, Eliza, 19, 32, 65
Sheffield, 10, 31, 32, 42, 43, 47, 65–6, 75, 157–8, 160
Sheridan, R. B., 5, 10–11
Sherwin, W. T., 16; *Weekly Political Register,* 16, 17, 20
Social Democratic Federation, xi, 69, 174–5
socialism, 174–8, 179–80; *for early socialism see* Owenism
Society for Constitutional Information, 8, 9–10
Society for the Suppression of Vice ('Vice Society'), 16, 23–4, 29, 31
South Shields, 112
Southwell, Charles, 41–3, 47, 48, 54, 56, 59, 60, 63, 64, 65, 139, 142, 191, 195, 196

Spencer, John, 97–8
Spinoza, B., 143–4
Stafford, 74
Standring, George, 86, 89
Stephens, Rev. J. R., 177
Stockport, 18, 19, 36, 40, 59, 75, 115–17
Stowell, Rev. Hugh, 41, 214

Taylor, Rev. Robert, 18–19, 34–6, 39, 89, 104, 123
temperance, 108, 113, 130, 159, 171
Thelwall, John, 5, 8
Todmorden, 75, 103
trade unionism, 39, 105
Trevelyan, Arthur, 59, 60, 64, 67
Truelove, Edward, 68, 70, 209
Turner, B., 121–2
Turton, Thomas, 32, 53

Unitarians, x, 36, 50, 52, 93, 95–6, 106, 191, 194–5
United States of America, x, xvi, 67, 107, 156; *see also* revolution
Urquhart, David, 63
utilitarianism, 123, 151

Vincent, Henry, 106
Volney, C. F., 32; *Law of Nature,* 142, 147–9; *Lectures on History,* 103; *Ruins of Empires,* x, 12, 13, 105
Voltaire, 3, 13, 14, 109, 112

Watson, James, xv, 39, 43, 54, 57, 60–1, 64, 68, 99–106, 187–8
Watts, Charles, 66, 67, 68, 85, 86, 121, 187, 188
Watts, John, 84–6, 166–8
Winks, J. F., 77, 78
women's rights, 60, 85, 153, 186–90
Wooler, T. J., 100, 116
Wright, Frances, 105
Wright, Susannah, 26, 28, 29–30, 32, 102
Wyvill, Rev. Christopher, 3, 4

Yorkshire, West Riding, 40, 64, 98, 115; West Riding Secular Union, 78–81

zetetics, xi, 17–20, 31, 38, 43, 71, 123